D0989363

# Freud as a Writer

LARRY E. FISHER
P.O. BOX 848
LATHAM, NY 12110

# Freud as a Writer

*Expanded Edition*

PATRICK J. MAHONY

Yale University Press
New Haven and London

Copyright © 1987 by Yale University.
All rights reserved.
This book may not be reproduced, in whole or in
part, in any form (beyond that copying permitted by
Sections 107 and 108 of the U.S. Copyright Law and
except by reviewers for the public press), without
written permission from the publishers.

Designed by James J. Johnson
and set in Palatino Roman type
by r/tsi typographic company, inc.
Printed in the United States of America by
Edwards Brothers, Inc.,

*Library of Congress Cataloging-in-Publication Data*

Mahony, Patrick, 1932–
　　Freud as a writer.

　　Includes bibliographies and indexes.
　　1. Freud, Sigmund, 1856–1939—Literary art.
2. Psychoanalysts as authors.　I. Title.
[DNLM:　I. Freud, Sigmund, 1856–1939.　2. Psychoanalysis
—biography.　3. Writing—biography.　WZ 100 F889MAA]
BF173.F85M247　1987　　808'.0092'4　　86–28912
ISBN 0–300–03781–3 (alk. paper)

---

*The paper in this book meets the guidelines for permanence
and durability of the Committee on Production Guidelines for
Book Longevity of the Council on Library Resources.*

---

10　9　8　7　6　5　4　3　2　1

Lo duca e io per quel cammino ascoso
intrammo a ritornar nel chiaro mondo;
e sanza cura aver d'alcun riposo
salimmo sù, el primo e io secondo,
tanto ch'i' vidi de le cose belle
che porta 'l ciel, per un pertugio tondo.
E quindi uscimmo a riveder le stelle.

—DANTE, *Inferno*, Canto 34

# Contents

# Foreword

AT A TIME WHEN AN EVER-INCREASING NUMBER OF BOOKS AND ESSAYS on Freud and psychoanalysis have appeared, we should pause and ask why. Has psychoanalysis existed long enough to have a history of its own? Has it now become sufficiently established to become the object of scrutiny, criticism, refutation, or confrontation? The answers to these and similar queries are speculative. But what is not conjectural are the many philosophical, historical, biographical, sociocultural, political, biological, and economic studies of Freud and psychoanalysis that have been published recently.

Employing a new approach, the present volume focuses on a heretofore insufficiently explored aspect of Freud: his outstanding ability to express himself clearly in writing and in speech. If speech and writing are an index of a creative mind, it is significant to examine Freud from this perspective. One may say that, in his writings, Freud understood the aesthetic aspects of his conceptual systems, as well as their scientific and clinical significance.

Professor Mahony observes that Freud's mode of thinking and intelligence were predominantly verbal. In his writings, as with the spoken word, he captured the attention and imagination of his audience, visually rounding out his lectures, essays, and monographs with the excellent use of imagery, metaphor, analogy, parallels, and models for purposes of explanation and illustration, and drawing upon his prodigious memory and thorough classical education. His language was simple and effective.

In similar fashion, Mahony writes clearly and simply, and presents his arguments and illustrations convincingly. Well aware, as was Freud, of the problems of translation, Mahony goes back to Freud's original language to indicate where alternative translations yield different concepts—some incorrect as a result of the translation choice. By using selections from Freud's works, Mahony offers the reader the opportunity to follow his literary and textual analyses and to note how these integrate with the conceptual analysis of the psychoanalytic classics he has chosen for in-depth study. Thus he invites the reader to share in an exciting intellectual exploration. Focusing on language, style, and form—a model of textual criticism used to examine other scholarly works—his approach yields new insights for the student, scholar, and psychoanalytic researcher.

As one carefully reads Mahony's monograph, one appreciates Freud as a writer who offers various blendings of form, style, and content. Freud's originality of expression and example, his use of poetic phrases, his brevity and sparkle make reading his contributions a pleasure as well as a gain in knowledge. Although Freud reads more naturally in German, he is still very expressive in English translation. (However, the problems of translating words, phrases, and colloquialisms from everyday Viennese life do not escape Mahony's attention.) I am certain that Freud's literary appeal served to influence the spread of his ideas. His receiving the Goethe Prize for literature is evidence that some of his essays were masterpieces of writing, although certainly Freud's readers were influenced by the content of his works as well as by their style.

Unfortunately, we cannot at first hand assess Freud's style of delivery, although some of his lectures were published as they were orally presented. But the magnetism of his presentation, the tempo, tone, and wit of his manner of speaking are lost to us.

Professor Mahony, an outstanding scholar and master of language, who is also a well-trained, practicing clinical psychoanalyst, has written a work that will soon become a classic. He has studied Freud and the significant commentaries on his work from an original and pioneering point of view. Sensitive to the nuances of his thesis, Mahony is objective and gives evidence for his assertions. His documentation and scholarship are first-class; his command of the Freud literature is admirable. His ability to synthesize the methods of literary criticism and psychoanalysis yields new awareness of Freud's style, content, and means of communication. His work is a model of interdisciplinary bridging.

In addition to studying Freud as a writer, Mahony's approach provides the reader with the means of studying the literary style of other psychoanalytic contributors, but, more important, his emphasis on style in writing can be applied to the study of the style, form, and language of the contents of the clinical psychoanalytic situation, e.g., free associations. My own clinical experience has led me to see a meaningful correlation between the style-form-content of the analysand's communications, the presenting psychopathology, the stage of psychoanalytic treatment, and the responses of the analyst. These vary at different times in the course of therapy and, when carefully noted, these variations in communication can be used as indicators of process and its vicissitudes. Mahony's approach can thus be seen not only as deepening our awareness of Freud's ideas and his manner of expression but as contributing to our understanding of clinical communications as well.

Finally, Mahony's emphasis on the relationship between Freud and his audience has implications that go beyond what he presents. When one considers, for example, the writer as performer and the reader as audience, the dynamic relations between drama and literature and the audience for which they are intended emerge more clearly. Extrapolating these dynamics to the psychoanalytic situation, one can view analysand and analyst in the shifting roles of performer and audience/observer. This "stage" orientation can thus lead to applying the theory of drama to the interaction of the psychoanalytic situation. This observation is only one of the several chains of thought elicited in me by Mahony's work, and the same may hold for those who participate in it as reader/audience.

This stimulating volume will provide the serious student and reader with much to discern, reflect upon, discriminate, and evaluate. Whatever the final appraisal—and I am confident it will be very positive—Professor Mahony is to be congratulated on a job well-done, and we must thank him for his contribution.

GEORGE H. POLLOCK, M.D., PH.D

# Preface to the Second Edition

I finished the manuscript for *Freud As a Writer* in 1979, although it was not published until 1982. Besides making a number of corrections for the new edition, I decided to add a postscript on "The Psychoanalytic Reading of Freud," which complements the subject of the earlier chapters and represents a considerable advance in my thinking over the past seven years.

I gladly thank Stephanie Jones and Gladys Topkis of the Yale editorial staff for their thoughtful considerations, and I express my deepest gratitude to Drs. Darius Ornston and Pierrette Senay for the endearing astuteness and empathy with which they read the Postscript.

*Montreal, July 1986*

# Acknowledgments

Grateful acknowledgment is made to the publishers for permission to quote material from the following:

"A Character Trait of Freud's," by Joan Riviere. In: *Psychoanalysis and Contemporary Thought*, edited by J. Sutherland. By permission of The Hogarth Press, Ltd.

*Dialectic*, by Mortimer Adler. By permission of Routledge & Kegan Paul, Ltd.

*Freud: Living and Dying*, by Max Schur. Copyright 1972 by Estate of Max Schur. By permission of International Universities Press.

*Freud: Master and Friend*, by Hans Sachs. By permission of Harvard University Press.

*The Interpretation of Dreams*, by Sigmund Freud. By permission of Basic Books, Inc., and George Allen & Unwin, Publishers, Ltd.

*Introductory Lectures on Psycho-Analysis*, by Sigmund Freud. By permission of Liveright Publishing Corp. and George Allen & Unwin, Publishers, Ltd.

*Life and Death in Psychoanalysis*, by J. Laplanche, translated by J. Mehlman. Copyright 1976 by J. Laplanche. By permission of The Johns Hopkins University Press.

*The Life and Work of Sigmund Freud*, Volumes 2 and 3, by Ernest Jones. Copyright 1955 and 1957 by Ernest Jones. By permission of

Basic Books, Inc., and The Hogarth Press, Ltd.

*Memories, Dreams, Reflections*, by C. G. Jung, edited by A. Jaffe, translated by R. Winston and C. Winston. By permission of Pantheon Books, a Division of Random House, Inc.

*Minutes of the Vienna Psychoanalytic Society*, 4 Volumes, edited by Herman Nunberg and Ernst Federn. Copyright 1962, 1967, 1974, 1975 by International Universities Press. By permission of International Universities Press.

*The Origins of Psycho-Analysis: Letters to Wilhelm Fliess, Drafts and Notes: 1887–1902*, by Sigmund Freud, edited by Marie Bonaparte, Anna Freud, and Ernst Kris, translated by Eric Mosbacher and James Strachey. By permission of Basic Books, Inc., and The Hogarth Press, Ltd.

*The Philosophy of Nietzsche*, by Friedrich Nietzsche; edited by W. Wright. By permission of George Allen & Unwin, Publishers, Ltd.

*Psychoanalysis and the Question of the Text*, edited by G. Hartman. By permission of The Johns Hopkins University Press.

"On Reading Freud," by Robert R. Holt. Published in *Abstracts of the Standard Edition of the Complete Psychological Works of Sigmund Freud*, edited by Carrie Lee Rothgeb. By permission of Jason Aronson, Inc.

"Recollections of Berggasse 19," by Franz Alexander. Published in *Psychoanalytic Quarterly*, 9:195–204. By permission of the *Psychoanalytic Quarterly*.

*Seventeenth Century Prose and Poetry*, edited by A. Witherspoon and F. Warnke. By permission of Harcourt Brace Jovanovich, Inc.

*Sigmund Freud and Lou Andreas-Salomé: Letters*, edited by E. Pfeiffer, translated by W. and E. Robson-Scott. By permission of Harcourt Brace Jovanovich, Inc., and The Hogarth Press, Ltd.

*The Standard Edition of the Complete Psychological Works of Sigmund Freud*, revised and edited by James Strachey. By permission of Sigmund Freud Copyrights, Ltd., The Institute of Psycho-Analysis, and The Hogarth Press, Ltd.

*Talent and Genius: The Fictitious Case of Tausk Contra Freud*, by K. R. Eissler. Copyright 1972 by K. R. Eissler. By permission of K. R. Eissler and Times Books.

*The Tangled Bank: Darwin, Frazer and Freud as Imaginative Writers*, by Stanley Hyman. Copyright 1974 by Stanley Hyman. By permission of Atheneum Publishers.

*From Thirty Years with Freud*, by Theodor Reik. By permission of The Hogarth Press, Ltd.

*Totem and Taboo*, by Sigmund Freud. By permission of W. W. Norton, Inc., and Routledge & Kegan Paul, Ltd.

"The Writer's Audience Is Always a Fiction," by Walter J. Ong. Published in *PMLA*, 90:9–21 (1975). By permission of the Modern Language Association of America.

# 1

# The Dimensions of
# Freud's Writing: An Overview

THIS WORK IS ONE OF THE HAPPY PRODUCTS OF A SIX-MONTH PERIOD during which I reread (as much as possible in chronological order) some forty volumes of primary source material fundamental to an understanding of Freud: the twenty-three text volumes of the *Standard Edition*,[1] the *Minutes of the Vienna Psychoanalytic Society* in four volumes, the biographies by Jones and Schur, and various collections of letters and personal accounts. But Freud, like many another great thinker, still awaits a complete and satisfactory edition. When all his correspondence is published, the corpus for appreciation will significantly exceed what we have today or any of his contemporaries could have had. Be that as it may, the documentation on Freud already amassed is said to surpass in specificity and depth of insight the extant material on any other human being in history.[2] This presents a formidable burden for anyone seeking to conduct original and comprehensive research on him, even within the topic I have chosen—Freud's specific identity as a writer—on which comparatively little has been written by him or anyone else. This lack is especially surprising in light of the fact that the only prize Freud received from Germany in his life was the Goethe Prize for literature. My aim in part is belatedly to establish further justification for conferring that distinction on Freud, whose knowledge of classical and modern literature excelled that of any other great modern scientist.³ In considering Freud's unique contributions, that fact is worth bearing in mind, as is the observation that "It would be hard to find in the history of ideas, even in the history of religion, someone whose influence was so immediate, so broad and so deep."⁴

Freud was not only the founder of psychoanalysis and its most brilliant theoretician; he also stands as the foremost writer in the discipline's history. His theories may be subject to important modifications—as in more recent psychodynamic conceptions of women, anthropological reconsiderations of the Oedipus complex, and the revolution in preoedipal-development models—but his style will remain unsurpassed. I use the term *style* in a comprehensive sense, referring not merely to the deployment of various figures of speech, but also including the other parts of classical rhetoric, such as manner of delivery, logical structure and organization, the assumed ethical stance of the speaker, and his emotional appeal to the audience. Literary style is not to be rigidly contradistinguished from content, but is rather the first and last elaboration of meaning; it partakes in the broader concept of cognitive style or "organized configuration of an individual's ways of taking in, processing, and communicating information about his world."⁵

Our knowledge of Freud is, naturally enough, overwhelmingly based on his writings, and of course he spoke much more than he wrote. Those who have remarked on his spontaneous oral style agree that it was simple, concise, and outstandingly fluent, as witnessed by the following three reports of acquaintances:

> He never said the same thing twice nor did he indulge in the beauty of words for the sake of rhetoric alone. The simplicity of his phraseology was its beauty.⁶

> Everything he said was practically fit for print; it was incisive, imaginative, filled with metaphors, analogies and stories—particularly Jewish ones—and it was not wordy. Freud talked like a book.⁷

> . . . sharp and accurate in his choice of words, sparing in gesture, natural and open in his facial expressions.⁸

So extraordinary were his conceptual power and ready verbal genius that when he lectured, he rarely prepared much, trusting the inspiration of the moment. On one occasion, for example, Jones asked Freud what his subject would be, and received the reply, "If I only knew! I must leave it to my unconscious."[9] For a time he avoided the obvious path of logical development in favor of elaboration led by "fancy."[10] And from Freud himself we know the startling way in which his five Clark lectures in 1909 were composed: during their regular walk, Ferenczi would sketch out a lecture which Freud would deliver half an hour later, much improved (*S.E.* 22:227). By far the most impressive performance occurred when, in response to Jung's request for a case history, Freud gave the small group of intimates present a spontaneous presentation, nearly five hours long, of the case of the Rat Man.[11]

Before passing on to Freud's writing, one final word about orality and psychoanalysis in a larger sense. That we have so little data on Freud as a speaker reflects the nature of psychoanalytic scholarship generally. In 1979 a pioneering article appeared postulating a sound image of the self that developmentally initiates the body image; and the author pertinently remarked that—in keeping with the neglect of problems in this area by Freud's commentators—the editors of the *Standard Edition* have not indexed such key terms as *voice, sound,* and *audition.*[12] For my own part, I doubt that this situation would have occurred if psychoanalysis had been invented in a tonal language such as Chinese or in an African language such as Khosi, which mixes words and a tongue-clacking that up to now has defied transcription. In such languages, psychoanalysts would be likely to devote more attention to nonverbal sounds and noises which, after all, increase as the treatment progresses (patients feel freer to make more noises as analysis goes on). I have searched the literature for a psychoanalytic article on patients whispering and can find none, despite the fact that verbalizations during lovemaking are almost always whispered. (Whispering, it should be noted, demands more muscular effort than simply lowering one's voice.)

Despite this neglect of sound phenomena, psychoanalysis as a 20th-century discipline stands out as an eminently *oral* praxis not only in the clinical setting and supervision of analytic candidates but also as it is steeped in oral history, as the Section on Oral History at the Annual Meeting of the American Psychoanalytic Association indicates. Analysts know too that our understanding of technique owes much more to the weight of oral tradition and elaboration than to the relatively few comments in Freud's written works. In what is yet an unwritten chapter in the history of psychoanalysis, the founding of the *Jahrbuch für psychoanalytische und psychopathologische Forschungen* in 1909 actually inaugurated in psychoanalytic circles a written tradition alongside the oral one. As Freud says in two remarks his commentators have completely overlooked, the *Jahrbuch* lightened the burden of transmission and, with its guaranteed regular audience, allowed him to pass over basic assumptions and eliminated the need to refute elementary objections in every paper.[13]

We have no chronicle of human consciousness that would place Freud's therapeutic lexicon in the context of the interaction between his personality and the history of the sensorium and of the media of communication. For example, although the primal scene is chiefly visual and auditory, why do we have no auditory counterparts for such pertinent terms as *voyeurism* and *exhibitionism?* Moreover, as George Steiner has described at length,[14] diverse eras and cultures have differed in the authority attributed to language; in the relations perceived between word and object; in the aggregate of silence and verbalization, and therefore in a redistributed "speech mass"; in their acceptance of new metaphors; and in the proportion of inward to public discourse. Psychoanalysis developed at a moment when in the European sensibility the techniques of meditation and introspection favoring inward discourse had wasted away; today, public verbalizing and publicity seem to have impoverished internal language further still.

For a man so prolific (even apart from the literally thousands of letters he composed during his lifetime), it is not surprising that the act of writing itself had especial significance. Thus when he yielded to a request to write in Latin rather than Gothic script, he felt his correspondence was impeded; he attributed fluency, inspiration, and a sense of personal intimacy to Gothic handwriting.[15] Freud ascribed an attack of writer's cramp in 1909 to prostatic hypertrophy, and in 1938 he felt that his urinary trouble spoiled his calligraphy.[16] Whatever its urethral significance, Freud found a symbolic paternal value in writing: "There is no doubt that the creative artist feels towards his works like a father" (*S.E.* 11:121). In Freud's case, the libidinal value of writing was not so uncontrollable and destructive as for the neurotic, for whom "writing, which entails making a liquid flow out of a tube on to a piece of white paper," becomes too strongly eroticized and inhibits ego-syntonic functions (*S.E.* 20:90). Even during the time Freud wrote letters to his fiancée and to Fliess to relieve tension in a way that none of his subsequent letters did,[17] he managed to compose scientific publications of enormous moment.

Freud's rhythm of writing was rather erratic. Weeks and months could go by without a line, followed by two or three lines a day and then a fury of production, the most outstanding of which was his composition of the five metapsychological essays in six weeks, a burst of activity that in the opinion of Jones has hardly been equaled in the history of science.[18] Without evidence we could hardly guess that Freud's creativity was highest when he was in a bad mood. But evidence for this surprising fact does exist. He wrote to his friend Fliess: "One strenuous night last week . . . I was in the stage of painful discomfort in which my brain works best";[19] if on the one hand a family worry could disincline him to write letters, it could on the other drive him to "look for distraction by writing [two essays]";[20] and when the Nazi invasion of Austria caused him to dismiss his two patients ("When the conscious mind is troubled, one cannot be interested in the unconscious mind"), he yet held that he could continue writing *Moses and Monotheism*, which contained "some connections with the situation in Austria."[21]

Probably Freud was like Goethe, who felt that he did not fully assimilate an experience until he had written about it. Another and crucial motivation for Freud to write was to engage in an active endeavor as a necessary means of self-preservation and counterreaction to the many hours of relatively passive psychoanalytic listening during the day.[22] One should not, however, jump to the conclusion that without the drain of an onerous clinical practice Freud could have produced more; the evidence is in fact to the contrary:

> A sudden drop in my practice is giving me almost more leisure than I wanted after working at full pressure for four months. However, such reliefs from work do not lead to any productivity with me.[23]

My practice is not quite complete, only seven patients so far. Consequently, I have not yet mobilized intellectually; for instance, I have not yet resumed my studies on religion.[24]

As might be supposed from his attitude to public speaking, Freud was inclined to write when prompted by impulse. When on one occasion he was asked if he found writing difficult, he answered:

> No, because I have usually not written until a thing was ripe and I felt a real compulsion to express myself. When I have had to write to order on the other hand—introductions and the like—it has always been hard.[25]

Consequently he judged that the essay "The Psycho-Analytic View of Psychogenic Disturbance of Vision" (1910), like everything he wrote to order, was inferior,[26] and it is worth noting that his *Autobiographical Study* (1925) originated not in some inner urgency but in the insistent request of a publisher.[27] When setting down *Totem and Taboo*, however, especially Part 4, Freud acknowledged that he was following "a crooked way in the order of my works . . . but it is the order of unconscious connections."[28] It was his typical procedure.

Like Shakespeare, Freud was known among his close associates for his facile pen. Alluding to the infrequency of corrections in Freud's writings, Hanns Sachs has left this memorable account:

> I asked him once how this was possible, since he was dealing with such difficult conceptions which needed the most careful formulation. I wondered whether he had never to search for the exact expression or if he did it by jotting down notes which were sifted and corrected until they could be used for the final draft. He answered that he was not in the habit of writing down anything before the final *draft* stage, not only the content and construction, but also the exact formulation of each sentence, before he put pen to paper. When he sat down to write, the process was almost automatic under the inner dictation of the prearranged sentences.[29]

An exception to this unrehearsed clarity is Freud's exceedingly difficult neurological study *Project for a Scientific Psychology*, the ideas of which only took clear shape as he set them down.[30] Yet thanks to its rigorous deductive method, exceptional within the Freud canon, his groping thoughts nevertheless do emerge in ready language. Kurt Eissler has expressed this idea with admirable insight, contending that the root of Freud's genius, however powerful his observation and judgment, lay rather in his language:

> A psychological explication of Freud's genius will, I think, have to center in his language. His power to observe, to judge, to draw inferences—indispensable as these were to the greatness of his work—nevertheless, in my opinion, have to take a secondary place to the genius of his language. I even anticipate the possibility that one day someone will be able to demonstrate that what Freud presented to the world in the organized form of his scientific papers—which seem to contain the results of innumerable as well as of single observations, of intensive meditation and deliberations, of subtle working through, checking and counter-checking, comparing and returning over and over again to the raw observational data—that all this was in the end the refined and scientifically correct presentation of what had been linguistically preformed earlier.[31]

Notwithstanding his verbal powers, Freud was painfully aware of the limping nature of language as a completely reliable instrument for clinical description. Just past the surface, dream interpretation becomes so voluminous in exposition as to be antiheuristic; not to mention that language imposes chronological sequence on the description of dream processes that in reality are simultaneous (*S.E.* 4:118; 5:405, 576). Freud came back again and again to the basic challenge psychic reality poses for exposition: psychic events are overdetermined and draw simultaneously from various strata, whereas in verbal exposition these superimposed strata are flattened out into a verbal string; if linearity is the essence of language, superimposition is the keynote of psychic events. In presenting the Dora case, Freud selected as an organizational principle two dreams; but even then, for purposes of coherence, his exposition occasionally altered the order of interpretation (*S.E.* 7:10; see also 18:160). Besides, to have presented not only the results of interpretations but also the process would have created utter confusion (*S.E.* 7:12–13), and the results would be equally unreadable if a case history attempted a full account not only of the structure of a neurosis but also of the management of analytic technique (*S.E.* 7:112; 10:156; 17:7–8, 44 fn., 104).[32] Apart from the discrepancy between exposition and clinical treatment, there is also a discrepancy, due to condensation, between the course of an analysis and the development of a neurosis (see *S.E.* 10:83). It follows that the development of a neurosis, the unfolding of its treatment, and the order of exposition are all at odds: exposition is a reconstruction subject to narrative constraints that in turn are based on the reconstruction and interaction within the clinical setting which thus slides away from the etiology of the neurosis by at least two vectorial removes.

As Freud passed from the Dora case (1905) to the Rat Man (1909) and the Wolf Man (1918), his expository powers grew. He no longer relied on the relatively simple compositional device of centering his account around two dreams; yet in the end he was overwhelmed by the extraordinary mass and structure of psychic material. It was with the Rat Man in mind that he avowed to Jung, "How bungled our reproductions are, how wretchedly we dissect the great works of psychic nature."[33] Aesthetically, then, the reporting therapist falls short of the inherent beauty of nature but also of the literary artist, whose profession allows a higher degree of abstraction and the omission of more cumbersome material (*S.E.* 7:59–60); Freud bemoaned this state of affairs and could not fully reconcile himself to it. Did he not lament—but I would not say wholeheartedly—that no matter what alterations he made in the Dora case, his desperate efforts at a realistic account would still be read by many as a *roman à clef* (*S.E.* 7:9)? At other times Freud was patently prepared to erase the line between his roles as case writer, clinical pathologist, and author of creative fiction. Thus, for instance, he ends the Schreber case wondering whether the future will decide if there is unexpected delusion in his own theory and truth in Schreber's delusion (*S.E.* 12:79); he acknowledged his essay on da Vinci to be "partly fiction"[34] and that some friends might evaluate it as a "psycho-analytic novel" (*S.E.* 11:134); and he wrote the first draft of *Moses and Monotheism* under the title *The Man Moses: A Historical Novel.* Indeed, the sundry comments on aesthetics in the da Vinci essay may be applied to the essay itself, which is self-reflexive, autobiographical, scientific, and aesthetic in nature.

Freud's writings fall into many genres, among them history, biography, autobiography, letters, lectures, dialogue, case-history narratives, scientific treatises on various subjects, and the Dreambook, which is *sui generis*. In all of them we encounter, again and again, Freud the skillful storyteller. His revelation to Stekel is little known yet hardly surprising: "Freud told me once, when we were walking in the forest of Berchtesgaden, 'In my mind, I always construct novels, using my experiences as a psychoanalyst; my wish is to become a novelist—but not yet; perhaps in the later years of my life.'"[35] Only once did Freud acknowledge finding a double—the Austrian novelist and dramatist Arthur Schnitzler.[36] Bleuler, the greatest psychiatrist of the day, told Freud that however outstanding his scientific accomplishments were, he was psychologically impressive as an artist.[37] (Curiously enough, when Havelock Ellis said the same thing, Freud was indignant.[38]) Jones, for his part, saw a combination of the two aspects—scientist and artist—strikingly combined: "If William James wrote textbooks of psychology as if they were novels and his brother Henry wrote novels as if they were textbooks on psychology, Freud may be said to have combined the two aims in an enchanting degree."[39]

It is around the designation of Freud as a scientist or artist that the most serious scholarship on his work as a writer turns, and a broad study of it is in order here. There have been numerous remarks on Freud as a writer, but the number of fully developed studies on this topic is quite limited; the number of major contributions is meager indeed. Foremost among the general continental commentaries are those by Schönau, Muschg, Schotte, and Roustang. These critics' positions can be placed in terms of two questions: First, is Freud above all a scientific writer whose aesthetic powers are subordinated to expository and persuasive ends? And second, does the supposed antithesis between science and art do injustice to the unique combination found in Freud's writings? The shifting definitions frequently assigned to the basic terms of discussion and Freud's own ambivalence toward his artistic identity do not help resolve these issues. We are familiar with his acknowledgments that aesthetic literature anticipated psychoanalysis in investigating the deep strata of the human psyche; we are familiar, too, with the fact that the early Freud won greater acceptance in literary than in scientific circles; and we recall his remark that his case histories read like novels (*S.E.* 2:160). Was Freud mostly an artist? Mostly a scientist? There is no shortage of champions for either position.

The sole book-length analysis on the subject of Freud as a

literary artist is Walter Schönau's doctoral thesis, published as *Sigmund Freuds Prosa: Literarische Elemente seines Stils*.[40] His main argument is that Freud's prose is above all scholarly and not artistic, and that Freud never cultivated artistic form as an end in itself but rather continuously subordinated form to the overriding intention to instruct and convince the public, as is manifest in every page (*aus jeder Textseite*) of Freud's work. Schönau's Freud, then, is a rhetorician characterized by the conscious and rational control of expository and persuasive techniques, and accordingly particularly fond of the lecture, which Schönau holds up as a general model of scholarly prose. At times Schönau sets off in a promising direction, as when he elaborates on Freud's inventive use of well-known mottos and quotations, distorting them into new meanings and thus departing from the traditional scholarly approach with its insistence on preserving the original context. But Schönau opens this door only a crack and most uneasily; he fails fully to exploit his distinction between a writer's intended or "target" public (*Zielpublikum*) and his actual readership and paints a portrait of Freud predominantly as a writer of secondary-process and rational procedure, conforming to a traditional style without originality or creativity of his own. Schönau does not appreciate that Freud's writing *produces* knowledge rather than merely describing it, a point I cannot stress too strongly.[41] Germanists were quick to answer. Accusing Schönau of putting the cart before the horse and of ignoring Freud's double nature that achieved great things both in art and science, Politzer stresses the difference between Freud's charismatic and multifaceted style from the scholarly diction of his predecessors, contemporaries, and successors; he proposes that the unique trait of Freud's style is metaphor; and points to the development of Freud's style from the wit of the 19th-century Jewish middle class in Vienna, which was much given to puns and ambiguities.[42] Another reviewer, Hans Mayer, with whom I am in agreement, goes further still: if Schönau concedes Freud's greatness only in science whereas Politzer extends it equally to verbal artistry, Mayer rejects the scientist-artist dichotomy even on theoretical grounds; the boundaries between fiction and nonfiction have become increasingly blurred, at least since Nietzsche, if not before.[43]

Walter Muschg's classic "Freud als Schriftsteller" was, at his own wish, slightly revised and abridged by his French translator Jacques Schotte, who added a series of detailed explanatory notes and an introductory essay that are eminently valuable in their own right.[44] Taking off from the rhetorical question, Who can doubt that Freud's need to write was more powerful than his need to speak?, Muschg's essay is a beautiful and impassioned tribute to Freud as a literary artist. Muschg admires the antithetic tension Freud often builds into his titles; the tranquil assurance of the definite article in *The Interpretation of Dreams;* the attention to the well-turned phrase; the aptness of image and metaphor; the care and awareness with which he guides the reader; the narrative skill and vivid presentation of character; and the delight in recurrent themes that keep appearing in new lights. The aesthetic richness of the Dreambook contrasts sharply with the typically tortured German of Freud's contemporaries in the medical profession (*Medizinerdeutsch*)—but so does the asceticism of the *Three Essays on the Theory of Sexuality.*

Pursuing this line a step further, rejecting a "scientific" and linear reading of Freud as too simplistic, and advocating a reading that combines multiple perspectives, Schotte emphasizes that Freud's theories and psychoanalytic explanations are but fragments of a process: properly understood, the knowledge of psychoanalytic theory must be recognized as essentially incomplete, undogmatic, and processive. Freud frequently refers to beginnings, origins, base, or ground (*Grund*). Freud's continual returns to himself run parallel to the advances in his theory, the history of which is a constant search for new vistas, shaped in equal measure by Freud the man, Freud the writer, and Freud the theoretician. His works read like clinical material, with nodal points, associations, retrospective glances at past remarks, and anticipations of what is to follow.

Limiting himself to Chapter 7 of *The Interpretation of Dreams,* Roustang makes a praiseworthy attempt to explore the psychoanalytic aspects of Freud's style.[45] My own approach in this vast field has a different focus, and I can only outline the major ideas of this compact study here (realizing full well that no summary can do justice to its wealth of concentrated detail and observation). At the outset four recurrent figures of style are brought forward: *concaténation*, or the repetition of words from the end of one paragraph at the beginning of the next; *chiasmus*, or repetition of words in reverse order (e.g., "the wish of dreams" and "the dreams of the wish"); *inclusion*, or repetition of the same words at the beginning and end of a paragraph; and *péricentre*, the placement of a word or words from the periphery of one paragraph at the center of a later one.[46] These four figures of style show Freudian syntax to be maintained by what Roustang defines as *parataxis*, the placement of words in a sentence or in a series of sentences independent of the syntactic connections expressed in prepositions, conjunctions, declensions, and conjugations. With all his syntactical subtleties, and in spite of them, Freud's style effects a paratactic regression in which traces of the infantile, the archaic, and the psychoneurotic come to the fore. But parataxis takes its movement from *diataxis*, the dynamic principle of Freud's style and theory, which interrupts the order of a sentence by introducing a new element and thereby instigates another arrangement. If at the limit syntax is on the side of secondary process and parataxis on the side of primary process, diataxis is the stylistic figure of interpretation that tips discourse over, turns it back, or makes it advance. Through diataxis, analytic theory assumes the particular status of style; in Chapter 7 of *The Interpretation of Dreams* the activity of the psychic apparatus is at once the style's subject and its object; the container and contained, form and matter, are inseparable and indeed interchangeable.

Roustang's critical model belongs to what may justly be called the "French" reading of Freud, according to which his poetics (which governs its general economy and ultimate import) is rooted in the theory of repression. Freud's poetics, then, is a metaphorics of discontinuity constantly in threat of being repressed.[47] Within the same context Jacques Lacan can deny the existence of a metalanguage; and the philosopher Jacques Derrida, analyzing one of Freud's nudity dreams (*S.E.* 4:243–244), can deny that there is any formal or semantic difference between the dream and the analytical commentary.[48] In the probing words of one literary critic:

What kind of discourse is literary criticism? What is the status of psychoanalytic discourse? Can these be honestly distinguished from the discourse they take for their text, from poetry or art or somatic writing? Or why does the work of art seem more lucid than the "ridiculous terminology" (Antonin Artaud's phrase) that claims to elucidate it? . . . In short, the logic of inquiry produces a text that raises a question about the text so produced. . . . Today, by many thinkers in France, and especially by the psychoanalytic movement associated with Jacques Lacan, the unconscious ego is identified with language, or the priority of language to meaning. Literary language (the "lack" or "gap" in meaning that leads to figurative supplementation or overdetermined and ambiguous usage) is not treated as specifically literary: it is said to characterize the very structure of the psyche.[49]

Much of the "French Freud" is based on the psychoanalytic premise that the entire ego is conflictual, whereas (to generalize) the Anglo-American psychoanalytic approach, influenced by ego psychology, postulates that a large part of the ego is autonomous and conflict-free. The rejection of metalanguage and the denial of a fundamental difference between fiction and nonfiction are consistent and harmonious with the advocacy of an entirely conflictualized ego; the belief in an autonomous ego, on the other hand, is compatible with maintaining firm distinctions between fiction and nonfiction. The interdisciplinary quarrel in Anglo-American circles whether psychoanalysis is an art or a science continues, of course, undiminished, as no doubt it will for years to come. In the chapters that follow, I shall explore the makings of Freud's style and let the weight of evidence accumulate as the basis for a later chapter, in which I confront the abiding issue head-on.

The most outstanding commentator in English on Freud's style is Robert Holt, who also (perhaps not by accident) sings the death of metapsychology and ego psychology.[50] Holt's Freud is one of the handful of scientists who keep one foot in art and in whose productive creative thinking the bonds of secondary-process thinking are loosened in a dialectic of freedom and control. Holt's essay "On Reading Freud"[51] concludes with a decalogue which should be hung on permanent display in classrooms of psychoanalytic institutes just as the alphabet used to be in grammar schools. Here are some excerpts:

1.  There is no substitute for reading enough of Freud to get

his full meaning, which is almost never fully expressed in a single paragraph on no matter how specific a point.

2. Don't take Freud's extreme formulations literally. Treat them as his way of calling your attention to a point. When he says "never," "invariably," "conclusively," and the like, read on for the qualifying and softening statements.

3. Look out for inconsistencies . . . take them as incomplete dialectic formulations awaiting the synthesis that Freud's cognitive style made him consistently draw back from.

6. Be benignly skeptical about Freud's assertions of proof that something has been established beyond doubt.

8. Though he was often right, it was not always for the reasons he gave, which are almost never truly sufficient to prove his case, and not always to the extent he hoped.

However these principles were intended, all could easily be invoked by the French commentators on Freud.

The few other English essays on our subject tend to be general appreciations that do not noticeably advance our knowledge.[52] One happy exception is the superb analysis of the Dora case by the literary critic Steven Marcus, who sees Freud as a major literary artist and the Dora case as an outstanding literary work combining an imaginative and cognitive performance of the highest order and constituting (along with Freud's other case histories) a new literary genre in which creative narratives contain their own analyses and interpretations. The Dora narrative is anything but unbroken, linear, or uninflected. It is a tissue of such novelistic devices as the double plot, reversal, and inversion. For the careful reader, moreover, the unraveling story reveals that the main character is not Dora but the narrator Freud, the seeker for patterns and understanding, the archaeologist of the psyche.[53]

At this stage, a rapid historical survey of Freud's style is in order. Ideally a book such as this one ought to include a comprehensive stylistic survey, but at this point in the history of Freud studies it would present a forbiddingly vast undertaking. So far, published comment on this specific topic has been rare. William Niederland, noting that certain words and concepts occur very sparsely in Freud's earlier writings, draws attention to the fact that the word *guilt* occurs neither in the Rat Man monograph (1909) nor in the one on Schreber (1911), and adds that the use of direct discourse with the reader seems to be less frequent in Freud's later works.[54] But these statements require modification: *guilt* or *guilty* appears six times in the Rat Man case; and the later Freud, starting from the *Introductory Lectures* (1916–17), makes richer use of a kind of Socratic dialogue, replacing the *I* with the communal solidarity of *we*.[55]

But we can make some other pertinent, if rather general, observations on the history of Freud's style. As a teenager in the *Gymnasium*, Freud already wrote in what his teacher called an "idiotic" style,[56] which must not be understood in its current pejorative meaning but rather according to its Greek etymology in the sense of "personal," "individual." Even in the hectic setting of the army, a commanding officer complimented him for his well-organized writing.[57] As individual and masterly as Freud's style was, it showed great variety throughout his long writing career. In the early essay "Über Coca" (1884) there is a tone of fondness found nowhere else in Freud's formal writings. His daughter finds that her father here "comes near occasionally to being enthusiastic"[58] and for Jones, it is as if the author "were in love with the content itself."[59] "A Reply to Criticisms of My Paper on Anxiety Neurosis" (1895), a fine early demonstration of Freud's persuasive skills, was written in the same year the *Project for a Scientific Psychology* took shape, which is unique in the Freudian corpus for its sustained, rigorous, and abstract reflection. We will have more to say later about *The Interpretation of Dreams;* suffice it here to state that the Dreambook ranges in style from the relatively arid initial historical survey to the blending of analytic powers, complex theorizing, and the oneiric processes of dreams themselves and their associations.

If we go along with Freud's dictum that unclear and convoluted thought is a slip that may betray the author's distraction by a multiple target (*S.E.* 6:101; cf. also p. x), we may regard the successive editions of *The Psychopathology of Everyday Life* (originally published in 1901) with its increasingly jumbled expository form as an example of parapraxis. The mass of new examples, supposedly added to confirm the proven, in fact end up needlessly interrupting or obscuring the line of argument; all in all, the text suffered not the ravages of temporal erosion but the damage of temporal accretion. Genetically the Joke Book and the *Three*

*Essays on the Theory of Sexuality* (1905) comprise a kind of diptych: during the time of their composition they were kept on adjoining tables and Freud worked on one manuscript or the other according to his mood,[60] and yet, however closely associated the two subjects may have been in Freud's mind, little sexual content dots the pages of the Joke Book and few of his works are so ascetic in descriptive style as the *Three Essays*. As for the article "Character and Anal Erotism" (1908), which has been criticized for its unhappy literary form, blunt statements, and lack of persuasive power,[61] its lack of persuasiveness could well be due to the combined unconscious influence of two traits treated in the context of anal eroticism: the need for order, and miserliness. The second remarkable diptych in the Freudian canon is *The Interpretation of Dreams* and *Totem and Taboo*, the first of which describes the wish to kill the father, the second, the actual deed.[62]

It is easy to agree with Freud that "Observations on Transference-Love" (1915) is the best of his papers on technique,[63] but all the later ones show a new trend in his writing, becoming "more honest, bolder and more ruthless" since the irreversible confrontation with Jung.[64] The change in style coincides with a shift to greater activity during the inspirational phase of writing: "My way of working used to be different, I used to wait for an idea to come to me. Now I go out to meet it, and I do not know whether I find it any more quickly because of that."[65] Also belonging to this period is *On the History of the Psycho-Analytic Movement*, which throughout its exposition and particularly in the last section is the most belligerent of all treatises (*S.E.* 14:4). It forms a tetralogy with the contemporary "On Narcissism," the Wolf Man case (1918), which dealt more calmly with the Jung-Adler controversy, and the even colder and more dispassionate historical account in *An Autobiographical Study* (1925).

In the last twenty years of his life Freud would no longer tell even his intimates what he was working on;[66] it can hardly be a mere accident that the highly imaginative and speculative *Beyond the Pleasure Principle* (1920) introduced this phase.[67] Freud dismissed his next effort, *Group Psychology and the Analysis of the Ego* (1921), as "close to banality . . . and badly written"[68] and thought that after *The Ego and the Id* (1923) he entered a regressive phase in which he said nothing essential or truly original (*S.E.* 20:72). Although contemporary judgment would not completely agree with this self-appraisal, one may speculate on the correlation between a reactive modification of creative output, his numerous operations, and a disruption of what the early Freud called "ideational mimetics," which are crucial not only in communication but also in endopsychic representation (*S.E.* 8:192–193). With this in mind, we can understand his personal physician's remarks in a new light:

> To listen to Freud's delivery of the spoken word was [a] . . . unique experience. Anyone who met him before his surgery was impressed by it. His manner of speaking blended with the content of what he said and with his facial expression and his eyes. A good deal of this was still left after the surgery, but what had been an easy, natural flow had become a painful effort, interrupted by movements which looked like mannerisms but in reality served to make some readjustments of the prosthesis to relieve the pressure.[69]

The writings of Freud's very last years are quite uneven. *Inhibitions, Symptoms and Anxiety* (1926) exhibits a noticeable lack of unity, and in a letter to Reik, Freud admits the careless architecture of his essay on Dostoevsky (*S.E.* 21:195). In his second prefatory note to *Moses and Monotheism* Freud acknowledges his diffidence in a vivid simile: the work, he says, is like a dancer balanced on a single toe (*S.E.* 23:58).[70] But despite its disunity, which is unparalleled in his writings, the book constitutes another important diptych: just as in the progress of social psychology the early Freud went from wish in the Dreambook to deed in *Totem and Taboo*, so the later Freud went from viewing religion as sheer illusion to postulating its historical truth. In the Postscript to *An Autobiographical Study* he writes:

> In *The Future of an Illusion* I expressed an essentially negative valuation of religion. Later, I found a formula which did better justice to it: while granting that its power lies in the truth which it contains, I showed that that truth was not a material but a historical truth [*S.E.* 20:72].

Last but not least is *An Outline of Psycho-Analysis*, written in his penultimate year. Unlike his other presentations of psychoanalysis, which were always aimed at a general public, the *Outline* is addressed to advanced students. Within the Freud corpus its concision, lucidity, and organization are unsurpassed.[71] The history of Freud's psychoanalytically relevant presentations is, roughly speaking, bracketed by the *Project* and the *Outline*, and although they both share an exceptional overall deductive arrangement, there is a great difference between them: the deduction of the *Outline* is based on over forty years of clinical induction.

Reviewing the wealth of Freud's psychoanalytic productions, we are overwhelmed by the vastness of his individual achievements and yet recognize at the same time that he always seems to have more to say. In this he consciously abided by what he held to be characteristic of the classical style, as indicated by an early comment on a work by Fliess: "Throughout one feels that there is more behind you, but that you are able to put your riches aside and confine yourself within the limits laid down. I think that is the hallmark of the classic style."[72] One of the greatest among innumerable tributes to Freud's style came from another of this century's giants, Albert Einstein: "I quite specially admire your achievement [and presently in *Moses and Monotheism*], from a literary point of view. I do not know any contemporary who has presented his subject in the German language in such a masterly fashion."[73]

In the interlacing chapters that follow I hope to expand Einstein's tribute. From here, I proceed as follows: Chapter 2 provides a detailed treatment of *Totem and Taboo*, Part 4, and *Beyond the Pleasure Principle;* Chapter 3 examines the problem of audience; Chapter 4, the ramifications of certainty; Chapter 5, the intertwinings of language and analogy; Chapter 6 offers a summary view of the workings of Freud's style; Chapter 7, finally, attempts to define psychoanalytic theory as style and parapraxis. On the level of macroanalysis, which is my chief subject, I quote from the *Standard Edition;* wherever verbal nuance is critical, however, I translate directly from the *Gesammelte Werke*. The charm, flexibility, and force of Freud's Viennese expression differs markedly from the typical rigidity of his German counterparts, as it does from the formality and would-be accuracy of the English translation.

Notes

1. *The Standard Edition of the Complete Psychological Works of Sigmund Freud*, 24 Volumes, translated and edited by J. Strachey (London: Hogarth Press and the Institute of Psycho-Analysis, 1953–1974). Cited hereafter in the text and notes as *S.E.*

2. An observation by H. A. Murray, cited by P. Roazen, *Freud and His Followers* (New York: Signet, 1971), p. 10.

3. G. Levin, *Sigmund Freud* (Boston: Twayne Publishers, 1975), p. 9.

4. R. Wollheim, *Freud* (London: Fontana, 1971), p. 9.

5. R. Holt, "Freud's Cognitive Style," *American Imago*, 22:163 (1965).

6. E. Simmel, "Sigmund Freud: The Man and His Work," *Psychoanalytic Quarterly*, 9:166 (1940).

7. A. Kardiner, "Freud: The Man I Knew," in *Freud and the 20th Century*, edited by B. Nelson (New York: Meridian, 1957), p. 49.

8. L. Binswanger, *Sigmund Freud: Reminiscences of a Friendship* (New York: Grune & Stratton, 1957), p. 3.

9. E. Jones, *The Life and Work of Sigmund Freud*, 3 Volumes (New York: Basic Books, 1953–1957), Vol. 1, p. 341.

10. Cf. letter of 1.10.10, in *The Freud/Jung Letters*, edited by W. McGuire (Princeton: Princeton University Press, 1974), p. 358; see also letter of 12.5.11 (p. 422).

11. Jones: 2:42.

12. D. Anzieu, "The Sound Image of the Self," *International Review of Psycho-Analysis*, 6:23–36 (1979).

13. Letters of 17.10.09 (p. 254) and 2.1.10 (p. 282), in *Freud/Jung Letters*.

14. *After Babel: Aspects of Translation and Language* (London: Oxford University Press, 1975), and "A Note on Language and Psychoanalysis," *International Review of Psycho-Analysis*, 3:253–258 (1976).

15. Jones 3:130.

16. Jones 3:236.

17. Jones 2:155.

18. Jones 2:185, 395.

19. Letter of 20.10.95, in *The Origins of Psycho-Analysis*, edited by M. Bonaparte et al. (London: Imago, 1954), p. 129; see also letter of 6.9.99 (p. 296), and Jones 2:352, 396. I have found one exception to these typical statements, the letter of 21.9.98 (*Origins*, p. 298): "You will see that my style will improve and my ideas be better when this town affords me a prosperous livelihood."

20. Letter of 23.7.22, in M. Grotjahn's "Collector's items from the Correspondence between Sigmund Freud and Otto Rank; and from the First 'Rundbriefe' of the 'Ring Holders,'" *Journal of the Otto Rank Association*, 6:15 (1971).

21. Journal entry for 1.9.38, in S. Blanton, *Diary of My Analysis with Sigmund Freud* (New York: Hawthorn, 1971), pp. 106–107.

22. Cf. letter of 3.7.12 to Abraham, in *A Psycho-Analytic Dialogue,* edited by H. Abraham and E. Freud (London: Hogarth, 1965, p. 120), and letter of 15.4.10 to Jones, in Jones 2:64.

23. Letter of 26.2.11, in *Psycho-Analysis and Faith: The Letters of Sigmund Freud and Oskar Pfister,* edited by H. Meng and E. Freud (London: Hogarth, 1963), p. 48.

24. Letter of 12.10.11, in *Freud/Jung Letters,* p. 447.

25. J. Wortis, *Fragments of an Analysis with Freud* (New York: Simon & Schuster, 1954). Journal entry for 21.1.35 (p. 152). For a stark contrast, compare the later Helene Deutsch's need to write in order to combat loneliness and "fill my depleted existence with the past. . . . The immense enhancement of my life that comes from writing these memoirs . . . lies in the memory process itself: the intense emotions that arise when we meet or confront once more the loved and hated figures of the past" *(Confrontations with Myself* [New York: Norton, 1973], pp. 14–15).

26. See letter of 12.4.10, in *Freud/Jung Letters,* p. 306.

27. Letter of 26.4.25 to Georg Groddeck, in his *The Meaning of Illness,* edited by L. Schacht (New York: International Universities Press, 1977), p. 92.

28. Letter of 9.8.11 to Jones, cited in Jones 2:350. Freud's *Autobiographical Study* contains a rare kind of statement in which the author traces at length the genetic development of the unconscious connections underlying *Totem and Taboo,* Part 4 (S.E. 20:67–68).

29. *Freud: Master and Friend* (Cambridge: Harvard University Press, 1945), p. 97.

30. Letter of 20.10.95 to Fliess, in *Origins,* p. 129. Traces of Freud's quest for clarification appear throughout the *Project,* e.g: "A first idea might be . . . Perhaps light will be thrown on this later . . . I can see only one way out of the difficulty: a revision of our fundamental hypotheses . . . The following description is still more satisfying . . . Thus we find ourselves quite unexpectedly before the most obscure problem . . . The time has now come to qualify a hypothesis made earlier" (S.E. 1:301, 310, 362, 369, 378).

31. *Talent and Genius: The Fictitious Case of Tausk Contra Freud* (New York: Quadrangle Books, 1971), p. 277; cf. also Jones 1:342.

32. For some broader implications of this problem, see M. Sherwood, *The Logic of Explanation in Psychoanalysis* (New York: Academic Press, 1969), and P. Ricoeur, "The Question of Proof in Freud's Psychoanalytic Writing," *Journal of the American Psychoanalytic Association,* 25:863 (1977): "My thesis here is as follows: *if the ultimate truth claim resides in the case histories, the means of proof reside in the articulation of the entire network: theory, hermeneutics, therapeutics, and narration."*

33. Letter of 30.6.09, *Freud/Jung Letters,* p. 238.

34. Letter of 7.11.14 to Hermann Struck, *Letters of Sigmund Freud,* edited by E. Freud (London: Hogarth, 1961), p. 312.

35. *The Autobiography of Wilhelm Stekel,* edited by E. Gutheil (New York: Liveright Publishing Company, 1950), p. 66.

36. Letter of 14.5.22 to Schnitzler, in *Letters,* pp. 344–345.

37. Alluded to in Bleuler's letter of 5.11.13 to Freud, in F. Alexander and S. Selesnick, "Freud-Bleuler Correspondence," *Archives of General Psychiatry,* 12:6 (1965).

38. Ellis's letter of 2.10.36 to Wortis, in *Fragments of an Analysis,* p. 176.

39. Jones 2:210.

40. (Stuttgart: J. B. Metzlersche Verlag, 1968). At the end of Schönau's thesis is a collection of scattered comments on Freud's style (pp. 257–275); they are precious for their discord: on the one side are those who accuse Freud of writing restlessly, confusedly, illogically, and with a wealth of metaphor, on the other, those who see his writing as sparse, clear, concise, and typically free of metaphor. Stefan Zweig's judgment (p. 264) that Freud wrote univocally and always in sentences that are easily understood shows that even renowned creative writers are capable of an egregiously schematized reading.

41. Let us cite Professor Leipmann from Berlin, who criticized *The Interpretation of Dreams* upon publication on the grounds that "the imaginative thoughts of an artist had triumphed over the scientific investigator" (Jones 1:361). His comment is paradoxical and parapractic; he was objecting really to the book's deeper level of truth; it was precisely regression in the service of the ego that Freud brought to bear upon his own writing, as well as on his clinical listening.

42. Book review, *The German Quarterly,* 42:739 741 (1969).

43. Book review, *Psyche,* 23:951–952 (1969).

44. "Freud als Schriftsteller," *Die psychoanalytische Bewegung,* 2:467–509 (1930); translated as "Freud écrivain," *La Psychanalyse,* 5:69–124 (1959), and introduced by Schotte's essay "La Lecture de 'Freud écrivain,' " pp. 51–68.

45. F. Roustang, "Du Chapitre VII," *Nouvelle Revue de Psychanalyse,* 16:65–95 (1977). My summary of this fine, dense essay (which is notable for its two apt neologisms, *diataxis* and *péricentre)* is stitched together from direct quotations.

46. We may fruitfully apply these figures of style to the development of Freud's theories in general. For such an application of chiasmus, see Chapter 5 below.

47. These notions are expertly elaborated by J. Mehlman in his "Translator's Introduction" to J. Laplanche, *Life and Death in Psychoanalysis* (Baltimore: Johns Hopkins University Press, 1976), pp. vii–x, and his editorial introductory essay to *French Freud: Structural Studies in Psychoanalysis (Yale French Studies,* 48:5–9) (New Haven: Yale University Press, 1972).

48. "Le Facteur de la vérité," *Poétique,* 21:99–100 (1973).

49. G. Hartman, editorial preface, *Psychoanalysis and the Question of the Text* (Baltimore: Johns Hopkins University Press, 1976), pp. viii–xi. A topic of parallel interest to Freud the writer is the topic of Freud as a reader. On the latter, see S. Kofman, *Quatre romans analytiques* (Paris: Editions Galilée, 1973) (n.b. p. 14: "It seems in fact that his readings of works of fiction are in their turn fictions themselves and veritable 'novels' "); and R. Gasché, "Psicoanalisi 'come' Letteratura," in *La critica freudiana,* edited by F. Rella (Milan: Feltinelli Economica, 1977), pp. 125–164.

50. "The Past and Future of Ego Psychology," *Psychoanalytic Quarterly,* 44:550–576 (1975).

51. Introductory essay, in *Abstracts of the Standard Edition of the Complete Psychological Works of Sigmund Freud,* edited by C. Rothgeb (New York: Jason Aronson, 1973).

52. I would like to single out for special mention two articles: M. Grotjahn's "Sigmund Freud and the Art of Letter Writing," *Journal of the American Medical Association,* 200:13–18 (1967), and E. Wolf's *"Saxa Loquuntur:* Artistic Aspects of Freud's 'The Aetiology of Hysteria,' " *The Psychoanalytic Study of the Child,* edited by R. Eissler et al. (New York: Quadrangle, 1972), 26:535–554 (1971). Observing that in his letters Freud tended to change his thought in midstream, Grotjahn seems to retreat from the import of his own remark, only to conclude with a startling defense: "Such sentences appear awkward and give the translator a new problem to deal with" (p. 13). Having made a semiotically dubious distinction between the *formal aspects* of the created work, relatable mainly to the transformation of narcissism, and the *content,* relatable mainly to the vicissitudes of object love, Wolf concludes that in Freud's essay "unconsciously the need to create a work of beauty took precedence over the need to persuade. An artistic work of science became a scientific work of art" (p. 549).

53. S. Marcus, "Freud and Dora: Story, History, Case History," in *Psychoanalysis and Contemporary Science,* edited by T. Shapiro (New York: International Universities Press, 1976), 5:389–442.

54. "Freud's Literary Style: Some Observations," *American Imago,* 28:17–23 (1971).

55. Muschg, "Freud écrivain," pp. 103–104.

56. Jones 1:20.

57. Jones 1:72.

58. *Cocaine Papers by Sigmund Freud,* edited by A. Freud (New York: New American Library, 1974), p. 49. (The essay is not in *S.E.)*

59. Jones 1:82.

60. Jones 2:12.

61. Jones 2:296.

62. Avowal to Jones, 2:354.

63. Letter of 4.3.15, in *A Psycho-Analytic Dialogue,* p. 213.

64. Letter of 29.7.14, *Dialogue,* p. 187.

65. Letter of 11.12.14, *Dialogue,* pp. 204–205.

66. Jones 2:409.

67. See *An Autobiographical Study* in *Beyond the Pleasure Principle, Group Psychology,* and *The Ego and the Id,* "I have given free rein to the inclination, which I kept down for so long, to speculation" (*S.E.* 20:57). For a similar idea, cf. the letter of 12.11.38 to Marie Bonaparte, in *Letters,* p. 451.

68. Excerpt from letter to Ferenczi quoted in Jones 3:99.

69. M. Schur, *Freud: Living and Dying* (New York: International Universities Press, 1972), p. 365.

70. I am inclined to believe that the very topic of Moses disoriented Freud

so as to have a negative impact on his style. If so, Freud's insecurity was activated also in his earlier essay on Michelangelo's Moses: "The 'Moses' is anonymous partly as a pleasantry, partly out of shame at the obvious amateurishness which it is hard to avoid in papers for *Imago*, and finally because my doubts about the findings are stronger than usual, and I published it only as a result of editorial pressure" (letter of 6.4.14, in *A Psycho-Analytic Dialogue*, p. 171).

71. Cf. Strachey's notes in *S.E.* 23:5, 143; and Jones 3:257.

72. Letter of 20.9.01, in *Origins*, p. 338.

73. Letter of 4.5.39, in Jones 3:243.

# 2

# Two Sample Texts

THE TWO TEXTS CHOSEN AS SAMPLES FOR ANALYSIS ARE IN SOME WAYS opposites within the Freud canon. In the first, Part 4 of *Totem and Taboo*, Freud is surveying an immense field of anthropological literature, assessing it, working through it, and finally bringing his psychoanalytic knowledge to bear on the whole. Freud thought that its harmonic marriage of content and form made *Totem and Taboo* his best-written work, and the sensitive reader will agree.[1] We might place the five metapsychological papers, which are characterized by their highly expository quality, at the apex of an isosceles triangle, whose base extends from *Totem and Taboo* to its counterpart at the other end, *Beyond the Pleasure Principle*, "the most fascinating and baffling text of the entire Freudian *corpus*."[2] Despite their differences, then, our "opposites" exhibit a continuum of style, and the ultimate difference between them is a matter of emphasis. True, its persuasive intention, awareness of the audience, and firm rhetorical control all set *Totem and Taboo* apart from the manifest oneiric quality of the inward spiraling *Beyond the Pleasure Principle*, for which the author seems to be his own chief audience. Yet *Totem and Taboo* contains the stuff of dreams, as is evident in the book's strong mimetic factor, and the clear impact of primary process, which we could only deny at the cost of grave critical injustice. *Totem and Taboo* and *Beyond the Plea-*

24

*sure Principle* may be viewed profitably as complementary works: *Beyond the Pleasure Principle* defines death as a drive, which we see retrospectively in the compulsive repetition of totems and taboos.

Argumentation and mimetic structure are the keynote of Part 4 of *Totem and Taboo* as Freud wrestles with an immense mass of anthropological documentation and the inherent chronological problems it presents in such aspects as origin, sequence, simultaneity, and discontinuity. As it contends with the subject of time, his text becomes a temporal artifact of narrative suspense in its own right: the objective chronological difficulties spill over into the diverse mappings of origins from mythology and secondary historical sources and into Freud's own theory and narrative elaboration of it. The imbrication of shifting time levels truly imitates the enmeshing of thought and deed which preoccupies Freud at the end of his text. To set out in a dozen lines or so the full roll call of those temporal complexities may be trying for the reader, yet an adequate impression requires the full roll call of Freud's topics. They are: phylogeny and ontogeny in general, and in particular, the origin and development of totemism and its relation to exogamy (antecedent? consequent? simultaneous?); the orientation to past, present, and future time within totemic practice itself; the originality and development of anthropological scholarship on totemism; developmental distortions in anthropological reflection (primitive races are old, not young, and their original ideas are now being distorted; given our psychic constellations, we are liable to misinterpret primitive races just as we do children); Frazer's erroneous conjecture based on Arunta practices that actually (*pace* Frazer) represent totemism not at its beginnings but in its final stage of dissolution; Freud's own reordering of the sequence of Frazer's scholarship and his acknowledgment that he, Freud, must condense secondary data and distort the time factor by abbreviation of his own reconstruction; the periodic retrospective and prospective references to other parts of *Totem and Taboo;* and finally the temporal complications inherent in such psychoanalytic conceptions as deferred obedience, the continuity of collective memory, and the chronological separability of thought and deed among neurotics and primitive men.

The temporal complexity extends to the reader's involvement. Freud's writing is a product of his own free-floating attention, but the level of its cognitive functioning is typically above average, analogous to the kind of analytic listening that goes on during a first session, the termination of treatment, or a period of crisis. In Part 4 of *Totem and Taboo*, high crests of synthesizing concentration are abundantly in evidence: they are followed by stretches of relaxed thinking and primary process. Freud makes explicit his expectation that the reader pay correspondingly intensified free-floating attention, hovering over the mass of detail, judging and remembering, and after a certain point gently calling the reader to account for it.

We are now prepared to follow the progression and structure of Part 4 of *Totem and Taboo*, beginning with the brief prologue (p. 100). With a rhetorical flourish, Freud reassures his audience that psychoanalysis will not overstep its bounds by reducing religion to a single source; surely its etiology must be complex, and be-sides, is it not psychoanalysis itself that first brought overdeter-minism to light? Then, with typical deterministic flair, in a maneuver to ward off offense at his treatment of the touchy sub-ject of religion, Freud carefully makes the case for the honor and moral responsibility of psychoanalysis: "psycho-analysis is compelled—and is indeed, in duty bound—to lay all the empha-sis upon one particular source," whose relative value among all possible sources he humbly leaves to the interdisciplinary re-search of the future to determine. His rhetorical stance is that of an ethical speaker, modest and committed to the truth. All in all, the tone is most appropriate for an opening.

Section 1 (pp. 100–108) presents us with a Freud who, charac-teristically, feels "obliged" by his purpose to deepen his investiga-tion, and who refers to Reinach's *Code du totémisme* for "reasons which will presently become clear." After enumerating Reinach's twelve principles, Freud announces that he will show the code to be defective. As an emerging corrective, he presents in over five pages (without commentary) two other detailed explanations of totemism (Frazer's and Wundt's), forewarning the reader of gen-eral chronological obstacles inherent in the subject. Using the editorial *we*, Freud now merges with the reader: "If we seek to penetrate to the original nature of totemism . . . the following essential traits yield themselves to us."[3] Only then does he specify Reinach's two shortcomings, appealing to the reader's hovering attention: "We shall now, perhaps, be struck by the fact that in Reinach's *Code du totémisme* one of the two principal taboos, that of exogamy, is not mentioned at all, while the belief upon which the second one is founded, namely descent from the totem animal, is only referred to in passing" (p. 107).[4]

In the section's closing sentence Freud explains his dialectical reason for using Reinach in the first place: "to prepare us for the differences of opinion between the authorities—differences into which we must now enter" (pp. 107–108). In this way, it is as if Freud the stage director, rather than presenting a stage already set at the rise of the curtain, had opted to arrange it with the curtain up, a technique I shall examine more fully in a later chapter. For now, be it said that in Section 1, as Freud goes about formulating the original nature of totemism, he takes Reinach as his straw man; consequently his retrospection and anticipation, instead of being merely expository, function within a dialectically argumentative framework.

Section 2 (pp. 108–126) is the longest and most complicated of the seven sections; it has its own prologue, followed by a subsection on "The Origin of Totemism" and two fused subsections entitled "The Origin of Exogamy and its Relation to Totemism."[5] The prologue itself advocates gaining a psychological and historical understanding of totemism and exogamy through a study of their origins. At this strategic point, Freud does not in fact chiefly discuss totemism and exogamy in themselves but rather the past and present scholarship, as well as the scholarly treatment that is to follow in his own treatises; thus the temporal complexities of the secondary literature sound a counterpoint to his own main subject matter.

The opening sentence shifts from past to present, and once more a pressing note is sounded:

> The more incontestable became the conclusion that totemism constitutes a regular phase in all cultures, the more urgent became the need for arriving at an understanding of it and for throwing light upon the puzzle of its essential nature. Everything connected with totemism seems to be puzzling . . . [p. 108].

Freud then goes on to say what a satisfactory explanation *should* do, tells his readers that they *will* be surprised by the variety and divergency of hypotheses, meanwhile underscoring the precariousness of advancing any generalization in the matter. Elsewhere Freud often anticipates his rational arguments; here he situates the reader differently, anticipating the audience's affective response of surprise. Everything is flux, and the mutable Frazer is quoted admiringly: "I have changed my views repeatedly, and I am resolved to change them again with every change of the evidence, for like a chameleon the candid inquirer should shift his colours with the shifting colours of the ground he treads" (p. 108 fn.).[6]

Grappling with the origin of totemism, Freud first treats the nominalist theories and initially elects a deductive procedure: "My accounts of these theories will justify my having brought them under the title I have adopted" (p. 110). The last theory to be considered is that of Andrew Lang, whose hypotheses contain psychological elements, and in the course of two short paragraphs Freud resorts once more to his favorite prospective and retrospective device:

> The second part of his theory goes on to try to explain how the names in fact originated; as we shall see, it is of a very different character from the first part. . . . The hypothesis that in the course of time the origin of these names was forgotten connects this part of Lang's theory with the other part which I have already discussed [pp. 112–113].

Following the nominalist theories come the sociological and psychological ones; let us dwell momentarily on the former. In the treatment of the sociological theories Freud reserves Frazer's for last. After a typical anticipation (the promise to deal with Frazer's psychological theory later) Freud artfully weaves Frazer's reasoning into his own sociological theory: "Two factors seem to have led Frazer to suppose . . ." "Frazer came all at once to see . . ." "Frazer accepted the Arunta tradition that each totem clan had originally eaten its own totem without restriction. But it was then difficult to understand the next stage in development . . ." "Frazer, however, makes no disguise of the difficulties . . . nor does he venture to suggest . . ." After this long rehearsal of Frazer, Freud's refutation is climactically swift: Frazer's hypothesis stands or falls on his presumption that Arunta totemic practices are the oldest form. But no, they seem rather to be advanced stages of totemism in dissolution.

Prefacing his examination of the origin of exogamy and its relation to totemism, Freud looks backward and forward yet again, expressing concern that his recital of theories thus far has suffered by compression but announcing that he must resort to even further condensation for the reader's sake. The style is marked by such typical features as animated determinism ("I cannot resist referring, too, to") and peremptory declarations in the place of reasoned refutation ("Thus the view . . . must be abandoned" rather than "Thus the view is refuted"). But the main purpose of his method at this point is to swamp the reader with conflicting views about exogamy, totemism, and incest, leading after several pages of summary, to this seeming impasse: "We are ignorant of the origin of the horror of incest and cannot even tell in what direction to look for it. None of the solutions of the enigma that have been proposed seems satisfactory" (p. 125). He closes with a dramatic, crescendo reprise of the very problem with which the section began: the section is encased in mutually reflecting mirrors: "It is a little difficult to bring these two points of view into harmony: according to the first theory exogamy would have originated before totemism, while according to the second it would have been derived from it" (p. 126).

Part Four of *Totem and Taboo* is entitled "The Return of Totemism in Childhood," but in fact Freud does not broach childhood until Section 3. (Bearing in mind that totemism issues from the Oedipus complex, we may read the book's heading the other way around: "The Origin of Totemism in Childhood.") The photic imagery with which the section begins and ends provides coherence: into the *"obscurity"* (p. 126) of totemism, psychoanalytic explanations of children's animal phobias by the Oedipus complex cast a single ray of *"light"* (pp. 126 and 132); time and time again Freud deftly calls attention to his own discourse and procedure, especially by his penchant for what we may call "metadiscourse," by means of which temporal markers point to the discourse's own temporal flow: "In order to pursue this possibility, we shall have, in the *following* pages, to study a feature of the totemic system (or, as we might say, of the totemic religion) which I have *hitherto* scarcely found an opportunity of mentioning" (p. 132; italics mine).

Section 4, like a contrasting musical movement, is in another key: there is no psychoanalysis, but merely the aim to explain and establish Robertson Smith's hypothesis that "the sacramental killing and communal eating of the totem animal, whose consumption was forbidden on all other occasions, was an important feature of totemic religion" (p. 139). Freud characteristically expresses his regret at having to omit details in his summary, which sporadically gives the impression of oral argument: "Let us now turn to the sacrificial animal. As we have heard. . . . We have heard how in later times . . ."[7]

The tempo steps up dramatically at the beginning of Section 5 in which Freud invites us to imagine the awesome spectacle of an ongoing totemic meal, shifting thence to a new contextual scene as he continues to trace the evolution of ideation:

> If, now, we bring together the psycho-analytic translation of the totem with the fact of the totem meal and with Darwin's theories of the earliest state of human society, the possibility of a deeper understanding emerges—a glimpse of a hypothesis which may seem fantastic . . . [p. 141].

But pursuing this line of thought ends in a stalemate; Darwin's primal horde does not resolve the question of beginnings, and Freud once more has recourse to the totem meal: "If we call the celebration of the totem meal to our help, we shall be able to find an answer." But now, instead of another imaginary staging and dramatization, he switches to discussion in the prose fictional mode, beginning with one of the most famous of all fictional formulas: *One day (eines Tages)*. The phrase is followed immediately by an exponential footnote reference. We do not continue but drop our eyes to the bottom of the page where we read: "To avoid possible misunderstandings, I must ask the reader to take into account the final sentences of the following footnote as a corrective to this description." What now? Do we continue to read the main body of the text with its inaccuracy hovering in our memory? Do we refuse to suspend our attention and race instead to the final lines of the subsequent footnote? Momentarily caught up between the fictive device and typographical byplay where one footnote prefaces another, we are nostalgically driven back to carry on after the fairy-tale opener. For analysts of a later generation the story has a familiar ring anyway, evoking Freud's primal-horde theory, his myth of the primal parricide. And then comes the literary, palinodic corrective of the footnote:

> The lack of precision in what I have written in the text above, its abbreviation of the time factor and its compression of the whole subject-matter, may be attributed to the reserve necessitated by the nature of the topic. It would be as foolish to aim at exactitude in such questions as it would be unfair to insist upon certainty [pp. 142–143].

This fictional mode gives way to a more expository kind of historical reconstruction centered on deferred obedience, by which the parricidal brothers forbade murder and incest and ambivalently founded totemic religion. After surveying this temporal complexity of deferral, Freud offers a one-sentence conclusion whose diversified elements majestically orchestrate a whole series of temporal complexities, embracing the time of Freud's own exposition, two different periods of anthropological scholarship, and the origin of totemism and exogamy (simultaneous with deferred obedience):

> Thus psycho-analysis, in contradiction to the more recent views of the totemic system but in agreement with the earlier ones, requires us to assume that totemism and exogamy were intimately connected and had a simultaneous origin [p. 146].

Section 6 begins with the author reflecting on his expository decisions:

> A great number of powerful motives restrain me from any attempt at picturing the further development of religions from their origin in totemism to their condition to-day. I will only follow two threads whose course I can trace with especial clarity as they run through the pattern: the theme of the totemic sacrifice and the relation of son to father [p. 146].

In saying that sacrificial activity "throws a searching retrospective light" and "confesses . . . to the fact," Freud seems to personify the activity as a collaborator or expositor who proffers aid and helps clarify the investigation.

The theanthropic sacrifice of the god, into which it is unfortunately impossible for me to enter here as fully as into animal sacrifice, throws a searching retrospective light upon the meaning of the older forms of sacrifice. It confesses, with a frankness that could hardly be excelled, to the fact that . . . [p. 151].[8]

Freud lightens the heaviness of the material by such rhetorical devices as merging with his audience and blending the logical and pathetical appeals:

> But we are relieved from the necessity for further discussion by the consideration . . . [p. 148].
>
> But in our attempts at understanding this situation we must beware of interpretations which seek . . . [p. 149].

The climactic Section 7 posits the Oedipus complex as the nucleus of religion, morals, society, and art. Additionally it postulates the central concept of the collective mind and the continuity of the emotional life of man,[9] and by virtue of that continuity, a creative sense of guilt that prevents repeated parricide. In the course of the description, cognitive processes are paraded in the arena of drives and determinism: "I shall *resist* the *temptation* of pointing out these traces . . ." ". . . this fact cannot *blind* us to the uncertainties of my premises or the difficulties involved in my conclusions. I will only mention two of the latter which may have *forced* themselves on the notice of a number of my readers" (italics mine). In keeping with this device, Freud tends to overpower the reader with suggestion: "No one could have failed to observe . . ."; ". . . direct communication and tradition—which are the first things that occur to one . . ."; "We are justified in believing . . ." (a favorite expression of Freud's as we shall see in the next chapter). But an even more prominent trait of the following pages is the display of a dialectical movement of starts, modifications, and resumptions, which makes Freud's prose itself suitably psychoanalytic. I have extracted evidence of this procedure from the closing pages of Section 7 (pp. 156–160):

> I will cut the discussion short and give a quick reply. . . . That being so, it is easy to understand. . . . One possible assumption is. . . . In particular, I have supposed. . . . I have supposed. . . . It must be admitted that these are grave difficulties; and any explanation that could avoid presumptions of such a kind would seem to be preferable. Further reflection, however, will show that

I am not alone in the responsibility for this bold procedure. . . .
A part of the problem seems to be met. . . . The problem would
seem even more difficult if we had to admit. . . . In this way we
should avoid the necessity for deriving the origin. . . . No damage would thus be done to the causal chain. . . . To this it may
be objected. . . . This is a powerful argument, but not a conclusive one. . . . And if it is further argued . . . this further objection carries just as little weight.

The ending of *Totem and Taboo* crests with declaratory acro-
batics. Whereas Freud hitherto had postulated that the primal
horde of brothers realized their first wish of killing their father but
had to abandon their second wish of becoming like him (p. 148),
in the last three pages of the book the relationship between the
primitives' wishes and deeds as compared to those of neurotics is
subjected to a series of revisions. First of all, he contrasts the
deed-oriented primitives to neurotics, who overvalue psychic
reality:

> The earliest moral precepts and restrictions in primitive society
> have been explained by us as reactions to a deed which gave
> those who performed it the concept of 'crime.' They felt remorse
> for the deed and decided that it should never be repeated and
> that its performance should bring no advantage. This creative
> use of guilt still persists among us. . . . [Among neurotics, how-
> ever we] find no deeds, but only impulses and emotions, set
> upon evil ends but held back from their achievement. What lie
> behind the sense of guilt of neurotics are *always psychical* realities
> and *never factual* ones [p. 159; italics added for the words *always*
> and *never*].

But suddenly this line of thinking takes an abrupt turn; alluding
to his previous demonstration that primitives are characterized by
their belief in the omnipotence of thoughts, Freud temporarily
assumes a similarity between primitives and neurotics, proceeding to defeat two mock counterarguments.

In the next paragraph, a veritable tour de force, Freud proceeds to undercut his analogy and its implications:

> Let us, then, examine more closely the case of neurosis—
> comparison with which led us into our present uncertainty. It is
> not accurate to say that obsessional neurotics, weighed down
> under the burden of an excessive morality, are defending them-

> selves only against *psychical* reality and are punishing themselves
> for impulses which were merely *felt*. *Historical* reality has a share
> in the matter as well. . . . The analogy between primitive men
> and neurotics will therefore be far more fully established if we
> suppose that in the former instance, too, psychical reality—as to
> the form taken by which we are in no doubt—coincided at the
> beginning with factual reality: that primitive men actually *did*
> what all the evidence shows that they intended to do [pp. 160–
> 161].

In sum, primitives and neurotics are now alike in that at the
beginning their psychic and factual reality coincided. The reader is
no sooner set in this position than unhorsed:

> Nor must we let ourselves be influenced too far in our judge-
> ment of primitive men by the analogy of neurotics. There are
> distinctions, too, which must be borne in mind. It is no doubt
> true that the sharp contrast that *we* make between thinking and
> doing is absent in both of them. But neurotics are above all
> *inhibited* in their actions: with them the thought is a complete
> substitute for the deed. Primitive men, on the other hand, are
> *uninhibited:* thought passes directly into action. With them it is
> rather the deed that is a substitute for the thought. And that is
> why, without laying claim to any finality of judgement, I think
> that in the case before us it may safely be assumed that in the
> beginning was the Deed' [p. 161].

Here Freud is caught up in the age-old (unoriginal) question about
origins, Which came first, the egg or the chicken?—if (in-deed)
the chicken came after.

If we consider the ending of *Totem* semiotically, we note the
irony between suspension of finalized judgment and the typographical finality of the last sentence which, in another reversal,
sends us back to the beginning. In other words, the text ends
with a return to the beginning of history, but this ending (and
also beginning!) is not conceived as being final. Thus the text is
"open-ended" just as the mythical origin of history is. Not granting his conclusion conclusiveness, Freud thrusts beyond both his
text and his proposed conception of history. In a narrow sense, he
lets himself and his text be woven by the loom of history itself,
and his final words on his subject are not his final thoughts. His
speculation grandly reaches back to the time before the deed,
beyond the historical principle.

In his outstanding essay "Legs de Freud," Jacques Derrida's main enterprise is to apply Freud's model to his own text.[10] Concentrating on Chapter 2 of *Beyond the Pleasure Principle,* Derrida shows with immense dexterity and sensitivity how as a piece of writing it is the product of repetition and detour. Four times in the chapter, Derrida explains, Freud attempts to explain the phenomenon of repetition, each time interrupting his train of thought and declaring his argument to be without any conclusive result. Moreover, "Down to the detail, we can see an overlapping between the description of the family grandson's *fort/da* and the speculative game, likewise so attentive and repetitive, of the grandfather writing 'Beyond' " (p. 96). Continuing in the same vein, Derrida observes that Freud "writes what he writes, he describes what he describes but also what he does, he does what he describes, namely what Ernst does: *fort/da* with his reel" (p. 111); the upshot is not only that the text of *Beyond the Pleasure Principle* has a mimetic structure but also that it is a performance in itself (pp. 98, 113).

Derrida's insights may be supplemented by considering Freud's text in terms of *three* movements: retrogressive, progressive, and a combination of the two. The instincts in general are conservative; they endeavor to restore an earlier state of things (I shall return to this notion below). The death instinct in particular drives on to reach its final aim as quickly as possible—the end is a time before the beginning; the representation of the traumatic past in repetition compulsion functions within the economy of the death instinct.

The complex movement of Freud's text starts with the first word of the title. Besides meaning "out of the reach and sphere of," the word *beyond* takes on the quality, as the text proceeds, of a linguistic "shifter." Shifters (such as the temporal and spatial adverbs *here, now, there, tomorrow*) assume part of their meaning by reference to the speaker who utters them. As a shifter *beyond* means "farther on" or "on the other side" as opposed to "on this side." In the middle of Chapter 1 we are told that the pleasure principle does not dominate the mental processes (p. 9). With all the examples of repetition, the text gathers its own momentum, and Freud says at the close of Chapter 2 that there is something "more primitive" than the pleasure principle, but he does not name it. His statement propels the reader on into Chapter 3, which names the compulsion to repeat, concluding that we must further meditate on the repetitive force which is *"more primitive, more elementary, more instinctual* than the pleasure principle . . . to which . . . we have *hitherto* ascribed dominance over the course of the processes of excitation in mental life" (*S.E.* 18:23; italics mine). The *beyond* is also a *before*. In a series of progressive stages Freud's text promises and refers to further clarification of the key concept; this concept is by definition retrogressive. What Freud finally arrives at is the most primordial; his destination is a point of radical beginning, arrived at by the monumental irony of his unfolding exposition. Hence, reflecting on the complete text, the reader sees that the very first word of the title, *Beyond,* is Janus-faced: it epitomizes a reversible movement which characterizes the text not only as exposition but also as performance, describable in terms of "acting out," a writing about and also a writing in and a writing out. And it is noteworthy that the word *beyond* not only appears in the title but is placed in the initial position, and hence is preceded by that arch-representative of death, an empty space.

Freud fittingly devotes Chapter 1 to what he regarded as the basis of metapsychology, economic theory; within economics, he goes directly to tension, its activating basis. "We believe . . . that the course of . . . events is invariably set in motion by an unpleasurable tension, and that it takes a direction such that its final outcome coincides with a lowering of that tension" (p. 7). Dealing with psychic beginnings, Freud's text dismisses, in a mimetic kind of counterthrust, the importance of textual precedent: "Priority and originality are not among the aims that psycho-analytic work sets itself." Found on the opening page of his own text, the statement recalls another text that deals with beginnings, "The 'Uncanny,' " which begins with Freud's announcement of his interest in a "remote" subject on which his research has been limited, especially with reference to "foreign" literature, so that he presents his paper to the reader "without any claim to priority."

Chapter 1 of *Beyond the Pleasure Principle* makes a powerful beginning, taking off from the first word of its title. It differs—appropriately—from the other chapters of the book in its freedom from imagistic analogies and its sparing use of references—indeed, there is only a single reference to other work; it is to

Fechner. As a conglomeration of returns, repetitions, detours, involutions, and in its mimicry of rational and affective processes, Chapter 1 serves as a model, a source of pattern or return, for subsequent chapters. When exposition involutes, turns in on itself instead of progressing, may it not be modified by primary process and the pleasure principle? Does not thought in its swift divergence show the influence of instinctual traces? Does this influence invalidate "reasoned" conclusions? Or does this particular verbalized kind of speculation concerning the instincts in fact mimic them? The answer is that such exposition eminently exhibits and stresses instinctual traces. But Freud's prose does not merely dramatize and mirror; it also has reflective, rational value. More than that of any other analyst, Freud's prose is bilateral, Janus-faced, amphibian, poised between showing and doing, between enactment and description, reflecting and giving witness, primary and secondary process, affect and rationality, impulse and analysis; it hovers between the conscious and the unconscious; it is a borderline prose, thus very authentically "psychoanalytic." Window and mirror *together* constitute the proper image for characterizing his speculative prose; and let us reflect that the word *speculative* comes from the Latin *speculum*, which means "mirror."

A fine early example of Freudian double take occurs in a passage that relates the principle of pleasure to the principle of constancy. The semantic value of these two terms, their scientific discovery, and the interwoven order in which Freud places them in his sentences give the startling impression of two opposite boomerang trajectories, one clockwise, the other counterclockwise, intersecting in midair:

> The facts which have caused us to believe in the dominance of the pleasure principle in mental life also find expression in the hypothesis that the mental apparatus endeavours to keep the quantity of excitation present in it as low as possible or at least to keep it constant. This latter hypothesis is only another way of stating the pleasure principle. . . . The pleasure principle follows from the prinple of constancy: actually the latter principle was inferred from the facts which forced us to adopt the pleasure principle [p. 9].

Yet the pleasure principle is not dominant; if it were, most of our experiences would either be pleasurable or lead to pleasure, "whereas universal experience completely contradicts such a conclusion." But a nuance is lost in translation: Strachey's adverb *completely* is a woefully inadequate equivalent for Freud's *energisch*, "energetically" (*G.W.* 14:5). The brilliantly allusive use of *energisch* fuses description with re-presentation; the *conception* of psychic reality as energy fuses with the *experience* of that reality as energy, whereby the energy theory is "energetically" confirmed.

If the historicizing Freud of *Totem and Taboo* closed with the observation that "In the beginning was the Deed," the metapsychological Freud focuses on the unpleasurable tension by action of which the psychic apparatus is set in motion. The total extinction of tension—as opposed to its mere diminution—leads to death; and to the degree that extinction is direct, the pleasure principle is immediately serviceable to the death instincts, whose aim is to follow the quickest path to the previous state of inorganicity (p. 41). But there are other paths, too: the detours, "the long indirect road," chosen by the reality principle, for example (p. 10); the "roundabout paths" traced by the return of the repressed (p. 11); and in general, the option of the life instincts for "circuitous paths" that "prolong the journey" (pp. 38–39, 41). In his borderline prose, Freud's subsequent examination of the death instinct itself courses via detours laid down by impulse and mentation. As he says much later, toward the end of the journey set in motion by the high-tension prose of Chapter 1, "it is impossible to pursue an idea of this kind except by *repeatedly* combining factual material with what is purely speculative and thus diverging widely from empirical observation. . . . One may have made a lucky hit or one may have gone shamefully astray" (p. 59; italics mine). We gain a further understanding of this unleashed, pulsating prose when we understand that it is a leashing of rational process onto impulse, a harnessing of the black horse of passion and the white horse of reason. The very talking about the pleasure principle, about its precedence and dominance, yields to repetition and resumption not merely conceptually but also on the lexical level:

> The facts which have caused us to believe in the dominance of the pleasure principle in mental life also find expression in . . . [p. 9].

It must be pointed out, however, that strictly speaking it is incorrect to talk of the dominance of the pleasure principle over the course of mental processes [p. 9].

To Derrida's masterful analysis of Chapter 2, I would like to add some supplementary notes. If Chapter 1 concentrates on economic theory, the elementary factor in Freudian metapsychology, Chapter 2 moves into the arena of clinical observation, opening with remarks on accidents of war and continuing, significantly, with a return to one of the earliest activities, child's play. Specifically, Ernst's repeated *fort/da* game with the wooden reel repeats his mother's absence; the game, repeatedly observed by his grandfather, was repeated in its variant of the mirror game (p. 15 fn.). These playful exercises of the one-and-a-half-year-old child prepared him to react well to future but more solemn reenactments of parental departure: his reaction at two and a half when his father went off to war, and at five and three-quarters when his mother died.

But let us return to the play of the child, the theories of which, Freud finds, "fail to bring into the foreground the *economic* motive," the "consideration of [or more literally, the looking back at (*Rücksicht*)] the yield of pleasure involved" (p. 14; *G.W.* p. 11). In Ernst's case, the game is related to his instinctual renunciation, and it is indifferent "from the point of view of judging the affective [*affektive*; hence not "effective," as in *S.E.* p. 15] nature of the game whether the child invented it himself or took it over on some outside suggestion." Yet the more intriguing question remains as to how the game based on an unpleasurable experience relates to the nature of the repetition compulsion. At this crucial point Freud's apparently lucid prose proves defiantly elusive: either the child was motivated to turn a passive situation into an active one and thereby achieve mastery, or his throwing away (*Wegwerfen*) of the reel was his way of sending his mother away (*weg*)[11] and thereby achieving revenge. For the rest of the long paragraph and throughout the next Freud elaborates on this divergence until he silently collapses the disjunction between mastery and revenge: "As the child passes over from the passivity of the experience to the activity of the game, he hands on the disagreeable experience to one of his playmates and in this way revenges himself on a substitute" (p. 17).

If we pursue further Derrida's notion that Chapter 2 is as autobiographical as it is heterobiographical, we may note the covert emergence of the grandfather's surname in his account of his grandson's "joyful" (*freudig,* G.W. p. 12) *da,* which constituted a game preliminary to the mother's "joyful" (*erfreulich,* G.W. p. 13) return. Yet the most spectacular and certainly subliminal presence of the surname announces itself in a microanalysis of Ernst's verbal play. The *f* and *t* of *fort* are unvoiced dental consonants; they contrast with the *d* of *da,* the word of presence. The phonation of the phonetically complex marked *d* involves going back and down in the mouth and vibrating the larynx; the resulting sound is thus "more present" in the body. Similarly, the *o* of *fort* calls the frontal organ of rounded lips into play, whereas the *a* of *da* is unrounded. The anterior and posterior vowels and consonants of *fort* and *da* are homologously related to the words' semantic content: Anteriority accords with absence (*fort*); posteriority, with presence (*da*). The *eu* of *Freud,* a diphthong phonated as a glide from back to front, is a phonetic mimesis of the act of tossing the reel away. For this reason, the grandfather's name is subliminally present in the grandson's game of absence and presence; this subliminal presence might constitute another, certainly unconscious, reason for the author's fascination with the boy's game.[12] All in all, these phonetic phenomena act out—or better yet, talk out—a central tenet of the entire essay, which states that we are caught in a *Zauderrhythmus,* vacillating between the retrogressive death drive and the forward detours taken by Eros.

Chapter 3 displays a more subdued tone, and we feel less authorial involvement. Chapter 2 was dominated by a family centerpiece; the example bore far-reaching meaning, but it was insufficient material for the scientific demonstration of a principle beyond the pleasure principle. Domestic observation of little Ernst now gives way to clinical observation of adult transference neurosis, the multiple manifestations of which confirm the compulsion to repeat. In the transference neurosis the patient by himself is blind to the fact that his repeated acts are a "reflection" (*Spiegelung*) of his forgotten past (p. 19; G.W. p. 17), this reflection being a refracted example of what he also might have done repetitively as a child, as Ernst continually looks at himself in a full-length mirror (p. 15 fn.; *Standspiegel*, *G.W.* p. 13 fn.). As though repetition itself were the message, Freud feels obliged to reiterate in the closing part of this section that the compulsion to repeat overrides the pleasure principle.

Starting with Chapter 4,[13] all the chapters, save the last, are much longer. This change is not just a matter of length; it is the consequence of a radical departure in procedure:

> What follows is speculation, often far-fetched speculation, which the reader will consider or dismiss according to his individual predilection. It is a further attempt to follow out an idea consistently, out of curiosity to see where it will lead [p. 24].

It is for no superficial reason that Freud does not postulate the death instinct until embarking on this self-abandonment and unbinding.

To understand how Chapter 4 will proceed, we must go back and reread the conclusion of the previous chapter:

> But if a compulsion to repeat *does* operate in the mind, we should be glad to know something about it, to learn what function it corresponds to, under what conditions it can emerge and what its relation is to the pleasure principle—to which, after all, we have hitherto ascribed dominance over the course of the processes of excitation in mental life [p. 23].

At this point, then, while staking out a claim for the dominance of the repetition compulsion, Freud looks back ("hitherto") to when he assigned that dominance to the pleasure principle. But how will Freud proceed? Where to after mapping out the reality of the repetition compulsion? The answer is surprising. For the first half of Chapter 4 Freud explains the dominance of the pleasure principle! Is this a contradictory move? Or does not this repetitive elaboration about the dominance of the pleasure principle, by virtue of its very repetition, somewhat subvert the overt statement? Does not the repetition in its own way reflect, however obscurely, the dominance of the repetition compulsion? It cannot be otherwise if we pause to reconsider the summary statement placed midway in the chapter:

> I have an impression that these last considerations have brought

us to a better understanding of the dominance of the pleasure principle; but no light has yet been thrown on the cases that contradict that dominance. Let us therefore go a step further [p. 29].

But let us return to the beginning of the chapter (which is the middle chapter of the book). Just after resolving to indulge in free speculation, Freud states the point of departure for psychoanalytic speculation: that consciousness may not be the most universal trait of mental processes. This concern for point of departure, being midway in the book, is part of a symmetrical structure, repeating the concern for point of departure which, with mimetic appropriateness, is itself the starting point of *Beyond the Pleasure Principle* as text, namely the proposition that the course of all mental events is set in motion by unpleasurable tension.

Carefully following Freud through this midway point, we notice that the psychoanalytic starting point of consciousness leads him to define consciousness as a function of the system *Pcpt.-Cs.*, which itself is a midway point, a Janus-faced element, but of spatial rather than temporal nature, like *beyond*: "It must lie on the borderline between outside and inside; it must be turned towards the external world and must envelop the other psychical systems" (p. 24). From here on, Freud reiterates his running concern with origins, this time the origin of consciousness. To explain that origin, Freud has recourse to the example of the most original living organism, an undifferentiated vesicle, and the subsequent origin of its protective shield against stimuli. Three times Freud begins to talk of the vesicle and its protective shield, and three times the subject is broken off to deal with the nature of consciousness. This repeated interruption of Freud's exposition in the first half of Chapter 4 mimetically anticipates the subject matter of the second half: the origin of traumatic neuroses, described as a break or breach (*Einbruch, Durchbruch*) in the psyche's protective shield against stimuli. And how may dreams psychically bind traumatic impressions? By obeying the compulsion to repeat. The wheel has come full circle.

Before proceeding further into the intricate coursing of Freud's repetition, we must briefly regain our bearings; and to do so, we can have no better recourse than to Jones's observation that Freud's "mode of writing" in *Beyond the Pleasure Principle* "in itself indicates that the ideas propounded must be transmuted from some personal and profound source."[14] Thus, although repetition compulsion has to do, strictly speaking, with repressed material, Freud's mode of repetitive writing in the text at hand is evidence of the repetition compulsion. Besides explaining the repetition compulsion with new material, Freud explains it by resuming a previous explanation; the effect recalls two facing mirrors endlessly reflecting each other. Here is a resounding instance:

> The manifestations of a compulsion to repeat (which we have described as occurring in the early activities of infantile mental life as well as among the events of psycho-analytic treatment) exhibit to a high degree an instinctual character and, when they act in opposition to the pleasure principle, give the appearance of some 'daemonic' force at work. In the case of children's play we seemed to see that children repeat unpleasurable experiences for the additional reason that they can master a powerful impression far more thoroughly by being active than they could by merely experiencing it passively. Each fresh repetition seems to strengthen the mastery they are in search of [p. 35].

The statement gives rise to the question whether Freud, like an analytic patient, remembers or repeats. Is he not, through his interlocking repetition, struggling for mastery over that "personal and profound source" Jones postulates?

In an effort to relate the repetition compulsion to the instincts, a relation "repeatedly" proposed by other authors (p. 36 fn.), Freud's own use of repetition is extraordinary. To trace the relationship he advances, it is best to look ahead to the passage where he speaks of the life of organisms being governed by a "vacillating rhythm" (p. 41; *Zauderrhythmus*, *G.W.* p. 43), according to which the ego instincts rush forward on the shortest path to their final aim while other instincts deliberately take detours— detours to which the text has repeatedly, though divergently, referred (pp. 37–40). This vacillating rhythm, this *Zauderrhythmus*, dominates Freud's "prose speech" on the subject of the vacillating rhythm of the instincts. He even vacillates in attributing a sole forward movement to the life instincts: these too have their countercurrents. In Freud's revolutionary composition the form and content of the discourse become undifferentiated in a mimetic structure; and since the mimetic structure is also performative, the gap between the act of writing and what is written vanishes, and the two are wrapped into one.

Let us now return for a closer look at the way Freud develops his italicized premise that an instinct seems to be *"an urge inherent in organic life to restore an earlier state of things"* (p. 36). The repetitive character of fish and bird migrations, the recapitulation of phylogeny in ontogeny, the regeneration of lost organs in animals—these examples bear witness to the truth of Freud's premise. Then Freud raises the objection that instincts may exist that contradict his notion, that "push forward" and progress to new forms and hence are not conservative. He concedes the seriousness of this objection, but defers treatment of it for later, acknowledging that it will modify his present assertions. (To use Roustang's fine term, the moment of diataxis has not yet come.) Meanwhile—ironically—Freud pushes forward with his theory of restorative instincts and develops it to its logical extreme. He announces his resolution in a repetitive quasi-catechetical formula:

> But for the moment it is tempting to pursue to its logical conclusion the hypothesis that all instincts tend towards the restoration of an earlier state of things. . . . Let us suppose, then, that all the organic instincts are conservative, are acquired historically and tend towards the restoration of an earlier state of things [pp. 37–38].

In the framework of this argument, all the instincts, although conservative, are subject to increasingly complicated detours before attaining their final aim of death. Again Freud turns to tension as a point of origin, this time as the origin of animate matter, which instincts try to cancel out. Over the next two pages, Freud circuitously develops the argument that the self-preservative instincts (*Selbsterhaltungstriebe*) are assimilated into conservative ones. Then, suddenly, we come upon two sentences that halt us as abruptly as an unexpected red light: "But let us pause for a moment and reflect. It cannot be so" (p. 39).

At this point in the argument, the previous union of detour, death, and the conservative instincts bifurcates: only the life and sexual instincts follow detours, yet in bringing back earlier states of life and by preserving (*erhalten*) life for a longer time they are conservative; the other instincts rush forward to attain "the final aim of life" (death) as rapidly as possible. Freud illustrates the action of the two instincts by the example of germ cells, which also bifurcate as they begin to develop and repeat the performance that gave rise to their own existence. The outcome is that "once again one portion of their substance pursues its development to a finish, while another portion harks back [*zurückgreifen*; literally: "reaches back"] once again as a fresh residual germ to the beginning of the process of development" (p. 40). Having corrected his previous position, Freud resumes his scrutiny with phraseology that is itself repetitive, thereby reducing the distance between theory and object:

> Let us now hark back [*zurückgreifen*] for a moment ourselves and consider whether there is any basis at all for these speculations. Is it really the case that, *apart from the sexual instincts,* there are no instincts that do not seek to restore an earlier state of things? [p.41].

Freud brings up the possible exception of an instinct toward perfection, only to say, with inevitable irony, that we must not preserve (*schonen*) such an illusion. Rather, he explains, the impulse for perfection results from a repressed instinct. This sudden somersaulting of reference—the singular impulse for perfection coming from a repressed instinct—restores to the text a vacillating rhythm (*Zauderrhythmus*) that now is partially aborted at another level. The repressed instinct ceaselessly strives for full satisfaction, which would entail a backward movement—repeating a primary experience of satisfaction. No matter what substitutive formation or sublimation is chosen,[15] a tension will persist that arises from the difference between the amount of pleasurable satisfaction that is demanded and the amount that is achieved. The resultant difference, aided by Eros, then "presses ever forward unsubdued."

Chapter 6 is in many ways the most involved and at times the hardest to follow as it resurrects and modifies key concepts: ego and death instincts, conservative instincts, and the repetition compulsion.

The direction of thought in the opening paragraph is dominated by the interplay of one group of instincts that presses ahead and the other group of instincts that pulls back and restores an earlier state; the accustomed distance between thought and instinct is narrowed down, and the two engage harmoniously in a kind of shadowboxing match. The paragraph has three major crosscurrents. First, the conclusions about the instincts reached thus far are summarized and differentiated. Second, a correction is offered: only the ego instincts are conservative and correspond to a compulsion to repeat; though the sexual instincts reproduce primitive states of the organism, their clear aim is the coalescence of two radically different germ cells. Third, Freud reaches the new position that if we cannot say what is repeated in sexual reproduction, the distinction between the instincts no longer obtains and the compulsion to repeat dwindles in importance.

This paragraph is in fact overloaded with ideas, and their lack of clarity, despite Freud's intention, is not resolved. Part of the problem has to do with his use of the comparative rather than the superlative. The instincts, we have often read thus far, restore *earlier* states; if the text read *earliest*, it would point to the state of inanimate matter, and thus the death instincts alone would be conservative, and would repeat compulsively. But even if the sexual instincts repeat only an earlier state, not the earliest, their superordinate aim is to coalesce with that which is different. Throughout the chapter Freud seems to be tiptoeing unsteadily through these distinctions.[16]

Beginning with a sentence that refers to past, present, and future, the style of the second paragraph continues in the dynamic *Zauderrhythmus* of the instincts themselves: "Let us *turn back*, then, to one of the assumptions that we *have already made*, with the *expectation* that we *shall be able* to give it a categorical denial" (p. 44; italics mine). The proposition Freud expects to deny—that death is an instinct—turns his attention to biology; yet after four pages of biological findings (pp. 45–49), he sees that his expectation has not been fulfilled. Reasserting his theory of two instincts, he finds an ally in the philosopher Schopenhauer. Philosophers, as we see and shall see again, tend to be more congenial to Freud's theories than biologists.[17]

Freud's procedure in the next paragraph of taking "another step forward" is consistent with its subject matter, which is cellular union as a means of "prolonging" life. After applying libido theory to this cellular activity, Freud concludes that such activity coincides with the Eros of poets and philosophers. At this point, instead of proceeding, Freud prefers "looking back" and tracing his slow development of libido theory in three steps (pp. 50–53).[18] The third step—the inclusion in Eros of the ego instincts alongside the death instinct—is taken at the moment of composition and corrects the position of an earlier chapter, in which the ego instincts were included among the death instincts. And now, to enrich his third instinctual theory, Freud resolves not to reject (*zurückweisen*) any promising idea. After lamenting his failure to derive (*zurückführen*) one basic polarity (life and death; love and hate) from the other,[19] Freud negates the differences between the turning of an instinct from the object to the ego and the opposite instinctual movement from the ego to the object, coming to postulate a primary masochism by reference to which all subsequent masochism or turning round of the instinct upon the ego would be "a return to an earlier phase of the instinct's history, a regression." The semantic and lexical variants of the motif of returning (some of which are occulted in the English rendering) repeat and surround each other like verbal babushka dolls.

With the theoretical advance of asserting primary masochism, a diataxis occurs, but what is more important is the kind of diataxis. Again it is a turning back; in Freud's own words: "Let us, however, return to the self-preservative instincts." Even within this reference, there is another return, the return to the example of the protista or protozoa, which was used unsuccessfully to establish the death instincts; and we should not fail to note that the example of protozoa brings Freud back to the earliest state of animate matter. The union of two protista introduces fresh stimulus, tensions or "vital differences" which then must be lived off (*abgelebt*). This logical argument leads Freud into a trap: he equates the pleasure principle with the Nirvana principle, and insofar as he sees them as the dominant tendency of mental life (a position earlier assigned to the repetition compulsion) in their effort to reduce, keep constant, or eliminate internal tension, he finds in them the most solid evidence for the death instincts. Surely Freud's prose, which in its own way here negates a vital difference between these two principles (he corrects himself elsewhere[20]), mimics its own content. True, the "vital differences" he has alluded to were in the order of chemical tensions, but they are not alien to those breaches, those events of breaking in or break-ing through (*einbrechen, durchbrechen*) that are proper to traumatic neuroses. The frequent diataxes in the prose of *Beyond the Pleasure Principle* are in their own way instances of *reducing* tension, exam-ples of mentation and the pleasure principle acting in unison.

Freud shows dexterity marshaling the pleasure principle into the court of the death instincts, but the case is otherwise for the repetition compulsion, which proves much more recalcitrant. Once more Freud falls back on origins, the repetition compulsion being quintessentially a concept of origins. True, embryonic devel-opmental processes are rich in the "phenomena of repetition," but sexuality may well not be very ancient protistan activity.[21] In the ensuing elaboration of sexuality, we come upon one of the most striking displacements to be found anywhere in Freud's writing. In the midst of his baffled attempt to pin down the origin of sexuality, he suddenly writes as if the death theory (which he established) rather than the life instinctual theory were threat-ened:

> The view of sexuality we have just mentioned is of little help for our purposes. The objection may be raised against it that it pos-tulates the existence of life instincts already operating in the simplest organisms; for otherwise conjugation, which works counter to the course of life and makes the task of ceasing to live more difficult, would not be retained and elaborated but would be avoided. If, therefore, we are not to abandon the hypothesis of death instincts, we must suppose them to be associated from the very first with life instincts [p. 57].

Actually what frustrates Freud, as we can see from this fresh perspective, is a certain elusiveness in the symmetry between Thanatos and Eros. The death instincts tend to restore an earlier state, but that is their aim, and so there is paradoxically a forward and backward movement. Eros prolongs life, but to what degree does it tend to restore an earlier state? Ineluctably, here as else-where, Freud is plunged back into the problem of origins. The scientific information about the origin of sexuality being so sparse, Freud resorts to the explanation the poet-philosopher Plato put in the mouth of Aristophanes in the *Symposium*. Freud tries to de-velop Plato's theory in a whole uninterrupted paragraph of groping questions, only to break off abruptly under the accumulating speculative tension: "But here, I think, the moment has come for breaking off" (*abzubrechen*).

"Not, however, without the addition of a few words of critical reflection," Freud suddenly answers himself. Doubtful about the truth of his previous hypotheses, he again explains that he threw himself into a line of thought and followed it out of scientific curiosity. And yet, there is the insistence that the characterization of the instincts as regressive is based on observed material "repeatedly" combined with the purely speculative. The intellectual upshot of such a procedure admittedly might be "widely diverging" from empirical observation, and thus might constitute, in its own way, an erroneous detour. Another detour arises from the roundabout language Freud feels forced to use, a language he fittingly describes in a roundabout fashion: we are obliged, he says, to use scientific terms, but they too are figurative; we would probably overcome any deficiency if we could use physiological or chemical terms, but in fact they too belong to figurative language.

As we read the last chapter of *Beyond the Pleasure Principle* we cannot escape the question, Why did Freud write it? Of its five paragraphs the first two, true to form, repeat previous matter, and the very opening sentence is echoed to an extent in paragraph 3, which introduces a distinction so hastily as to leave a trail of disturbing obscurity; the last two paragraphs, for their part, offer new questions that could easily have been integrated into a previous chapter. Freud's chief concern in the final pages returns to economic issues, which constituted the subject of Chapter 1. But with the new questions Freud seems to carry into a speculative sphere the disruptive clamor of the life instincts. But has he not broken out of the repetitiveness of a smaller circle to discover himself caught in a larger one? Repetition compulsion is manifest in Freud's very need to write the seventh chapter. Building on Schur's remark that Freud's preoccupation with numbers had the intensity of a deep compulsive symptom, Shengold quotes two letters in which Freud explains that his life is marked by seven-year cycles; there is evidence also that his having seven brothers and sisters specifically influenced one of his dreams; and on a much later occasion Freud linked up seven with death prediction and the fight of his seven internal organs to bring his life to an end.[22] And, I might add, *Beyond the Pleasure Principle* is not unique in the Freud canon in having seven chapters. So do *The Interpretation of Dreams, Jokes and Their Relation to the Unconscious,* "The Unconscious," *The Question of Lay Analysis,* and *New Introductory Lectures.* The first two of the *Three Essays on the Theory of Sexuality* each have seven sections, as does Freud's own favorite among his works, Part 4 of *Totem and Taboo.* The *Introductory Lectures* number twenty-eight, which is a multiple of seven. It is not without significance that Freud's regular correspondence with Fliess lasted nearly fourteen years, his correspondence with Jung nearly seven years. The ring holders in the Secret Committee of the psychoanalytic movement numbered seven. The city of Rome with its seven hills was so fascinatingly forbidden to Freud that for years he could not bring himself to visit it; once he did, as we read in Jones, he returned for a total of seven visits.[23]

Recognizing that his inquiries have achieved limited scientific advance, Freud concludes by urging patience and readiness "to abandon a path again that we have followed for a time"[24] if it proves useless. Significantly his final words are a poetic quotation: "What we cannot reach flying we must reach limping. . . . The Book tells us it is no sin to limp" (p.64). Conceiving of life as a series of detours, Freud's essay ends unexpectedly with the image of the muscular "detour" of a limp.

Looking back on *Beyond the Pleasure Principle,* we may suddenly be seized by a wish that this difficult work, which as late as 1923 Freud judged to be well written and rich in ideas,[25] be rearranged in logical order. But if such a wish were realized, it would vitiate the essence of the text as a repetitive act executed in vacillating rhythms. In the order of its statements (and here the *order* constitutes a message), Freud's repetitive exposition mimics his grandson's *fort/da,* and thereby constitutes a masterful acting out in the writing in.

### Notes

1. See Strachey's note to *Totem and Taboo, S.E.* 13:xi. Further references in this chapter for *Totem and Taboo (S.E.* 13; *G.W.* 9) and *Beyond the Pleasure Principle (S.E.* 18; *G.W.* 13) will give only page numbers.

2. Laplanche, *Life and Death in Psychoanalysis,* p. 106.

3. The latter part of the phrase appears here in my own translation, and

shows how Freud's style enlivens quasianimate objects, as Strachey's phrase—"we find that its essential traits are these" (p. 107)—does not.

4. For a parallel text, see Freud's reference to difficulties inherent in his final position: "I will only mention two of the latter which may have forced themselves on the notice of *a number* of my readers" (p. 157; italics mine). In the very next sentence Freud takes up the first of the shortcomings: "No one can have failed to observe, in the first place, that I have taken as the basis of my whole position the existence of a collective mind." The potentially disruptive jump from a positive particular ("a number") to a negative universal ("no one") is swirled over by the uncommon, indeed unique, fluency and headlong rush of Freud's prose, which defies the attempt to pause and trace the current's leaps and turnabouts. It is instructive to compare this passage with p. 140. At midpage, Freud expatiates on the totemic festiveness after mourning; in the third paragraph he asks what we are to make of the prelude of mourning; and in the next paragraph, rather than answer, he goes back to the subject of rejoicing, thereby putting off the reply until further on.

5. This section contains a good example of Freud's technique of summarizing another's argument and then, with a sleight of hand worthy of Kafka, intermittently telescoping the distance between himself as author and the cited authority: "Frazer accepted the Arunta tradition that each totem clan had originally eaten its own totem without restriction. *But it was then difficult to understand the next stage in development, at which the clansmen became content with assuring a supply of the totem for others, while themselves renouncing its enjoyment almost completely.* He supposed that this restriction had arisen, not from any kind of religious deference, but perhaps from observing that animals never fed upon their own kind. . . . *Or it might be that by sparing the creatures they hoped to conciliate them*" (pp. 115–116; italics mine).

6. Hardly a better description could be found for Freud himself. Candidly inquiring, he shifts colors like a chameleon with the ground and grounding of his discourse—*grounding* is a key word here. His style should no more be conceived as an external yet responsive medium than should, say, a guitar, for does not the vibration we hear dwell in the strings of that in-strum-ent?

7. Note that Part 4 opens with an aural ring ("we heard" [p. 100]); however, another phrase on the same page ("As we have heard") does not have the same aural reference in the original German ("*Wir wissen*" [G.W. p. 122]). But see p. 140 in *S.E.*, where "As we have seen" should literally be "As we have heard" ("*Wir haben gehört*" [G.W. p. 170]).

8. See also in the last paragraph of this section: "But at that point the inexorable law of ambivalence claims its right" ("*fordert . . . seine Rechte*" [G.W. p. 186]). Strachey's consistent use of the past tense in this paragraph robs the original of its immediacy, to say nothing of his very loose rendering of *fordert seine Rechte* as "stepped in."

9. Strachey (p. 158) neglects to translate these last eight words; see G.W. p. 190: "*einer Kontinuität im Gefühlsleben der Menschen.*" On p. 157 Freud speaks of man's father complex and in a footnote offers an alternative: "*Respektive Elternkomplex*," literally: "Or parent complex." Strachey unjustifiably offers an editorialized translation: "Or, more correctly, their parental complex."

10. *Etudes Freudiennes*, 13/14:87–125 (1975). English readers may consult a translated, but unfortunately abridged, version entitled "Coming into One's Own," in *Psychoanalysis and the Question of the Text*, pp. 114–148. In "Freud's Masterplot: Questions of Narrative," Peter Brooks argues that *Beyond the Pleasure Principle*, with its exposition about repetition, detour, beginnings, and ends, is a master-plot for narration (*Yale French Studies*, 55/56:280–300, 1977). He does not, however, apply that model to Freud's own text except in one intriguing but undeveloped remark: "*Beyond the Pleasure Principle* is itself a plot which has formulated that dynamic necessary to its own détour" (p. 294).

11. Are these acts of throwing away and sending away detours (*Umwege*)? One can hardly doubt it; but that would put the repetition compulsion off onto the track followed by Eros, whereas Freud's text elsewhere designates the repetition compulsion as the quintessential myrmidon of the death instincts, which pursue their course silently and unswervingly.

12. I am impelled to note that the psychoanalytic literature completely neglects one of the paramount linguistic features that characterizes psychoanalytic treatment and sets it apart from other kinds of intimate, emotional, secret-sharing discourse: Within the clinical hour, an analyst would hardly ever address a patient by name. Freud was, however, well aware of the general importance of names. In *Totem and Taboo* he asserts: "Even a civilized adult may be able to infer from certain peculiarities in his own behaviour that he is not so far removed as he may have thought from attributing importance to proper names, and that his own name has become to a very remarkable extent bound up with his personality. So, too, psycho-analytic practice comes upon frequent confirmations of this in the evidence it finds of the importance of names in unconscious mental activities" (*S.E.* 13:56). Claudius, a shrewd politician, flatters Laertes by repeating his name five times in a mere handful of lines (*Hamlet*, I, ii, 42–49 and 62). Naming confers identity as well as recognition by another. For the patient in the clinical setting, the absence of naming is a narcissistic privation that helps trigger and mobilize the most personal memories and intense fantasies. Vast research remains to be done on the way names are phonetically fragmented and dispersed throughout one's dreams and associations—much as Freud's is in the *fort/da* episode.

13. Strachey's translation of this chapter is negligent on several points. For instance, he left out the words that here appear in small caps:

a) ". . . it is in *them* that its traces, ON WHICH MEMORY IS BASED, are left" (p. 25; G.W. p. 24: "*auf welche sich die Erinnerung stützt*").

b) "It seems best FOR THE TIME BEING, however . . . (p. 27; G.W. p. 26: "*vorläufig*").

Much more serious is Strachey's silent "clearing up" of Freud's loose use of *Tendenz* in one passage, especially in light of Freud's express attempt in Chapter 7 to introduce a sharper distinction between *tendency* and *function*. Here is the passage marred by Strachey's tinkering: "Thus it would seem that the function of dreams, which consists in setting aside any motives that might interrupt sleep, by fulfilling the wishes of the disturbing impulses, is not their *original* function. . . . If there is a 'beyond the pleasure principle,' it is only consistent to grant that there was also a time before the purpose [*Tendenz*] of dreams was the fulfilment of wishes. This would imply no denial of their later function. But if once this general rule [*Tendenz*] has been broken, a further question arises" (*S.E.* pp. 32–33; *G.W.* p. 33).

14. Jones 3:266.

15. Cf. p. 11: In certain instances, if the repressed instincts are able by detours to struggle through to a direct or substitutive satisfaction, that possibility for pleasure is felt as unpleasureful by the ego.

16. We get a better idea of Freud's groping if we take a look at his views beyond the sixth chapter. In the beginning of the seventh, he simply states that to restore an earlier state of things is a universal trait of the instincts. In 1923, he asserted that both instincts are conservative and seek to restore an earlier state (*S.E.* 18:259; 19:40). But in the *New Introductory Lectures* he questioned whether Eros, as it strives toward a synthesis of living things into greater entities, may be seeking to restore an earlier state (*S.E.* 22:107–108); by the time of the *Outline*, that question evoked a definite no (*S.E.* 23: 148).

On the other hand, texts before and after *Beyond* ascribe the compulsion to repeat to all the instincts (*S.E.* 17:238; 20:57, 265). Notwithstanding the major identifiable shifts in the evolution of Freud's theory, the constant change in the definition of so many key concepts triggers an elusive movement in any text.

17. Hence it is not surprising that medical analysts overwhelmingly reject Freud's theory of the death instinct. But they should be aware of the most likely constrictions that may result from their training and remember Freud's repeated profession that philosophers and poets, not scientists and physicians, were the true precursors of his discovery of the unconscious.

18. It is remarkably in keeping with the repetition in this chapter that Freud closes with a footnote resuming the development of his libido theory, and that the next year he grafted on another one whose purpose is to reword that development more clearly.

19. In the first six sentences of the paragraph where these polarities appear (pp. 53–54) verbs alternate from present to past in yet another variant of *Zauderrhythmus*.

20. Cf. "The Economic Problem of Masochism" where the Nirvana principle expresses the trend of the death instinct; and the pleasure principle, the demands of the libido (*S.E.* 19:160–161).

21. One should note the oxymoronic aspect of Eros, which, although striving to unite, consists of "extraordinarily violent instincts" (p. 56). On a different plane, cf. *Totem and* Taboo: "Sexual desires do not unite men but divide them" (*S.E.* 13:144).

22. See L. Shengold, "A Parapraxis of Freud's in Relation to Karl Abraham," *American Imago*, 29: 148–152 (1972).

23. Jones 2:19.

24. Strachey omitted the word *again (wieder* [*G.W.* p. 69]). Is his parapraxis a reaction to Freud's repetitiveness?

25. Cf. Freud's letter to Ferenczi, referred to by Jones 3:99.

# 3

# The Fulfilling Appeal
# to the Audience

HAVING ANALYZED TWO SAMPLE TEXTS AND PLOTTED THEIR GENERAL structural properties in the previous chapter, we may turn to other crucial issues, the first being Freud's relation to his audience. I know of no writer-psychoanalyst who combines to nearly the same extent such freedom and power of communication with such sensitivity to a reader's receptivity. Granted that for Freud writing was above all else a self-satisfaction and that in a handful of essays the reader feels like an eavesdropper—but even then (and contrary to possible expectations) Freud maintains an engaging openness of expression. One of his rhetorical strategies, used both in his writing and for public speeches, was to single out one or more followers and mentally address them, thereby relaxing himself and also narrowing the distance between himself and the other. Although there are passages of obscurity in Freud's work, he never cultivated it or paraded it. Rational understanding was uppermost with him; despite cocaine consumption that lasted over a decade, he never developed an addiction to this primary-process stimulant, although throughout his life he greatly relied on nicotine, which increased his attention span and eased secondary-process thinking.[1]

Freud fondly quoted the French maxim *"Pour faire une omelette il faut casser des oeufs"* ("You can't make an omelette without breaking some eggs"), and this Gallic note may serve as a heuristic link to the French psychoanalyst Jacques Lacan, whose attitude toward his audience contrasts so sharply with Freud's. Lacan's style is deliberately polysemous and ambiguous, attempting to capture as much as possible of his unconscious and to deposit it before the reader. Intentionally elliptical and poetic, his writing aims to defy rational interpretation, demanding that the reader sink into the text and add new unconscious meanings. Lacanian style is thus a kind of "happening," in which the unconscious "hangs out." Rhetorically speaking, the ethical stance that goes with this style is (at least potentially) highly disagreeable and egocentric. It can easily degenerate to exhibitionistic eccentricity and quickly smacks of autoeroticism in group rather than reflecting a mature mutuality. The Lacanian style risks too often being a disturbing acting out of the unconscious; Freud, by contrast, mobilized unconscious processes, filtering them through ego functions bent chiefly on elucidatory rather than obscurantist communication.[2] This trait in Freud's work, which is the subject of our elaboration in this chapter, is described with succinct accuracy by Joan Riviere in the following:

> Its general character is not only direct and plain-spoken—simple statements without padding—but in particular it conveys vividly an awareness of his readers or hearers, as if he were speaking directly to them, and were concerned to put forward his views in a form intelligible to *them*. . . . He had developed this special capacity for presenting his conclusions as if he were bent on enabling the reader to take them in—so much so that it colours his whole style and gives the presentation a simplicity and lucidity (often when the content is obscure) that is peculiar to him and most rare in such work.[3]

This abiding awareness of his audience and his responsiveness to it is evident in all Freud's writings, and characteristically has the effect of making the audience seem not vaguely present but vividly and immediately so. We read with pleasure so many pieces cast in the form of lectures for real or imaginary audiences; and even in those that are not, elements of dialogue, direct or disguised, habitually extend to the reader a gracious invitation and welcome to the text. The *New Introductory Lectures* were never orally delivered, yet present an outstanding example of responsiveness to the audience, for in imagination Freud placed himself in the lecture hall so as "not to forget to bear the reader in mind" (*S.E.* 22:5). On the other hand, in the preface to the published version of the earlier *Introductory Lectures,* first delivered to a live audience, Freud apologizes for the repetitions he says are unavoidable if one wishes to keep an audience's attention over the course of a two-hour lecture (*S.E.* 15:9).

Freud's private correspondence manifests a remarkable ability to adapt his style to the addressee,[4] from the romantic letters to Martha during their courtship and the insecure, soul-searching ones to Fliess, to those distinctive, respectful missives to James Putnam, which offer an unusual glimpse of their author in a self-conscious, prolonged exchange with a man ten years his elder, and in which he abandons the predominantly patriarchal note (however various) characteristic of his other post-1900 correspondence. We need a comprehensive study of Freud's correspondence, but it will have to await the publication of the full text of all his letters. Up till now, of the major published collections of Freud's letters, only the correspondence with Jung and Fliess fulfills this prerequisite for a complete understanding of the intellectual and emotional drift of each letter. A case in point is Freud's revealing description of his correspondence with Bleuler: "At the end of my letters nature always asserted itself and I started to fume. I am no great diplomat. . . ."[5]

Still, in spite of the responsibility Freud always felt toward his audience and his resulting commitment to clarity and intelligibility, he wrote primarily for himself. Jones reports:

> Freud once said, evidently speaking for himself but expressing it generally: "No one writes to achieve fame, which anyhow is a very transitory matter, or the illusion of immortality. Surely we write first of all to satisfy something within ourselves, not for other people. Of course when others recognize one's efforts it increases the inner gratification, but nevertheless we write in the first place for ourselves, following an inner impulse."[6]

On another occasion Freud explained that he was spurred on by curiosity to see what those inner impulses would reveal: "When I sit down to work, and take my pen in hand, I am always curious about what will come forth, and that drives me irresistibly to work."[7] So focused was Freud on choosing a sublimating satisfaction for his drives, giving them external realization, and mastering them that when the motive for writing was externally imposed on him, as in the case of the reluctantly penned "Why War?" (1933),[8] his typical stylistic vibrancy is noticeably lacking.[9] In several atypical works, however, the sense that Freud is writing for himself is so remarkable that the reader at times feels cast into the role of eavesdropper. In these works his style ranges from the loosely logical, as in *Inhibitions, Symptoms and Anxiety*,[10] to the oneiric, as in *Beyond the Pleasure Principle*,[11] and, as Freud intimated to Fliess, in large sections of *The Interpretation of Dreams*.[12] But even here, where Freud's style might be expected to harbinger Lacan's, it is quite different: there is no striving for the flashy effect, no deliberate ellipsis or ambiguity, no wanton indulgence in obscurity—just grudging tolerance for its inevitable occasional appearance. Even when Freud surrenders his musings to the public, he nonetheless maintains a constant grip on his authorial responsibilities toward the reader; and secondary process was so highly mobilized in him that even his quasiprivate efforts to pursue and clarify meaning are highly communicative. However much this salient trait of Freud's so-called "private" writing drew on innate disposition and talent, it was certainly enhanced in his self-analysis: in the early stages, words played only a minor role in his dreams, a typical dream structure being comprised of a visual first part (thing representation) and a second verbal part (word representation); from August 1898 onwards, verbal elements became ascendant.[13]

As we have seen above, when Freud addressed an audience other than himself, and especially when speaking before a group of people, he would pick out one friendly listener who, in his mind, constituted not merely his prime but his sole audience. Referring to a letter from Freud, Theodor Reik best enlightens us about this intriguing habit:

> He once wrote to me that when he lectured he chose one sympathetic person from among the audience and imagined that he was addressing this person alone. If this person was absent from among his listeners, he would not feel at ease until he had found someone to understudy, so to speak. This attitude explains the

direct address form of his lectures and the manner in which he anticipated objections, formulating the doubts and questions of his audience as he could their minds.[14]

There are explicit indications that when Lou Andreas-Salomé attended the meetings of the Vienna Psychoanalytic Society in 1912 and 1913, it was she who comprised Freud's target audience and source of confidence:

> I missed you in the lecture yesterday and I am glad to hear that your visit to the camp of masculine protest played no part in your absence. I have adopted the bad habit of always directing my lecture to a definite member of the audience, and yesterday I fixed my gaze as if spellbound at the place which had been kept for you.[15]

> I am very sorry that I have to answer your letter in writing, i.e., that you were not at my lecture on Saturday. I was thus deprived of my point of fixation and spoke uncertainly.[16]

We can hardly exaggerate the import of the second passage, which clearly confirms our previous observation on Freud's style: his discourse is a special combination of primary and secondary process in which intellectual power and unconscious influence have complementary sway. It seems that Freud, somewhat anxious about exteriorizing his ultimately undefinable unconscious (however filtered through secondary process) experienced a degree of personal insecurity and sought containment in a projected psychic space bounded and defined by good object relations. I believe that such dynamics partly explain Freud's shying away from oratory and choice of an intimate conversational style by which he brought himself close to his listeners.

Freud's focus on a single member within a larger audience even carried over into his scientific writing. The "private" audience of *The Interpretation of Dreams* included both Fliess and Minna;[17] *Gradiva* was composed especially for Jung's pleasure;[18] *Leonardo da Vinci*, for a limited group of friends and followers;[19] *Totem and Taboo*, for four or five faithful;[20] and it is probably Pfister who was the imagined interlocutor in the two final chapters of *The Future of an Illusion*.[21] Freud's desire for communicative intimacy is also manifest in his ease with the genre of dialogue (in which he excelled), with its frequent Socratic overtones,[22] which feature prominently in Freud's exchanges with his fictitious interlocutors in *The Future of an Illusion* and *The Question of Lay Analysis* (the inconsistent "Impartial Person," *S.E.* 20:208), as well as with the less explicitly fictitious audiences of the *Introductory Lectures* and *New Introductory Lectures*.[23] The rationale for imagining an interlocutor is spelled out in *The Future of an Illusion:* if successfully done, it heightens the accuracy of reflection:

> An enquiry which proceeds like a monologue, without interruption, is not altogether free from danger. One is too easily tempted into pushing aside thoughts which threaten to break into it, and in exchange one is left with a feeling of uncertainty which in the end one tries to keep down by over-decisiveness. I shall therefore imagine that I have an opponent who follows my arguments with mistrust, and here and there I shall allow him to interject some remarks [*S.E.* 21:21].[24]

In two important instances Freud apparently adopted the dyadic form for other strategic reasons. In "Screen Memories," Freud put his personal experiences into the mouth of a young male interlocutor; the fictive device is in itself an artistic screen that mimics the dynamic memory screen. In a later piece, "A Comment on Anti-Semitism," Freud responds to an essay by a bigot, plainly a straw man invented out of thin air (cf. *S.E.* 23:289).

Even outside an explicit lecture format Freud occasionally makes direct appeals to us as readers:

> I can only advise those of my readers who have not as yet themselves conducted an analysis not to try to understand everything at once . . . [*S.E.* 10:65].

> I cannot tell whether my presentation of the case has made any impression on the reader and whether it has put him in a position to take an interest in these minute details [*S.E.* 19:96].

> If the reader feels inclined to shake his head at my credulity, I cannot altogether blame him . . . [*S.E.* 20:34].

> In the course of this discussion the reader will have felt certain doubts arising in his mind; and he must now have an opportunity of collecting them and bringing them forward [*S.E.* 17:245].

A delightful twist on this device occurs in the case history of Little Hans. The main text reports a dialogue between Hans and his disapproving father in which Hans protests that his wish to be alone with Mommy is good, as is whatever else he may think; footnoting this exchange, Freud injects himself into the reported dialogue, directly addressing one of the interlocutors in the manner of an 18th-century novelist: "Well done, little Hans! I could wish for no better understanding of psycho-analysis from any grown-up" (*S.E.* 10:72 fn.).

The dyadic quality in Freud's prose is often achieved through the familiar use of the editorial *we* and a self-revelatory use of *I:*

> But what is there in common between the technique of the first group (condensation with substitute-formation) and that of the two others (multiple use of the same material)?
>
> Well, something very simple and obvious, I should have thought. . . . It is true that here we should not find that condensation would meet the case; but if instead of it we take the more inclusive concept of economy . . . It is easy to point out what we save in the case of Rousseau [*S.E.* 8:42–43].

As this example shows, Freud does not require a full-blown dialogue format to achieve the dialogue's feeling of immediacy. He often suggests it indirectly, by the dyadic manipulation of personal pronouns.

Freud was so intent on audience contact that he insisted that the papers delivered over the years in the Vienna Psychoanalytic Society be delivered from memory or from notes, the motivation being that a paper read out loud thwarts intimacy with the audience. For similar reasons, Freud was against verbatim case reports:

> Nevertheless it must be borne in mind that exact reports of analytic case histories are of less value than might be expected. Strictly speaking, they only possess the *ostensible* exactness of which 'modern' psychiatry affords us some striking examples. They are, as a rule, fatiguing to the reader and yet do not succeed in being a substitute for his actual presence at an analysis [*S.E.* 12:114].

Two outstanding models of psychoanalytic writing and commitment to audience are the writings of Anna and Sigmund Freud. The daughter's style, a paragon of lucidity and simplicity, is imitable (although few analysts have successfully done so). The father's richer, looser, and more allusive style has been equaled by no one.

Having surveyed pertinent comments about audience from throughout the Freud canon, let us analyze in detail the role of the audience in a specific work. For such an analysis, we could choose no better text than the *Introductory Lectures* (*S.E.* 16–17), which are unique in showing how Freud responded to a public audience over a two-year period (1915 to 1917), although we must keep in mind that, as Freud acknowledged years afterwards, the lectures of the first half of the series were extemporaneous, and not written out until right after they were publicly delivered, whereas the lectures of the second half were prepared during the intervening summer (*S.E.* 22:5). Before considering the twenty-eight lectures, I should like to dwell a moment on the notion of reader, for as Walter Ong says in the title of his suggestive essay, "The Writers Audience Is Always a Fiction," and in fact, "[the] history of the ways audiences have been called on to fictionalize themselves would be a correlative of the history of literary genres and literary works, and indeed of culture itself."[25] There are some things, says Ong, every writer must assume that every reader knows (Shakespeare is a poet); there are other things which not every reader knows, but is assumed to know anyway, to avoid insult (thus the assertion "Jung was a Swiss psychiatrist" may be implied in the phrase "the Swiss psychiatrist Jung"); and finally, there is knowledge which the author may safely presume his readers do not know. It has been my observation again and again that most analysts when writing have considerable difficulty in managing these three levels,[26] and I suspect that the underlying problems are not simply pedagogical.

Freud's handling of the audience in his *Introductory Lectures* is extremely subtle, all the more so when we consider that at the time they were written, Freud bore in mind two levels of reception: his original audience at the University of Vienna and the new readership at large. The *Lectures* progress in three developmental patterns: there is the constant reference to the history of psychoanalytic discovery and the present state of knowledge;[27] there is the frequent description of the development of the analytic patient's knowledge and self-awareness; and there is, finally, the gradual education of Freud's own audience and readership about the principles and tenets of analysis. These three patterns of development are masterfully orchestrated, and blend at times for moments of brilliant, even dramatic, harmony. And there is the added drama that arises from the challenges to the analytic teaching, brought forward by objectors, imaginary or real, some of them actually present in Freud's audience.

We appreciate an artistic technique worthy of the best fiction as we follow Freud's gradual unfolding to his audience of theory that intersects with the development of symptoms and the patient's reaction in treatment on one hand and the historical advance of psychoanalytic knowledge on the other. The following passage, concerning the past and present movement between his own exposition and the dynamics of symptoms, partially illustrates this technique:

> Let us now go back to the symptoms. They create a substitute, then, for the frustrated satisfaction by means of a regression of the libido to earlier times, with which a return to earlier stages of object-choice or of the organization is inseparably bound up. We discovered some time ago that neurotics are anchored somewhere in their past; we know now that it is at a period of their past in which their libido did not lack satisfaction, in which they were happy. . . . In some way the symptom repeats this early infantile kind of satisfaction . . . [S.E. 16:365].

Someone may object that this is sheer coincidence, that it just so happened that Freud interwove a retrogressive movement in his exposition, analytic discovery, and account of neurotic fixation— in sum, a serendipity of collateral actions having little to do with mimesis or art. In our commitment to fairness we cannot dismiss offhand such a worthy objection, and so we should now proceed to see how it stands up under the weight of textual analysis.

The stage is set at the very beginning of the *Introductory Lectures* when Freud asks his listeners not to be annoyed if he treats them the same way as his neurotic patients; just as he is at pains to tell the starting patient the great difficulties inherent in analytic treatment, he hastens to stress how radically psychoanalysis will challenge the education and habits of thought of his listeners (*S.E.* 15:15). Similarly, as he resumes the lecture series the following year, Freud once more asks his listeners to assume a benevolent skepticism (*S.E.* 16:244). The dream of the three theater tickets, the principal dream of the *Lectures*, treated on six separate occasions, affords an outstanding example of the way the progress of Freud's audience mimics that of a patient. As he concludes the first description of the dream along with its analysis and clinical setting, he declares:

> As regards the meaning of the dream and the dreamer's attitude to it, we might point out much that is similarly surprising. She agreed to the interpretation indeed, but she was astonished at it. She was not aware that she assigned such a low value to her husband; nor did she know *why* she should set such a low value on him. So there is still much that is unintelligible about it. It really seems to me that we are not yet equipped for interpreting a dream and that we need first to be given some further instruction and preparation [*S.E.* 15:125].

Subsequently, having demonstrated with fragments the meaning of dreams as a fulfillment of wish, Freud divines that his audience wants a complete dream but advances an objection that psychically weaves together the audience and his subject matter: "But the difficulties that stand in the way of the fulfilment of your wish are too many" (*S.E.* 15:184). This interweaving also occurs when Freud, dealing with the subject of suggestion, aptly intensifies his technique of imagining or prompting audience comments:

> But here I will pause, and let you have a word; for I see an objection boiling up in you so fiercely that it would make you incapable of listening if it were not put into words: 'Ah! so you've admitted it at last! You work with the help of suggestion, just like the hypnotists! . . .'
> What you are throwing up at me in this is uncommonly interesting and must be answered. But I cannot do so to-day; we have not the time. Till our next meeting, then. I will answer you, you will see [*S.E.* 16:446–447].

In continuation Freud opens the next lecture with direct suggestion:

> Ladies and Gentlemen,—You know what we are going to talk about to-day. You asked me why we do not make use of direct suggestion in psycho-analytic therapy, when we admit that our

influence rests essentially on transference—that is, on suggestion; and you added a doubt whether, in view of this predomi-
nance of suggestion, we are still able to claim that our
psychological discoveries are objective [*S.E.* 16:448].

In reply Freud stresses that the transference or suggestion comes
from the patient; immediately thereafter, with breathtaking agility,
he explains, indeed suggests, to the audience what it is saying to
him:

Thus it becomes possible for us to derive an entirely fresh advantage from the power of suggestion; we get it into our hands. The
patient does not suggest to himself whatever he pleases: we
guide his suggestion so far as he is in any way accessible to its
influence.

But you will now tell me that, no matter whether we call the
motive force of our analysis transference or suggestion, there is a
risk that the influencing of our patient may make the objective
certainty of our findings doubtful [*S.E.* 16:451–452].

The theme of sexuality likewise permits Freud to apply psychoanalytic findings to his audience:

What we inferred from these [adult] analyses was later confirmed point by point by direct observations of children. . . . You
are committing the error of confusing sexuality and reproduction
and by doing so you are blocking your path to an understanding
of sexuality, the perversions and the neuroses. This error is,
however, a tendentious one. Strangely enough, it has its source
in the fact that you yourselves were once children and, while
you were children, came under the influence of education [*S.E.*
16:310–311].

On another score, Freud's references to "stopping-places" and
"firmer footing" link up fixation and regression with the audience's need to understand these concepts in order to progress
further:

Consider that, if a people which is in movement has left strong
detachments behind at the stopping-places on its migration, it is
likely that the more advanced parties will be inclined to retreat to
these stopping-places if they have been defeated or have come
up against a superior enemy. . . . It is important for your understanding of the neuroses that you should not leave this relation
between fixation and regression out of sight. This will give you a

firmer footing in facing the question of how the neuroses are caused . . . [*S.E.* 16:341].

Freud's conclusion to the *Lectures*, presented as a series of fragments, is a text that turns in upon itself and reflects the audience. Citing three concurrent limitations, he asserts that psychoanalytic knowledge is incomplete; that his condensed summary (which by its nature *had* to be incomplete) has fallen short of the intended aim of presenting an adequate account; and that ideally, it should have merely enlightened the audience rather than imparted the comprehensive knowledge of experts:

> I undertook to give you an account of a subject which is still incomplete and in process of development, and my condensed summary has itself turned out to be an incomplete one. At some points I have set out the material on which to draw a conclusion and have then myself not drawn it. But I could not pretend to make you into experts; I have only tried to stimulate and enlighten you [*S.E. 16:463*].

The power of this conclusion is matched by only one other passage: the conclusion to the first series of *Lectures*, where, in an elaborate orchestration of time references Freud explains that months and years of work are required to show the sense of a patient's symptoms whereas a few hours suffice to demonstrate the sense of dreams and thus to confirm basic psychoanalytic doctrine, whereupon he invites us to consider simultaneously the analogy between dreaming and neurosis on the one hand, and the rapid transition from dreaming to a reasonable waking state on the other. The purpose of this telescoping of time and subject matter is to induce us "to arrive at a certainty" with similar speed, and the cascading ending sweeps us onward to the conclusion with no less speed. Some shaky logic notwithstanding, the ending is spellbinding and merits being quoted in full:

> There is nothing else from which one can so quickly arrive at a conviction of the correction of the theses by which psychoanalysis stands or falls. Exacting work over many months and even years is called for to show that the symptoms of a case of neurotic illness have a sense, serve a purpose and arise out of the patient's experiences in life. On the other hand, only a few hours' effort may be enough to prove that the same thing is true of a dream which is, to start with, confused to the point of being

unintelligible, and thus to confirm all the premises of psychoanalysis—the unconscious nature of mental processes, the peculiar mechanisms which they obey and the instinctual forces
which are expressed in them. And when we bear in mind the
sweeping analogy between the structure of dreams and that of
neurotic symptoms and at the same time consider the rapidity of
the transformation which makes a dreamer into a waking and
reasonable man, we arrive at a certainty that neuroses too are
based only on an alteration in the play of forces between the
powers of mental life [*S.E.* 15:239].

Let us now go into greater detail on some other aspects of
Freud's rhetorical relationship to his audience. As we have seen,
along with the dialogue markers *I* and *you*, Freud regularly uses
the collective *we*; such pronouns and their possessive forms take
the edge off a magisterial tone and narrows the distance to the
audience. This technique admits the audience into an intimate
quasisharing in the direction both of the lectures and of psychoanalytic treatment. For an initial illustration, here is the Seventh Lecture:

Ladies and gentlemen, as you see, we have not unprofitably
studied faulty actions. Thanks to these efforts we have . . . .
acquired two kinds of things. . . . I now propose to you that a
change be introduced into our nomenclature which should facilitate our maneuverability (*G.W.* 11:111, my translation; cf. *S.E.*
15:113].

Merging with his audience, Freud then enters into analytic dream
technique and indeed into the clinical setting itself. After spelling
out the rules for interpreting dreams, he continues:

I know, however, of something else that will make things
easier—something, moreover, which lies along our path. Instead
of starting on the interpretation of whole dreams, we will restrict
ourselves to individual dream-elements and track down in a series of examples how these are are clarified by the use of our
technique (*G.W.* 11:116, my translation; cf. *S.E.* 15:118).

Freud goes on to narrate in full the central dream of the three
theater tickets; in the evocation of the clinical setting that follows,
he fuses the audience with himself as analyst:

The first thing the dreamer reports to us is that the precipitating

cause of the dream is touched on in its manifest content. . . .
And the absurd notion of taking three tickets for only two people? She has nothing to say to that, and refuses to report any
further ideas or information [*S.E.* 15:122–123][28]

In the last three lectures the referential complexity of the *we* acquires a new dimension. In Lecture 26 Freud recapitulates what
we, he and his audience, have dealt with so far. Gradually the
reference of the pronoun changes as Freud shifts to the history of
what we, the analysts, have discovered; yet having followed the
previous lectures the audience can now associate pronominally
with the analyst—via Freud's *we*—in the last two lectures, which
deal with analytic technique.

Freud takes care to appease his audience with the reasonable-
ness of the form and arrangement of his subject matter; this too is
an appeal.[29] The lectures did more than merely introduce psychoanalysis; they were the forum in which the greater part of its
discoveries were presented to the public (p. 11). Although addressing a mixed audience of nonmedical and medical people
with varying knowledge of psychoanalysis, Freud, as we are surprised to hear, starts out with two fictions. First, the announced
title in the academic prospectus, "Elementary Introduction to
Psycho-Analysis,"[30] obliges him to fabricate an audience who
knows nothing of psychoanalysis but that it is a treatment for
neurotic patients;[31] the appeal then to the lowest common denomi-
nator is dictated not by the constituency of the audience itself but
rather by a commitment made a priori to give an elementary
introduction. Second, as we have seen, Freud treats this fictive,
ignorant audience in the same way as he does his neurotic patients. Indeed, he outdoes himself. At the outset of treatment he
only presents the patient with the difficulties. Here he goes so far
as to plead with his Viennese audience not to return to the lecture
hall a second time, dissuading all from entering into a permanent
relationship with psychoanalysis; ending with a rhetorical flourish, he nevertheless welcomes the return of any who remain un-
dismayed by his discussions.

After the preliminary lecture Freud shrewdly starts with the
most amenable material: not with postulates but with an investigation; not with exclusively psychopathological phenomena but

with parapraxes, which are observable in any healthy person. Having answered an imagined objection from the audience that such events are trivial, he triangulates in the face of weightier objections and proposes to the audience (whom he has assumed to know nothing about psychoanalysis) to summon up an objector knowing nothing about psychoanalysis: "Let us now call in someone who knows nothing of psycho-analysis, and ask him how he explains such occurrences" (*S.E.* 15:27). Sharing his rationale for proceeding by degrees of complication, Freud next treats dreams, which, though occurring in normal people, are neurotic symptoms and comprise the best preparation for the investigation of neuroses (*S.E.* 15:83; see also 16:338, 389).

Freud's educational project is not long under way before he feels forced to reexplain its title: the introduction is atypical of introductions in that it purposely reveals its own gaps and uncertainties, and Freud challenges his listeners once again, begging those not to return who find the project too laborious and too lacking in firm foundations (*S.E.* 15:102).

As he ends his course on dreams, we again hear him justifying his procedure: dreams are the best preparation for studying neuroses (although a full appreciation of the former is impossible without a knowledge of the latter); besides, dreams supply the most immediate evidential support for psychoanalytic doctrine (*S.E.* 15:239). The way is cleared for the following year's elaboration of neuroses: though less accessible phenomena, Freud will soon reveal their kinship to parapraxes and dreams. Assuming a new instructive stance, he says that he cannot continue as in the previous year, when he never proceeded without the audience's agreement and assent based on the supremacy of "common sense."[32] And yet, in a self-critical and self-ironic way quintessential to his manner of expression, Freud in the opening pages of Lecture 24 (*S.E.* 16:378–379) attacks his own previous justifications for the title and content of his lecture series: the third part of the lecture series, the theory of neuroses, constitutes the psychoanalysis proper and is ill-served by the misnomer "Introduction"; his previous explanations were abstract, long-winded, antiheuristic in the use of undefined concepts, and so on and so forth.[33] Freud arrives at a kind of diataxis, and we cannot help suspecting that his rationale is overcast by unconscious motives and primary process. In his abiding, responsible commitment to understandable communication Freud reveals his own dilemma; his words call to mind T. S. Eliot's dictum in his essay on Coleridge— that if one cannot explain reality, one should be content to describe it:

> I am not so enamoured of my skill in exposition that I can declare each of its artistic faults to be a peculiar charm. I think myself that it might have been more to your advantage if I had proceeded otherwise; and that was, indeed, my intention. But one cannot always carry out one's reasonable intentions. There is often something in the material itself which takes charge of one and diverts one from one's first intentions. Even such a trivial achievement as the arrangement of a familiar piece of material is not entirely subject to an author's own choice; it takes what line it likes and all one can do is to ask oneself after the event why it has happened in this way and no other [*S.E.* 16:379].

On second thought, however, we need not be surprised at this remarkable avowal; after all, Freud explicitly rejects any polemic or eristic intentions, and repeatedly asks his readers and interlocutors to suspend judgment so as to let the material work on them (cf. *S.E.* 15:12, 79; 16:243–244, 431). Thus, with a wave of his hand, Freud has brought a scene of public discourse, where speaker and receptor communicate across a powerful barrier, into the intimacy of the clinical setting, where analyst and patient commonly attend to the emerging voices of the unconscious. No wonder Freud speaks of meaning as an event that "dawns" on us (*S.E.* 16:378, 380; the German words are *einleuchten* and *aufdämmern*, *G.W.* 11:392, 394).[34]

The *Introductory Lectures* are partly a *Bildungsroman*, like Goethe's *Wilhelm Meister*, tracing the education of the hero. Following Freud's series of gradual steps through the material of psychoanalysis, the reader-listener grows.[35] We need only compare the beginning, when the very presence of psychoanalysis elicits audience resistance (p. 48), to the end of the series the following year, when the meaning of symptoms and repression dawns upon the audience. Thus the development of the lectures is to a degree a history of the audience working through its own resistances, comprising a series of staged replies and intrusions from the audience—"What is it you want to ask me? . . . I am particularly interested, however, in your next question. . . . You will break off at that, but only to take up your resistance again at another point. You proceed . . ." (*S.E.* 15:44–49)—interruptions that eventually diminish. In sum, the text is a weaving of pedagogy and guided working through. Beyond that, Freud was well aware that the printed version of the lectures did not have the calmness of a scientific treatise. Quite aware, too, that he had to maintain the audience's attention for a two-hour stretch, he was forced into a certain number of repetitions, interruptions, and recapitulations (p. 9).

A comment of Freud's completely overlooked in the psychoanalytic literature gives us a fuller appreciation of his technique and effect in the *Introductory Lectures*. Criticizing Bleuler's paper "Freud's Psychoanalysis: A Defence and Some Critical Remarks" for being too hard on the adherents of psychoanalysis and too easy on its critics, Freud remarked that Bleuler, the author of *Affectivity* (1906), "ought not to be surprised if the influence of a work is determined not by the strength of its arguments but by its affective tone" (*S.E.* 14:41). With these words in mind, we should be attentive to the tone of earnestness and propriety in the *Lectures*, and for that matter in all his writings. The number of times that *correct*, *right*, and their derivatives appear is amazing. A brief selection from the first two lectures: *justified* (berichtigt), *right*, *claim* (Anrecht), *direction* (Richtung), *training* (Unterricht), *correctness* (Richtigkeit), *untrue* (unrichtig), *gone astray* (nicht auf der richtigen Spur), *procedures* (Verrichtungen), *rightly* (mit Recht).[36] Repeated throughout Freud's works, these words convey an overall impression of truth and dignity, appealing to the ego and superego individually or collectively (justification; correctness).

Looking back on the *Introductory Lectures* and summarizing their rhetorical complexity, we marvel at the delicate balance of meshing interrelationships: the audience's relation to Freud the speaker; the audience's relation to and evolution through his discourse; Freud's relation to his discourse and appeal to the audience on the level of feelings, and of ego and superego considerations. As the audience is represented as objecting or as lowering its resistances, Freud modulates his distance and his tone. On several occasions Freud declared himself to be more interested in making discoveries than in curing others; still, faced with this evidence, we can hardly deny that he was eminently committed to exposing those discoveries to *others*.[37] In the next chapter we shall see how Freud went beyond his commitment to communicability to fulfill a further desire: the desire to communicate an evaluation of his discoveries.

## Notes

1. See Schur, *Living*, p. 412.

2. The most incisive remarks on Lacan's style are to be found in E. Bär, "Understanding Lacan," in *Psychoanalysis and Contemporary Science*, edited by L. Goldberger and V. Rosen (New York: International Universities Press, 1974), 3:473–544; and *Semiotic Approaches to Psychotherapy* (Bloomington: Indiana University Press, 1975), Chapters 1 and 2.

3. "A Character Trait of Freud's," in *Psychoanalysis and Contemporary Thought*, edited by J. Sutherland (London: Hogarth, 1958), pp. 145–146.

4. See Schur, *Living*, p. 292 fn.

5. Letter of 31.10.10, *Freud/Jung Letters*, p. 365. Another unwritten chapter in the history of analysis concerns the rhetorical complexity of the unpublished 460 or so *Rundbriefe* or circular letters sent around Freud's Secret Committee from 1920 to 1924. From Vienna Rank wrote in the person of *we* for himself and Freud; from Berlin Abraham wrote for himself and Hanns Sachs and Max Eitingon; and the London-based Jones and Budapest-based Ferenczi spoke in their own persons—four letters, then, completing one round or set. The *Rundbriefe* were regularly written on the first, eleventh, and twenty-first of each month, and supplemented by private correspondence and visits among the seven members; the eventual outcome in 1924, according to one of Ferenczi's *Rundbriefe*, was that "correspondence splintered up into a number of private correspondences, while the circular letters were degraded into a formality without content" (see the pertinent articles in the *Journal of the Otto Rank Association*, Vol. 8 [1973–1974]: M. Grotjahn, "Notes on Reading the 'Rundbriefe,' " pp. 35–38, and E. Salomon, "Reactions to Reading the 'Rundbriefe,' " pp. 89–91).

These *Rundbriefe* suggest another extremely fruitful area of research. Grotjahn refers to a letter by Jones citing his patients' fees in guineas and explaining that it creates a bad impression to speak in pounds since the use of the monetary designation *guineas* stresses the difference between tradespeople and professionals (p. 59). This simple but weighty fact hints at a field that is wide open for an economic history, which, whenever written, should not neglect the datum that Freud "strictly banished" his sons from becoming medical doctors (M. Freud, *Glory Reflected* [London: Angus and Robertson, 1957], pp. 23, 160)—a detail of far-reaching implications not recorded in the biographies by either Jones or Schur.

6. Jones 2:397.

7. The remark was made to Braun, Grand President of the Austrian District of B'nai B'rith; see H. Knoepfmacher, "Freud and the B'nai B'rith," *Journal*

*of the American Psychoanalytic Association,* 27:447 (1979). Freud was curious about what would flow from his pen, but his manuscripts rarely show any verbal corrections; these facts, taken together, bear out Eissler's splendid assertion that Freud's genius is eminently linguistic (see Chapter 1, fn. 31).

8. See Strachey's commentary (*S.E.* 22:198).

9. See Riviere, "A Character Trait of Freud's," p. 146: "I suppose I had mentioned some analytic explanation that had occurred to me. [Freud] said: 'Write it, write it, put it down in black and white; that's the way to deal with it; you get it out of your system'. . . . This idea [years later] then linked up in my mind with his former remark to me: 'Get it out, produce it, make something of it—*outside you,* that is; give it an existence independently of you.' " Cf. also his letters of 24.1.10 to Pfister, in *Psycho-Analysis and Faith,* p. 33; and of 29.6.14 to L. Andreas-Salomé, in *Sigmund Freud and Lou Andreas-Salomé. Letters,* edited by E. Pfeiffer and translated by W. and E. Robson-Scott (London: Hogarth Press, 1972), p. 17.

10. Cf. Jones 3:254: "It is a rather discursive book, with little of the incisiveness we expect from Freud, and it was evidently written for himself, to try to clarify his own ideas rather than as an exposition of them." Of all Freud's works, I find this the most plodding and lacking in artistic touch. Even the title, consisting of three nouns, stands off from most of the Freudian corpus in which the titles are highlighted by two main words: *Studies on Hysteria, Totem and Taboo, Moses and Monotheism,* etc; I hold this titular polarity—like the duality so characteristic of Freud's theories—to be a drive derivative linked with the triangulation of the Oedipus complex (in this context, see Jones 3:267, and Chapter 7, below).

11. Cf. Jones 3:266: "It is very evident that while writing it Freud had no audience in mind beyond himself; it was written in the hope of clarifying some problems that had long puzzled him. It is somewhat discursively written, almost as if by free associations, and there are therefore occasional gaps in the reasoning." We should refine Jones's statement, since at the beginning of Chapter 4 Freud explicitly serves notices that "what follows is speculation" that the reader is free to accept or discard (*S.E.* 18:24). The rampant speculation out loud continues for three chapters; it concludes, as it were with a closing bracket, with Freud's resubmission to the reader (p. 59).

12. See Freud's letter of 20.6.98 to Fliess, in *Origins,* p. 257: "The psychology is going curiously; it is nearly finished, was written as if in a dream, and certainly is not in a form fit for publication—or, as the style shows, intended for it."

13. D. Anzieu, *L'Auto-analyse de Freud et la découverte de la psychanalyse* (Paris: Presses Universitaires de France, 1975), 1:258, 282, 356; 2:468.

14. *From Thirty Years with Freud,* translated by R. Winston (New York: Farrar & Reinhart, 1942), pp. 10–11. See also Schur, *Living,* p. 306.

15. Letter of 10.11.12, *Letters,* p. 11.

16. Letter of 2.3.13, *Letters,* p. 13.

17. N.B.: not just Fliess (*S.E.* 4:116 fn., 297 fn., and 20:65) but Fliess *and* Minna (Jones 2:6 and 387). See also my article "Friendship and Its Discon-

tents," *Contemporary Psychoanalysis,* 15:55–109 (1979). *The Interpretation of Dreams* was undoubtedly influenced more by the oral interview style than by the formal lecture style of his hero Jean-Martin Charcot. As opposed to the formality of his lectures, hidebound by tradition, Charcot in his famous "Leçons du Mardi" exhibited his ongoing processes of thought, with its doubts and hesitations, and thereby "sought to narrow the gulf between teacher and pupil" (*S.E.* 3:18).

18. Jones 2:341.

19. Letter of 6.3.10, *Psycho-Analysis and Faith,* p. 34.

20. See Jones 2:99 and letter of 13.5.13, in *A Psycho-Analytic Dialogue,* p. 139.

21. Schur, *Living,* pp. 399, 403.

22. F. Wittels, *Sigmund Freud: His Personality, His Teaching, and His School,* translated by E. and C. Paul (London: George Allen & Unwin, 1924), p. 130: "Freud was fond of using the Socratic method. He would break off his formal exposition to ask questions or invite criticism. When objections were forthcoming, he would deal with them wittily and forcibly."

23. These texts point to an evolving sophistication in Freud's involvement with the reader and thereby force us to modify Niederland's speculation that Freud's direct discourse with the reader seems to be less frequent in his later writings ("Freud's Literary Style," p. 22).

24. This is further borne out by Franz Alexander's recollection: "Freud had strong convictions but he never became dogmatic and when uncertain he always admitted it. This made conversation with him delightful, especially the discussion of problems which puzzled him. To a suggestion he would respond with a question or with a 'perhaps,' spinning the idea further and waiting for the other to take up the thread again and offer some new suggestion. One had the feeling that one and Freud were working out something together" ("Recollections of Berggasse 19," *Psychoanalytic Quarterly,* 9:197 [1940]).

25. *PMLA,* 90:9–21 (1975). I cannot refrain from including one of the many rich ideas in Ong's article: "The present inclination to begin a story without the initial definite article, which tacitly acknowledges a range of existence beyond that of the immediate reference, and to substitute for the indefinite article a demonstrative pronoun of proximity, 'this,' is one of many indications of the tendency of present-day man to feel his lifeworld—which is now more than ever the whole world—as inclose to him, and to mute any references to distance. It is not uncommon to hear a conversation begin, 'Yesterday on the street this man came up to me, and. . . .' A few decades ago, the equivalent would very likely have been, 'Yesterday on the street a man came up to me, and . . .' " (p. 21 fn.9).

26. For further treatment of these questions, see R. DeMaria, "The Ideal Reader: A Critical Fiction," *PMLA,* 93:463–474 (1978). In a careful analysis, DeMaria contrasts the ideal readers assumed by Samuel Johnson, John Dryden, and Samuel Coleridge in their literary criticism; a long annotated bibliography is appended.

27. Cf. Gerald Levin's remark that Freud's joining his writing "to the

moment of discovery is a way of keeping track of origins and of preventing insight from disappearing into impersonal and reductive formulations" (*Sigmund Freud*, p. 62).

28. I follow Strachey's translation except in transposing his past tense into the present, to conform with the German and to restore the original immediacy between Freud and his audience.

29. It is valuable to note that all the lectures but one start with the direct address, "Ladies and Gentlemen." The one exception, beginning merely "Gentlemen," is Lecture 21, entitled "The Development of the Libido and the Sexual Organizations." Halfway through the previous lecture, which deals with the general sexual life of human beings, Freud also switches to the vocative "Gentlemen," but one is surely justified in the suspicion that its concentrated use reflects the shame about public discussions of sex on the part of the female Viennese audience.

30. We must not overlook a third fiction here of another order: The title for the orally delivered lecture series was "Elementary Introduction"; in the printed version, whose public is more various, the *Elementary* is dropped.

31. Among these "uninstructed" auditors were Schur, Fenichel, and Reik; see Schur, *Living*, p. 306; Sachs, *Master and Friend*, p. 39 fn; and Reik, *Thirty Years*, p. 17 fn.

32. For another penetrating and more rational self-critique, see "A Reply to Criticisms of My Paper on Anxiety Neurosis" (*S.E.* 3:124).

33. Such a statement is just one more indication of a fictionalized audience, for Freud had already asked those to leave who could not agree with him (see *S.E.* 15:101–102).

34. Compare Freud's advice in the Little Hans case: "I can only advise those of my readers who have not as yet themselves conducted an analysis not to try to understand everything at once, but to give a kind of unbiassed attention to every point that arises and to await further developments" (*S.E.* 10:65).

35. Comparing the first two parts of the *Introductory Lectures* (on parapraxis and on dreams), Freud wrote: "I expect, however, that in Part II, on Dreams, you will soon find that I have not succeeded in maintaining this kind of preparatory, indirect approach, which educates rather than instructs the audience" (letter of 27.7.16, *Andreas-Salomé: Letters*, p. 51).

36. In the clause "would push every other consideration into the background" (*S.E.* 15:36), Strachey neglects to translate the adverbial prepositional phrase *mit Recht* (*G.W.* 11:29).

37. Cf. the following two statements: "the technique of the treatment necessitates our subordinating dream-interpretation to therapeutic aims" (*S.E.* 15:184), and "My discoveries are not primarily a heal-all. My discoveries are a basis for a very grave philosophy. There are very few who understand this, *there are very few who are capable* of understanding this" (H. Doolittle, *Tribute to Freud* [New York: McGraw-Hill, 1975], p. 18).

# 4

# Proportions of Certainty

FREUD'S POWER AS A WRITER IS ALL THE MORE IMPRESSIVE IN LIGHT OF the fact that he rarely supported his claims with rigorous proof based on cross-validation. The development of the discipline he founded nearly single-handedly testifies to his high tolerance for inconsistency and uncertainty, and an irrational self-confidence capable of fending off self-doubt and despair in the face of psychic phenomena that were elusive and often contradictory.[1] This intriguing personality structure prompts us to a further appreciation of his style based on inquiry into the correlation between the quintessential elusiveness of psychic phenomena; Freud's particular gifts of imagination and analysis; and his aversion to precise, constrictive definition. And we shall see that his recurrent indications of his degree of certainty (*definitely, possibly, probably,* etc.) need not strictly remain a scientific praxis but can assume an aesthetic character.

Focusing on the topographic system, Freud drew a memorable and vivid distinction between the possibility of locating physical and psychic contents. Since it is not physical, spatial fixity but dynamic in-betweenness and virtuality that characterize the phenomena of mental life, the dangers of the topographic analogy may be avoided by recollecting that ideas, thoughts and psychical structures in general must never be regarded as localized in organic elements of the nervous system but rather, as one might say, *between* them, where resistances and facilitations [*Bahnungen*] provide the corresponding correlates. Everything that can be an object of our internal perception is *virtual*, like the image produced in a telescope by the passage of light-rays [*S.E.* 5:611].

In line with this perspective, Freud observed in his Clark lectures of 1909 that psychic processes, like dream work, "occur in the unconscious, or rather, to put it more accurately, *between* two separate psychical systems like the conscious and unconscious" (*S.E.* 11:36); in a similar vein, Freud cautioned against positing a strict demarcation between the ego and id (*S.E.* 19:24 and 20:97) and stressed the elasticity of instincts (*S.E.* 20:57). Even more generally, he warned that whereas clear-cut, broad concepts may exist in physics and chemistry, they are both superfluous and impossible in psychoanalysis (*S.E.* 20:57–58), so that "one should refrain from definitions when psychic phenomena are concerned."[2] Much to Jones's regret, such avoidance of precise definitions could at times give rise to confusing ambiguities.[3] I, for my part, would suggest that Freud's self-analytical openness and responsiveness to the vitality of psychic phenomena made his placement of them fluctuate. For example, he variously postulated that secondary revision took place during dream work, after the dream work proper, and after awakening.[4] While insisting that the advance of science in general does not require rigid definitions, he argued that psychoanalysis should be prepared to modify or replace its basic nebulous and hardly imaginable concepts, thereby foregoing the discipline of speculative theory, which proceeds within a tight, logically faultless system (*S.E.* 14:77, 117). Further instances of vacillation occur in Freud's placement of censors either between or within systems, and in his various identifications of the *Cs.* as an apparatus of the *Pcs.* or as a mere coordinating system.[5] These vacillations, we may suspect, bear witness to the flexibility of Freud's observing ego; they hardly suggest some fixated Olympian ego surveying psychoanalytic vistas from detached and lofty heights.

When following his natural bent, Freud was apt to roam freely in his thoughts to see where they would lead him; he was aware of spontaneous bursts which produced some elliptical obscurity (and moments of frustration for his translators) that he called *"pure Schlamperei"* or sloppiness.[6] Freud's spurning of exact definitions made his prose a particularly appropriate instrument for describing the vitality of mental events. It is also true that his wonderful ease of expression and his masterfully articulated syntax make his writing appear, at first blush, clear and less ambiguous than it is.

Freud's typical scientific procedure was cautious; he advanced tentative findings, labeling his opinions as inconclusive and modifying his position as scientific knowledge progressed (*S.E.* 4:xxv and 18:254). He was guided by such axiomatic principles of his early master Charcot as *"La théorie, c'est bon, mais ça n'empêche pas d'exister,"* and "What is probable is not necessarily the truth and . . . the truth is not always probable" (*S.E.* 23:17). At the same time Freud admired Charcot the practitioner, who would put aside his authority and examine unfamiliar cases before his students, on the spot, honestly sharing his doubts and hesitations (*S.E.* 3:18). Throughout Freud's writing, Charcot's influence is present to varying degrees; to disregard it is to mangle Freud's work in a procrustean bed of pseudoscientific presupposition and distortion arising from our own projections of infantile assurance needs.

Freud regarded it as critical that scientific researchers be content largely with varying degrees of probability, since necessary truths are very few.

> Science has only a few apodeictic propositions in its catechism: the rest are assertions promoted by it to some particular degree of probability. It is actually a sign of a scientific mode of thought to find satisfaction in these approximations to certainty and to be able to pursue constructive work further in spite of the absence of final confirmation [*S.E.* 15:51].

A most incisive remark by Marie Bonaparte gave Freud the occasion to elaborate on his position. When she observed that "Those who thirst before everything for certitude do not really love truth," he responded:

> I have said that too somewhere, in another way. Mediocre spirits demand of science a kind of certainty which it cannot give, a sort

of religious satisfaction. Only the real, rare, true scientific minds, can endure doubt, which is attached to all knowledge. I always envy the physicists and mathematicians who can stand on firm ground. I hover, so to speak, in the air. Mental events seem to be immeasurable and probably always will be so.[7]

Smiley Blanton was told:

In developing a new science one has to make its theories vague. You cannot make things clear-cut. But when you write, the public demands that you make things definite, else they think that you do not know what you are saying.[8]

Besides, while the public might accept unsolved problems in other sciences, it would not do so in the case of the budding science of psychoanalysis, by which the constitutional unsuitability of mankind for scientific research is exposed as well as its demands for kinds of satisfaction that have nothing to do with the advance of knowledge (*S.E.* 22:6). In view of this position, let us repeat that Freud preferred patients to undertake treatment with a degree of skepticism, for complete belief at the start is suspect, and convictions arduously arrived at are stronger and better able to weather subsequent resistance (*S.E.* 16:243–245).[9] Hence unlike physicians who reassure a patient about a new treatment, underplaying its inconveniences to increase the probability of success, Freud would indicate to psychoanalytic patients the sacrifices of treatment and warn them that its outcome was uncertain and dependent on their own cooperation (*S.E.* 15:15). We have already remarked on Freud's justified skepticism about so-called "exact reports" of case histories, since even verbatim records offer but an "ostensible" exactness to clinical events in their full context (*S.E.* 12:114). All in all, therefore, there were, apart from the personal traits that made for a certain carelessness in Freud's writing, scientific determinants for his imprecision and lack of clear definitions. In contrast to philosophy, which offers a world picture without gaps and incoherence (*S.E.* 22:160), science in Freud's view focuses chiefly on the external world and is characterized mainly by such traits as yielding to truth and rejecting illusion (*S.E.* 22:182). We marvel when we reflect that Freud's style, for all its excellence, was yet restrained by his concern for truth and precision, a concern properly uppermost when writing in the service of science, although he was convinced it detracted from the aesthetic power of his pen: he would sacrifice unity, coherence, and completeness for accuracy.[10]

It is worthwhile to trace further Freud's ability to rest with less than a high degree of certainty. He explicitly confessed that a "certain aversion of my subjective tendency of granting the imagination too free a rein has always held me back,"[11] a dislike no doubt reinforced by his reaction to Breuer, his father figure, and their peculiar collaboration in *Studies on Hysteria*. Whereas Freud proceeded mainly by induction and clearly labeled his rare uses of deductive logic, Breuer's theoretical chapter indulged in speculation, reasoning by analogy, and ideas deduced from highly abstract theories.[12] On the other hand we know that Freud was attracted by the unleashed imaginative daring of such younger men as Fliess, Ferenczi, Jung, and Groddeck, whose age permitted him to regard them in a filial light. By his own account, Freud kept any inclination to speculation in check until the works of his later years: *Beyond the Pleasure Principle, Group Psychology,* and *The Ego and the Id* (*S.E.* 20:57). In the later *Moses and Monotheism*, Freud deftly unbridled his imagination by a metaphorical algebraic manipulation:

> I have already laid stress on the factor of doubt in my introductory remarks; I have, as it were, placed that factor outside the brackets and I may be allowed to save myself the trouble of repeating it in connection with each item *inside* them [*S.E.* 23:31].

Ten pages later, Freud again calls attention to his proceeding in spite of the lack of certain knowledge, as if his personal identification with Moses demanded that the subject be worked out in detail:

> Once again I am prepared to find myself blamed for having presented my reconstruction . . . with too great and unjustified certainty. . . . this criticism . . . finds an echo in my own judgement. . . . On the whole my predominant impression is that it is worth while to pursue the work in the direction it has taken [*S.E.* 23:41].

Having given free rein to speculation, speculation spurs him on a course of extravagance.

Freud's imaginative flights were contingent on his sporadic

inspiration. As Freud explained to Lou Andreas-Salomé in connection with his delayed metapsychological work, "The systematic working of material is not possible for me; the fragmentary nature of my experiences and the sporadic character of my insight do not permit it."[13] Elsewhere he said: "I have a special talent for being satisfied with the fragmentary;"[14] "Often, it seems, I can go for a long while without feeling the need to clarify an obscure point, and then one day I am compelled to by the pressure of facts or by the influence of someone else's ideas."[15] On another occasion, he acknowledged his reliance on countertransferential inspiration: "Any kind of systematic work is inconsistent with my gifts and inclinations. I expect all my impulses from the impressions in the intercourse with the patients."[16] Freud's toleration of the fragmentary went hand in hand with his feeling that the inductive nature of psychoanalysis as an empirical science was a great burden, going as it did against his deeper inclinations and forcing him reluctantly to enter into prolonged logical demonstration.

> I can see from the difficulties I encounter in this work [the study of totemism, etc.] that I was not cut out for inductive investigation, that my whole makeup is intuitive, and that in setting out to establish the purely empirical science of ψA I subjected myself to an extraordinary discipline.[17]

A further peculiarity of Freud's makeup is that his intuitive gift was combined with a decided preference for analysis over synthesis:

> I so rarely feel the need of synthesis. The unity of this world seems to me so self-evident as not to need emphasis. What interests me is the separation and breaking up into component parts of what would otherwise revert to an inchoate mass. . . . In short, I am of course an analyst, and believe that synthesis offers no obstacles once analysis has been achieved.[18]

This preference, stemming from character traits, extended to Freud's external evaluation of the primacy of analysis—and it contrasts sharply with the view of such a critic as Pfister, who was prone to place synthesis first and foremost in psychoanalytic treatment.[19]

Throughout the entire corpus of pertinent primary source

literature, I have found but two passages that elucidate the fantasmal underpinnings for this preference of analysis over synthesis. In her journal entry of February 23, 1913, Frau Lou recounts her visit to Berggasse 19 and Freud's criticism of any rational need for a definitive unity of things not only on the grounds that such a need can hamper scientific research but also because it stems from highly anthropomorphic sources and customs. Years later, in a letter, Freud contrasted the disorder of his own work with Lou's tidiness, which he regarded as a feminine trait. We may speculate from this evidence that Freud's unconscious body image is at the root of his linking of analysis with maleness and synthesis with femaleness:

> For the first time I have been struck by something exquisitely feminine in your intellectual approach. When in my annoyance at the eternal ambivalences I am prepared to leave everything higgledy-piggledy, you tidy up everything, put everything in order and show that it is possible to be quite comfortable in that way too.[20]

In the context of Freud's avoiding both definition and analysis and his hyperbolic tendency to pursue ideas to their limits, we derive profit as soon as we turn our attention to a highly significant, though neglected, feature of his writing that stands out in psychoanalytic literature: the continual placement of the content at a particular level of certainty. Again and again, in this dance of judgment and ego functioning, we come across qualifiers like *rather likely, probably, certainly,* and countless others. Freud's knowledge of philosophy included but did not go beyond epistemology, which is reflected in the epistemological cast of his writing, the precise word choices of which never fail to specify the immediate *quality of knowing* (key words include: *obvious, guess, assume, evident, recognize, suspect, suppose,* etc.).[21] Thus the reader shifts effortlessly from the highest to the lowest degrees of certainty, experiencing an intellectual satisfaction due in part to a self-awareness of his own rapid adaptability and the flexibility of his judging ego. These factors contribute to the dialectical traces in Freud's work, traces we can best appreciate when we bear in mind that controversy only becomes dialectical when it attends not to facts but to the meaning of facts.

Freud's free-ranging powers of mind, his avoidance of special pleading, and his relative impartiality give his prose a certain note of lightness and a self-irony that recall that singular instance of humor in which the superego, abandoning its customary, flagellating role, comforts and is kind to the ego (see "Humour," *S.E.* 21:159–166). How far from the overseriousness and rigid self-defense of so many psychoanalytic authors is the tone of their great precursor, who could even contest his own mastery. Gently turning the tables on himself (as we have seen) at the end of his Schreber study, he floated the possibility that his analysis of the case might itself be a delusion, and did he not entertain the notion that his study of Leonardo might be merely "a psychoanalytic novel" (*S.E.* 11:134)? Going still further, Freud held elsewhere:

> I am myself a heretic who has not yet become a fanatic. I cannot stand fanatics, people who are capable of taking their narrowmindedness seriously. By holding on to one's superiority one can do a lot of things which are against the tide.[22]

Schur aptly remarked that Freud's self-ironical style enabled him to express the most subtle variations in mood.[23]

It is fruitful to compare Freud's expository procedure and dialectical orientation with Plato's. The mind that has been rightfully tempered by impartiality and the freedom of the exigencies of practice

> is able to experience the apparent tragedy by being thoroughly and relentlessly dialectical, and also to stand apart from it, unhurt, untouched, only smiling. In its impartiality before all ideas, in its freedom from what is really special pleading, in its ability to entertain any notion whether or not it be true or credible, such a mind enjoys the dialectical insight which makes controversy and reflection sane pursuits, and has those moments of quiet laughter which makes them what Plato called a "dear delight." . . . The play of thought! In so far as thinking is dialectical it is playful in the sense of a game taken in the comic spirit and serving impractical ends. . . . Perhaps all thinking is playful in this sense, but dialectic most certainly is.[24]

The "dear delight" is not to be understood as some casual feature of Freud's prose, which plays freely and roams through various levels of certitude. Kris lamented the general neglect of Freud's insight (in the Joke Book) that under certain conditions the activity of the psychic apparatus could be pleasurable in itself.[25] With great sensitivity, Kris contrasts the stereotyped variations of psychotic art with the free variations of truly creative art, where freedom marks the shifts in psychic levels, from conscious perception to preconscious elaboration to the reverberations of the id. Freud too, like the creative artist, maintains no rigid psychic distance from his material; he plays with it in the most constructive sense. Thus we may apply Kris's notions of aesthetics to Freud's writing—as well as to our own ideal reaction to it. As Kris points out, when psychic distance is minimal, our reaction to a work of art will be pragmatic rather than aesthetic. It is an even more ambitious and complex question, says Kris, whether we should restrict our aesthetic attitude exclusively to our reactions to art.[26] The implications of this question for Freud's work are immense, for the "traditional" approach, misguided by a particular attitude to science, has sought more assurance than Freud can really give. Put another way, when the psychoanalyst can allow himself to follow Keats and enter a sparrow to pick about the gravel; when he can follow Coleridge, willingly suspending disbelief; when he can remove himself from distorting infantile needs of assurance; when he can relaxedly follow the groping, turning, and self-correction and self-modification of Freud's thought from sentence to sentence; when he can permit himself to delight in the orchestration of the unconscious and conscious material Freud relates and evaluates, shifting with breathtaking unexpected frequency among the many levels of certainty—then he will appreciate that wonderful play of dialectical delight, aesthetic power, and intellectual insight Freud's prose gives through its varied unison of conscious and unconscious derivatives.

In this context, we do well to remember that the unconscious knows neither negation, doubt, nor "degrees of certainty" (*S.E.* 14:186). Consequently, in dream analysis, "the whole scale of estimates of certainty shall be abandoned and . . . the faintest possibility that something of this or that sort may have occurred in the dream shall be treated as complete certainty" (*S.E.* 5:516). Dream thoughts, that is, know no doubt or uncertainty, which arises from censorship governing dream work (*S.E.* 18:78 fn.). In light of this, we may appreciate within the upper and lower reaches of Freud's psychic activity the mobility of his attention, the dance and play of his intellect to roam from one realm of certitude to another, to juggle an array of concepts, to train his eyes on the changing position of each one relative to all others, and resist any tempting, immediate explanation for contradictory phenomena.[27] Such mastery over complex matter holds not only momentarily; it was with Freud throughout his life, permitting him easily to change opinions, as he frequently did in his life. He cherished this capacity; and approvingly quoted the self-commentary by Frazer already cited in these pages once before; the passage fittingly traces Freud's own chameleon movement:

> That my conclusions on these difficult questions are final, I am not so foolish as to pretend. I have changed my views repeatedly, and I am resolved to change them again with every change of the evidence, for like a chameleon the candid inquirer should shift his colours with the shifting colours of the ground he treads [*S.E.* 13:108 fn.].

The reference to ground leads us on to Freud's distinctive use of travel imagery to indicate levels of certainty and simultaneously to describe the progression of his argument. The subject of imagery will be discussed at length in my next chapter; for now, suffice it to say that such expressions as "firm footing," "a bold step forward, "shaky ground," "clearer path," etc., are liberally scattered through Freud's discourse. His recourse to his personal experience of mountain climbing and staking trails gave him an ideal linguistic instrument for alerting the reader to the changing judgmental and logical terrain from sentence to sentence and paragraph to paragraph. We can hardly find apter images for the variations of certainty than those from Freud's outdoor pastime with its moment-to-moment gropings, hesitations, tentative probings, and cautious steps forward. Glancing briefly at the first half of Chapter 6 of *Beyond the Pleasure Principle* we observe a unifying image that may recall our own experiences climbing:

> Let us turn . . . arrived at along a different path . . . in any direction . . . offer us a firm footing . . . in contrary directions . . . a bold attempt at another step forward . . . an opportunity

for looking back . . . the next step was taken . . . we are venturing upon the further step . . . [*S.E.* 18:44–52].

On a deeper level, Freud's use elsewhere of more creative metaphors, which depart from the rigidity and confining precision of
literal language, by virtue of their restless polarity between image
and idea, more closely approximates the dynamic character of
psychic processes. When Freud uses the mechanistic term *psychic
apparatus*, for example, he counteracts its technological connotations by the animation of its inhabitants—the id, ego, and
superego—that quasi-oedipal triangle that constitutes the
"edifice" complex of the structural theory.

All too often, commentators paraphrasing Freud leave out the
figure of speech, the *what if*, the *possible* or *probable*, by which his
own statements are qualified, thus obscuring the suppositional
character of the original. The causes for such unconditional interpretations may lie in the boundary-blurring, unitive force of analogical speech itself, in the exegetes' resistance to the compulsive
practice of labeling as hypothetical or figurative every Freudian
explanation they mention, or in still other factors. The frequent
result, in any case, is that qualifiers are winnowed out in the
exegetical enterprise, or, to put it more concretely, that the anvil,
usurping the forger's place, stamps a new forgery of its own. At
times, however, the difficulty is inherent in Freud's text itself, for
his exposition is typically a working through of meaning. Sometimes he ends a series of his own assertions by undercutting
them, as in the self-ironical, self-critical remarks in the final pages
of the Schreber and da Vinci treatises. Sometimes the procedure is
reversed: he begins with a series of qualified statements and suddenly leaps to a startling generalization. Roustang (p. 90) dwells
on one among many fine examples of the latter practice in Chapter 7 of *The Interpretation of Dreams*. Freud writes: "I think it is
highly doubtful whether in the case of an adult a wish that has
not been fulfilled during the day would be strong enough to
produce a dream" (*S.E.* 5:552). Several lines later this doubt assumes the form of a general opinion: "But in general, I think, a
wish that has been left over unfulfilled from the previous day is
insufficient to produce a dream in the case of an adult." By the

next paragraph this general opinion becomes a full-blown psychoanalytic law: *"a wish which is represented in a dream must be an infantile one."*[28] The escalation and de-escalation of universal statements is clear evidence of the amplitude of primary process and affective intensity in Freud's most speculative thought processes. His texts must be read with the utmost care and tact; we must beware of a-fortiori and post-hoc-ergo-propter-hoc arguments and of general proofs supported by a single striking example; and we should note, too, that his conscious penchant for hyperbole and antithesis imposes on us as readers the task of tailoring down or harmonizing many of his universal and partially contradictory statements.[29] Freud's expository style is genuinely dyadic, demanding the reader's understanding participation in constructing, reconstructing, and deconstructing the text.

For a detailed appreciation of the aesthetic play of Freud's judgment in exposition, we can choose no better text than the late short essay, "The Acquisition and Control of Fire" (*S.E.* 22:187–193). Recalling that degrees of certainty may be indicated not only by such obvious markers as *probably* and *surely* but also by modals (*must, might, could, did,* etc.) and indeed the sentence type as a whole (interrogative, declarative, etc.), let the reader experience at first hand Freud's adroit movement among levels of certainty. The following passage is from the ninth paragraph.

> A water-dragon subdued by fire—that surely makes no sense. But, as in so many dreams, sense emerges if we reverse the manifest content. . . . Heracles, then, extinguishes this brand of fire with—water. (The immortal head is no doubt the phallus itself, and its destruction signifies castration.) But Heracles was also the deliverer of Prometheus and slew the bird which devoured his liver. Should we not suspect a deeper connection between the two myths? It is as though the deed of the one hero was made up for by the other. Prometheus (like the Mongolian law) had forbidden the quenching of fire; Heracles permitted it in the case in which the brand of fire threatened disaster. The second myth seems to correspond to the reaction of a later epoch of civilization to the events of the acquisition of power over fire. It looks as though this line of approach might take us quite a distance into the secrets of the myth; but admittedly we should carry a feeling of certainty with us only a short way [pp. 191–192].

Put metaphorically (but the metaphor is imperfect, implying a division that does not exist), Freud's keenly balanced intellect is hunched over, running, ever ready to swerve and veer off in pursuit of the dodging subject matter, *all the while* (and this is the remarkable feat) judging and labeling the trustworthiness of the new terrain chosen by the subject matter in its flight. Even more remarkably, we witness again and again how certainty *increases* as Freud's thought goes forward. To grasp what I mean, I ask my reader to read patiently and responsively through the following selected list of illustrative phrases drawn from the essay at hand:

> I think my hypothesis . . . can be confirmed by an interpretation of the Greek myth of Prometheus, provided that we bear in mind the distortions. . . . If we were interpreting a dream we should be inclined to regard such an object as a penis symbol, although the unusual stress laid on its hollowness might make us hesitate. But how can we bring this penis-tube into connection with the preservation of fire? There seems little chance of doing this, till we remember. . . . it must have something to do with the matter; but for the moment I shall not attempt an interpretation. On the other hand, we feel on firm ground. . . . Well, if, through all its distortions, it barely allows us to get a glimpse of the fact . . . at least it makes no secret of the resentment which the culture-hero could not fail to arouse. . . . And this is in accordance with what we know and expect. . . . It is difficult to resist the notion that . . . and that, if this is so. . . . The bird which sates itself on the liver would then have the meaning of a penis. . . . A short step further brings us to the phoenix. . . .

The flexibility of judgment and self-monitoring in this impressive array of examples from an essay of fewer than a dozen paragraphs is indeed extraordinary.[30]

But it is most fitting that this chapter culminate in a close look at "The 'Uncanny' " (*S.E.* 17:219–256), which is shot through and through with certainties and uncertainties *about* certainties and uncertainties. The best commentary on it to date is by the French critic and writer Héléne Cixous,[31] whose argument runs roughly as follows: The text, being a play or replay with uncertainty, proceeds as its own metaphor; the uncanny comprises the object, essence, and the very methodology of the text. Moreover, the uncanny bespeaks its opposite, the familiar, and indeed the phenomenon of doubling dominates the essay. The protagonist,

Freud, is also part of the doubling: the scientific writer, he sees in himself a fictional writer, so that Hoffmann, one of the writers he alludes to, becomes his double. Along the same line, Freud at the outset avows that the feeling of the *uncanny* has long been *strange* to him. The object of his analysis is a doubling, constituted by the repressed and the surmounted, which are examined in their appearances both in life *and* in literature. This text on doubt raises doubt in the reader about itself, partly on account of the organization of the text, which is uncanny: the themes of the canny and uncanny are sometimes joined, sometimes separate, pairing off and splitting apart. A heightened instance of the pairing lies in the fact that since the *uncanny* is the name for that which remains hidden, Freud's initial lexicographical undertaking is undermined by the text as a whole, which functions as a metaphor of its own setting. Finally, Cixous argues, Freud is a novelist, and "The 'Uncanny' " is a theoretical novel, dramatically distributing suspense, surprise, and false leads.

My own commentary, following in the line of this stimulating analysis, goes further into the formal elements of Freud's essay which, appearances to the contrary, is a difficult and elusive piece of writing in all its three parts. Like many of his writings, "The 'Uncanny' " presents in its third part a synthesis and refinement of conclusions, suggesting that his purpose in writing is to work through complex ideas. Hence for purposes of analytic clarity, I begin with a diagrammatic outline of Freud's conclusions, all drawn from the third part, which will enable us to return to the beginning and trace the tentative paths of Freud's thinking.

There are two types of the uncanny:

I. The uncanny in real life, associated with an involuntary suspension of reality-testing; of this type there are two subtypes:

   A. The uncanny that we imagine or read about; thus, a matter of psychic reality. This type of the uncanny is something secretly familiar and repressed (infantile complexes such as the castration complex or womb fantasies); it returns with a frightening affect.

   B. The uncanny that we experience; hence, a matter of material reality. This subtype of the uncanny consists of primitive, animistic beliefs (omnipotence of thoughts, secret powers, return of the dead) eventually suppressed or surmounted that seem again to be confirmed. Thus reality-testing is shaken, and a conflict arises over whether the things surmounted or held to be incredible are in fact possible after all. It is interesting further to note that whereas the belief in the *material* reality of animistic beliefs has at one time been surmounted, in the case of the repressed, we have never ceased to believe in the reality of such a content [p. 249].

II. The uncanny in the realm of fictional literature, associated with the deliberate suspension of reality-testing, and consisting of two subtypes:

A. The uncanny concerning surmounted forms of belief. Whereas there is no uncanny effect in the outright authorial adoption of animistic beliefs as in fairy tales, the uncanny obtains when, while pretending to move in the world of common reality, the writer keeps us in the dark for a long time (or even for good) about his presuppositions about the supernatural.

B. The uncanny arising from repressed complexes. Here the literary impact is similar to the impact of repressed complexes in real life, except in cases when the creative author places us in a point of view *different* from that of the protagonist fearing the uncanny experience.

We should first of all notice that in talking about the uncanny or its opposite, Freud uses descriptive and expository terms intimately associated with his subject matter: thus the canny is echoed in such terms as *obvious, naturally, evident, familiar;* the uncanny, in *foreign, remote,* and *rarely.* In shifting gradations of uncertainty and certainty Freud's text pursues the theme of certainty, and its investigative method weaves into the object of investigation, as we can glimpse in the following sample list of indicators:

easily guesses . . . unhesitatingly recognized . . . not yet rightly understood . . . become intelligible . . . further doubts are removed . . . undeniable instances of the uncanny . . . we find ourselves on familiar ground . . . certainly not complete. . . . But that would be to open the door to doubts about what exactly is . . .

This terminological doubling runs parallel to the obvious character doubling and the less obvious element of returning in its various forms. There is the narrative episode of Freud returning to the same Italian red-light district three times, the returning of the readers' doubts (p. 245), and Freud's own expository return to material as yet not fully explained (p. 252).

Reversal and inversion are other pertinent phenomena, whether in logic or in other realms. Freud logically asserts:

> Naturally not everything that is new and unfamiliar is frightening, however; the relation is not capable of inversion [p. 220].

> It may be true that the uncanny [*unheimlich*] is something which is secretly familiar [*heimlich-heimisch*], which has undergone repression and then returned from it, and that everything that is uncanny fulfils this condition. . . . our proposition is clearly not convertible [p. 245].

In contrast there may be developmental reversion, as in the case of the ancient Egyptians who made images of the dead to achieve immortality but with the state of mortality surmounted, "the 'double' reverts its aspect" and turns into an uncanny harbinger of death (p. 235). But apart from such historical accidents, the existential nature of the uncanny in life is the reverse of its nature in art, so that *"a great deal that is not uncanny in fiction would be so if it happened in real life; and in the second place . . . there are many more means of creating uncanny effects in fiction than there are in real life"* (p. 249). A baseline of these various reversibilities is the evolution of the word *heimlich* itself, which developed in the direction of ambivalence only to coincide with its opposite, ranging in meaning from *familiar, intimate, secret* to *hidden* and *dangerous*. Threading throughout Freud's essay, then, is an uncanniness and uncertainty about ideas, the organization of those ideas, and the very terms used to describe them.

The organization of the opening paragraph of Section 1, which is mainly lexicographical, already contains a glimpse of the uncanny. The first sentence and the third (and last) mention the psychoanalyst's *rare* investigations in some *remote* province of aesthetics; these two statements bracket the central assertion, which refers to his usual, *familiar* activity. So the very arrangement of sentences mimics the content of the return of the uncanny.

Next come oxymoronic statements that the uncanny *undoubt-*

*edly* relates to the frightening and that, *equally certainly,* the term
has not always been used in a *clearly* definable way. In light of the
fact that World War I kept Freud from consulting any foreign
literature on the subject and therefore from claiming priority of
ideas, we are curious about Freud's feeling that his ideas might
already be *familiar* in a *strange* literature. What he was *able* to
consult was a monograph by Jentsch, in his native German. Pursuing an idea in that monograph, Freud confesses the feeling of
the uncanny has long since been strange to him, so that he must
imaginatively put himself into that state (*sich hineinversetzen*). To
elaborate on the concept of the uncanny, Freud sees two possible
courses: to trace the history of the word, or to collate instances of
the uncanny for purposes of inference. In his actual investigation
Freud began with the second, inductive approach, yet he writes,
very significantly for our analysis, that his exposition will follow
the "reverse course," i.e., the lexicographical one. Beginning with
the German word, he breaks off to deal with the way the concept
of the uncanny is rendered in other languages which, Freud tells
his German readers, tell us "nothing new, perhaps only because
we ourselves speak a language that is foreign." After a brief survey of foreign terms, Freud doubles back: "Let us therefore return
to the German language." The subsequent quotation from San-
ders's dictionary constitutes a reversal within a reversal, since the
entry for *heimlich* goes on for two and a half pages before arriving
at the negative derivate *unheimlich.* Finally, turning to Grimm's
dictionary, Freud, true to reverse form, cites only the entry
*heimlich.* The stage is now set for Section 2 and its examples for
induction, which were to be the first step in Freud's investigation;
and we as readers are already half-disoriented by the various
reroutings, textual and extratextual, of the uncanny.

In Section 2 the disorienting polysemy of doubling continues
to proliferate to such a degree that even terms of singularity start
to partake of paradox. Thus Hoffmann is hailed as the unrivaled
(*unerreicht*) master of the uncanny who achieved an incomparably
(*unvergleichlich*) uncanny atmosphere in his story "The Sand-
Man." Freud assumes the role of protagonist-expositor, attempting to pin down the uncertainty that pervades the story with a
self-reassuring rearrangement of the narrative episodes; in his
further role as apologist for psychoanalysis, he conjures up as a

possible double an unbeliever, who, he says, would be hard put to deny that the anxiety about the Sand-Man's threat to the eyes has a deep connection with the castration complex. The rest of Section 2 presents a series of doubles in various forms on which Cixous has commented superbly (see especially pp. 538–539). The story of the doubles comprises four different clusters, occurring simultaneously "in a spatio-temporal emancipation worthy of fiction": the first cluster centers on general manifestations of the double (cleavage, substitution, etc.); the second cluster, on the researchers of the double (Rank, Hoffmann, Freud, etc.); the third cluster, on a series of anecdotes; the fourth cluster, on the recognition that each theme is a double of another theme (dream language, Egyptian art, etc.).

To these clusters I would add the following: Coursing throughout Section 2 are the themes of death (a derivative of which is castration) and the return to mother and uterine existence; and death and this return are of course doubles too, and as such the very ground of all doubt and uncertainty. If in the context of "The Sandman" Freud can speak freely about the castrating father in Nathaniel's childhood, he avoids (as he tends to do throughout his work as well) the topic of the castrating mother, although it is very prominent in the story. Freud recounts from his own life a repetitive occurrence "undoubtedly" uncanny in feeling: Lost in a provincial Italian town, he returned three times to a district whose disreputable character could not long remain "in doubt." Without saying so, he was actually returning to a threatening and forbidden mother. He next conjectures that it would be uncanny to spot the number 62 over and over again in a single day. The number is, in fact, far from being innocent or idly chosen: it alludes to Freud's age a year before when (not for the first time) the vision of dying had powerfully welled up in him. In rapid step, Freud goes on to repetition and infantile psychology, which, he remarks without further specification, he treated in another work. That work is *Beyond the Pleasure Principle* with the famous and unforgettable episode in Chapter 2 that deals with the repetition compulsion and little Ernst's symbolic game about his absent mother.

We may quickly skip over the intervening pregnant references and proceed to Freud's closing statement that neurotic men often feel there is something uncanny about the female genitalia. I doubt today whether any analyst would accept Freud's male-chauvinist position that the Oedipus complex is completely dissolvable in some men but not in any women at all. Recognizing that traces of at least the Oedipus and castration complex remain in all men, we must regard Freud's qualifier about neurotic men as defensive; he too feels there is something uncanny about the female genitals, and having been there he can posit an undecipherable (let us say "uncanny") navel in every dream. But it is worthwhile spelling out Freud's own associations about the female pudenda:

> It often happens that neurotic men declare that they feel there is something uncanny about the female genital organs. This *unheimlich* place, however, is the entrance to the former *Heim* [home] of all human beings, to the place where each one of us lived once upon a time and in the beginning. There is a joking saying that 'Love is home-sickness'; and whenever a man dreams of a place or a country and says to himself, while he is still dreaming: 'this place is familiar to me, I've been here before', we may interpret the place as being his mothers genitals or her body. In this case too, then, the *unheimlich* is what was once *heimisch*, familiar; the prefix *'un'* ['un-'] is the token of repression [p. 245].

On the narrative level, Freud's erring in an Italian red-light district ends up at a home, a home subject to repression and negation. We suddenly remember that in the subsequent article "Negation" Freud recommended translating a patient's denial that he dreamt of his mother into the realization "So it *is* his mother." Here, we should apply this insight to himself: he is speaking of his own mother.[32] Thus Freud completes an uncanny cycle, from the uterus, mother, and mother substitutes to repression and negation and finally to death and the repetition compulsion. If this explanation itself is uncanny, it is as it should be, for psychoanalysis can become uncanny by unveiling hidden forces (p. 243).

The third and last section of "The 'Uncanny' " is devoted to clearing up remaining doubts and investigating further into the uncanny in life and in literature, its double. Attempting now *not* to be uncanny about the uncanny, he vows not to conceal (*verschweigen*) that nearly every example he adduces for his hypothesis has its negating counterexample. He readily admits, too, that his distinction between the *repressed* uncanny and the *surmounted* uncanny, which concerns primitive beliefs, is often not really clear since primitive beliefs and infantile complexes are deeply related. Hence disorienting unclarity persists through the canny and the uncanny. True to form, the essay ends with a reference (Freud's third in this text) to further explanation in another of his works (or doubles).

Freud never grappled with uncertainty and the uncanny more directly than here, nor will we go astray in using this text to clarify some of his other familiar ones. Perhaps such clarification begins best at the end, with the posthumously published essay "Splitting of the Ego in the Process of Defence," which starts out:

> I find myself for a moment in the interesting position of not knowing whether what I have to say should be regarded as something long familiar and obvious or as something entirely new and puzzling. But I am inclined to think the latter [*S.E.* 23:275].

Such intimacy in his writing, which was second nature to Freud, gives us the strange feeling of being right at home.

### Notes

1. See Robert Holt's insightful essay "Freud's Cognitive Style."

2. Scientific meeting of 23.10.07, in *Minutes of the Vienna Psychoanalytic Society*, 4 volumes, edited by H. Nunberg and E. Federn (New York: International Universities Press, 1962–1975), 1:222.

3. Jones 1:371, 396; and 2:282. In the words of Freud's best lexicographers to date: "Si Freud écrivain s'est montré inventif, il a été peu soucieux de la perfection de son vocabulaire. . . . La polysémie et les chevauchements sémantiques n'en sont pas absents; plusieurs mots n'appellent pas toujours des idées trés différentes" (J. Laplanche and J.-B. Pontalis, *Vocabulaire de la psychanalyse* [Paris: Presses Universitaires de France, 1968], p. vi).

4. See S. Breznitz, "A Critical Note on Secondary Revision," *International Journal of Psycho-Analysis*, 52:407–412 (1972).

5. M. Gill, *Topography and Systems in Psychoanalytic Theory. Psychological Issues*, Monogr. 10 (New York: International Universities Press, 1963), pp. 32–33, 100.

6. Jones 1:33–34; 2:401.

7. Jones 2:419.

8. Journal entry for 6.3.30, in *Diary of My Analysis*, pp. 47–48.

9. Similar advice was given to Joseph Wortis (*Fragments of an Analysis*, p. 137). In his own private life Freud greatly disliked helplessness; he habitually resisted the attempts of others to influence him, and he was appreciative of his wife's resistance to him (Jones 1:129; 2:428–429, and 1:122, respectively).

10. Letters of 25.5.16. (p. 45), 7.10.17 (p. 63), and the letter of about 10.7.31 (p. 196) in *Andreas-Salomé: Letters*.

11. Letter of 12.11.38 to Marie Bonaparte, in *Letters*, p. 451.

12. N. Schlessinger et al., "The Scientific Style of Breuer and Freud in the Origins of Psychoanalysis," *Journal of the American Psychoanalytic Association*, 15:404–405, 410, 421 (1967).

13. Letter of 2.4.19, *Andreas-Salomé: Letters*, p. 95. For similar statements, see letters of 9.11.15 (p. 35) and 1.4.15 (p. 28).

14. Letter of 17.4.21 to Groddeck, in *The Meaning of Illness*, p. 58.

15. Letter of 17.12.11 to Jung, in *Freud/Jung Letters*, p. 472. See also Holt's introduction in *Abstracts of the Standard Edition*, p. 66.

16. Letter of 5.2.10, Jones 2:65.

17. Letter of 12.12.19, *Freud/Jung Letters*, p. 472.

18. Letter of 30.7.15, *Andreas-Salomé: Letters*, p. 32.

19. See letters of 9.10.18 (p. 62), and 22.10.27 (p. 113), in *Psycho-Analysis and Faith*; also, letter of 23.3.30, *Andreas-Salomé: Letters*, p. 185.

20. Letter of 9.5.31, *Andreas-Salomé: Letters*, p. 193.

21. See the letter of 30.3.14 to James Putnam: "As you know, I comprehend very little of philosophy and with epistemology (with, not before), my interest ceases to function" (*James Jackson Putnam and Psychoanalysis: Letters between Putnam and Sigmund Freud, Ernest Jones, William James, Sandor Ferenczi, and Morton Prince, 1877–1917*, edited by N. Hale [Cambridge: Harvard University Press, 1971], p. 170).

22. Letter of 28.11.20 to Groddeck, in *The Meaning of Illness*, p. 56.

23. Schur, *Living*, p. 429; see also p. 449 fn.: "Freud used to point out that when a patient could recognize the humorous aspect of a situation, accept a joke or make one himself about it, this indicated a shift toward the dominance of the ego. That Freud could end this letter [written in the depth of sickness in 1933] with a joke indicated that he had been able, this time at least, to master his depressive mood in spite of all the odds against him." Like Schur, Walter Jens also appreciated the self-irony (*Selbst-ironie*) in Freud's letters (*Zueignungen: 11 literarische Porträts* [München: Piper, 1962], p. 66).

24. M. Adler, *Dialectic* (New York: Harcourt, Brace, 1927), pp. 134, 139.

25. See *Psychoanalytic Explorations in Art* (New York: Schocken Books, 1964), esp. pp. 61–63, 253–257.

26. Let us here recall Freud's idea that in obsessional neuroses, the sexual pleasure attached to thought contents is transferred onto the very act of thinking (*S.E.* 10:245).

27. In this as in other respects Freud is indebted to Charcot, who taught him that "one should not mind meeting with contradiction on every side provided one has worked sincerely" ("Letter to *Le Disque Vert*," *S.E.* 19:290).

28. Holt too quotes this sentence ("On Reading Freud," *Abstracts*, p. 53),

which he reads as an indication that Freud was unaware that his empirical propositions should be refutable if they are to be considered seriously.

29. Holt, pp. 42, 55.

30. The *Gesammelte Werke* prints the essay in eleven paragraphs; the *Standard Edition* silently reduces it to ten.

31. "Fiction and Its Phantoms, A Reading of Freud's *Das Unheimliche* (The 'Uncanny')," *New Literary History*, 3:525–548 (1976).

32. J.-M. Rey, *Parcours de Freud* (Paris: Editions Galilée, 1974), p. 131.

# 5

# Resources of Figurative Language

TO FREUD'S LIST OF THE COMPONENTS OF A HEALTHY LIFE—WORK and love—we should not hesitate to add play. His writing, too, contains all three: it bears witness to love of language, sensitively working and playing with it, both on the figurative and the literal level. Like his treatment of audience and the levels of certainty, Freud's figurative discourse skillfully enlists primary and secondary process to create majestic artifacts of conscious and unconscious production. After experiencing Adler's vague, ego-shadowed vocabulary and Jung's mystical, superego-inspired terminology, we turn for refreshment to Freud, whose unique language, constantly marked by physical and organic references, is never alienated from the id. Venturing into the vast terrain of Freud's figurative language, we encounter countless obstacles and pitfalls, and our footing is always insecure. In and around the field of metaphor terminological obscurities and complexities abound: the very instruments we survey with are of doubtful reliability. I begin, therefore, with a leisurely tour of literary history.

Renaissance rhetoricians categorized over two hundred figures of speech, divided into two general types: tropes and schemes. Tropes are figures that literally "turn" or change the meaning of a word, e.g., metaphor and irony; schemes have to do

97

with arrangement of words and sounds apart from their semantic content, e.g., alliteration and anaphora.[1] In the history of rhetoric, critics of various persuasions have accorded a privileged status to particular figures. The Anglo-American New Critics, such as William Empson, T. S. Eliot, I. A. Richards,[2] Ezra Pound, and others, saw the essence of poetry as residing in only a few of the two-hundred-odd figures catalogued by Renaissance rhetoricians: paradox, irony, metaphor, ambiguity, and one or two others. On the other hand, such Structuralists as Roman Jakobson and Roland Barthes regard only two tropes as preeminent: metaphor and metonymy. In fact, Jakobson sees in these the fundamental organizational principles of *all* human verbal and nonverbal sign systems from kinship, magic, and language to clothing, furniture, and countless others. Metonymy is a *combinatory* operation based on a relation of *contiguity;* metaphor is a *selective* operation based on a relation of *similarity.* Thus a menu, for instance, is organized along both metaphoric and metonymic axes, with a contiguous line of courses, each of which offers a possibility of selection.

The figures of speech have also a critical history within the particular domain of psychoanalysis. In 1950, Lionel Trilling offered the pioneering definition that the whole of psychoanalysis is "a science of tropes."[3] Subsequently, the eminent linguist Emile Benveniste designated *The Interpretation of Dreams* a compendium and inventory of stylistic figures.[4] Rieff has given us some fine pages orienting Freud's theory in terms of synecdoche.[5] Applying the structuralist grid to psychoanalysis, Jacques Lacan has equated metaphor with condensation and metonymy with displacement; and has further interpreted desire as metonymy and symptom as metaphor.[6] Harold Bloom has made an ambitious attempt to establish a homology between rhetorical tropes and the various defenses.[7] Figurist interpretation has achieved full vindication with the appearance of a recent issue of the prestigious *Diacritics: A Review of Contemporary Criticism* (Spring 1979) entitled "The Tropology of Freud."

Metaphor and metonymy are immensely useful concepts for psychoanalysis, but there is another figure whose far-reaching potential in this area has yet to be truly appreciated. In Chapter 1, I mentioned that Roustang recognized chiasmus as one of the hallmarks of Freud's style. But as Roustang describes it, chiasmus is no more than a localized stylistic manifestation of primary process. However, chiasmus may also trace out patterns of the effects of primary process on a much broader scale. If I were to simplify somewhat the change in the life of the Metaphysical poet John Donne, for example, I might postulate two Donnes: the first, a young man about London, wrote erotic poetry with a subcurrent of religious reference; the second, older and reformed, an Anglican preacher, composed religious verses shot through with erotic imagery.[8] That chiastic development could be expressed this way:

Chiastic dynamics similarly characterize the sadomasochistic elements in Richard Crashaw, a poet of the next generation. The prefatory couplet of Crashaw's "Saint Mary Magdalene" reads:

> Lo! where a wounded heart with bleeding eyes conspire,
> Is she a flaming fountain, or a weeping fire?

More striking examples abound in "The Flaming Heart," as in the following passage where the reader is invited to "correct" the image of Saint Teresa beside a dart-wielding seraph:

> Do then as equal right requires
> Since his the blushes be, and hers the fires,
> Resume and rectify thy rude design;
> Undress thy seraphim into mine.
> Redeem this injury of thy art;
> Give him the veil, give her the dart. . . .
> Love's passives are his activ'st part.
> The wounded is the wounding heart.
> O heart! the equal poise of love's both parts,
> Big alike with wounds and darts . . .

The dynamics of chiastic relations have yet to be fully worked out; but obviously chiasmus relates to such various phenomena as splitting, projection, ambivalence, and reversal into the opposite, as well as many others. Whatever its sources, chiastic patterning is markedly present in Freud's scientific production both early and late. Consider the example of *Studies on Hysteria*, in which Breuer intended to treat the subject along strictly psychological lines, yet wound up talking of intracerebral excitations and parallels with electric circuits, while Freud, who was after purely physiological and chemical explanations, yet concluded with the admission that his case histories read like fiction and that his analyses were psychological (see Strachey's note, *S.E.* 2:xxiv). In *The Future of an Illusion* there is a further chiasmus, in the exchange of roles between Freud and his imagined interlocutor, who gains the upper hand with his claim that he is reasonable and skeptical and his accusation against Freud as an enthusiast when he postulates a future time free of illusion (*S.E.* 21:51 ff.). A much more complicated chiasmus exists between the canny-familiar and the uncanny-unfamiliar, especially in view of Freud's comment that the prefix *un* is both the mark of repression and the operator that makes possible intellectual judgment. Freud's development displays chiastic patterning on an even grander scale. As Laplanche has brilliantly suggested, "If we place face to face the terms constituting the constant pairs of opposites in Freud's thought, that genealogy takes the form of a strange chiasmus whose riddle we, as Freud's successors, are beginning to decipher." The chiasmus is as follows:[9]

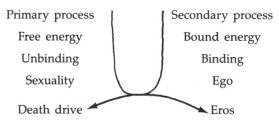

| Primary process | Secondary process |
|---|---|
| Free energy | Bound energy |
| Unbinding | Binding |
| Sexuality | Ego |
| Death drive | Eros |

Let us return to other forms of figurative language, the general family of analogy and metaphor, Freud's appropriation of which into general explanatory models has occasioned much recent critical debate. The advocates of metaphor in psychological and psychoanalytic thinking advance a dual argument: they point to the intrinsic advantages of metaphor on the one hand and the limitations of literal language on the other. For one commentator, the very instability of metaphor widens the scope of an idea beyond the limits of the given. Based as it is both on similarity and difference, and containing hidden connotations and traditional meanings, metaphor has greater potential for stimulating thought than sheer technical terminology.[10] Metaphor offers a subjective understanding of experience, and is thus superior to purely abstract terms for the purposes of the analyst, who must attend not only to ideas but mostly to the feelings of his patients.[11] We may postulate that the attack on metaphor in theory formation stems from a philosophy of radical empiricism, which is incapable of doing justice to the discipline of psychoanalysis; and we may insist that the use of metaphor in science is inevitable, that indeed all science is the systematic application of metaphor, and that accordingly, even if metaphors are not reified (remaining latent and therefore subversive), they remain indispensable for true scientific creativity. *"Alles Vergängliche ist nur ein Gleichnis"* sings the Chorus Mysticus at the close of Goethe's *Faust:* "Everything transient is merely a metaphor"—a poetic support for our apologies, which Susanne Langer buttresses further: "Every new experience, or new idea about things evokes first of all some metaphorical expression."[12] We may add here that no metaphor in any scientific context is completely neutral. The vehicle or image has a life of its own; spillage occurs, enhancing or devaluing the idea. In fact the problem is even more complicated and pervasive: scratch practically any word and you'll find a metaphor.

In their article summarizing the literature on the anthropomorphic brand of metaphor, Grossman and Simon[13] note that introspectable psychic life is anthropomorphic and that Freud tends to use his own terms metaphorically, particularly the structural ones. Accepting an anthropomorphic language for explanations of meaning and motive, they endorse a different language for causation, and look forward to the development of a superordinate schema in which both kinds of discourse could be coordinated. The attitude of Holt and Schafer toward Freud's anthropomorphism is much more circumspect.[14] Holt cautions against the dangers of reification in structural as well as in topographic theory; he sees Freud as grappling unsuccessfully with two traditions from which he emerged: the mechanism of Helmholtzian physicalistic physiology and the vitalism of *Naturphilosophie.* Schafer's attack stands out as the most sustained argument against metaphorical language used for psychoanalytic purposes: Freud's use of spatial analogies might be sufficient for preliminary phases of thought, says Schafer, but it is no substitute for proper theorizing. He argues further that by using action language instead of inert metaphorical disclaimers in the clinical context, we neither split off emotion from the controlling agent nor substantiate emotions and defenses, which gives us an advantage.

At any rate, we may not conclude that the suppression of metaphor can guarantee scientific prose. Two continental critics have brilliantly demonstrated the action of rhetoric in an apparently blankly factual article on the endocrinological functioning of the hypothalamus.[15] Gusfield reached similar results in his study of the rhetoric of a "scientific" report in one of the soft sciences; he answers the naive "windowpane theory," according to which scientific language is supposed to be easily detachable from its content, with an illuminating passage from Northrop Frye's *Anatomy of Criticism*:

> Anything which makes a functional use of words will always be involved in all the technical problems of words, including rhetorical problems. The only road from grammar to logic, then, runs through the intermediate territory of rhetoric.[16]

When we turn to Freud's own comments on and practice with figurative language, we find a series of subtle perceptions that might do honor to a master architect. To make such conceptions as "psychical locality" more intelligible, analogies are justified, says Freud, as long as we "do not mistake the scaffolding for the building" (*S.E.* 5:536). Justifying the use of spatial imagery to denote psychic locality in *The Interpretation of Dreams*, Freud has recourse to other clarifying spatial imagery. Yet feeling uneasy that such imagery might be "misleading," he returns to the problem of depiction, opting for a dynamic representation over a topographic one, and introducing his famous figure of endopsychic perception as resembling the virtual image inside a focusing telescope (*S.E.* 5:610–611). The root of the problem of representation is that "What is psychical is something so unique and peculiar to itself that no one comparison can reflect its nature" (*S.E.* 17:161). The next sentences of this passage are especially rich in imagery. Freud suggests four analogies to psychoanalytic work: the work of a chemist, of a surgeon, of an orthopedist, and of an educator. Thematically the ready interchangeability of these figurative analogies anticipates and mimetically paves the way for what Freud will say about the nature of the symptom: "Whenever we succeed in analysing a symptom into its elements, in freeing an instinctual impulse from one nexus, it does not remain in isolation, but immediately enters into a new one." Said in other words, the form of Freud's analogy—its tetradic multiplicity is the latent anticipation of the content of a statement about the vicissitudes of symptoms. Perhaps Freud's most sustained analogy is that of stratified structures figuring forth the trends of free association, a subject "which has never yet been represented" (*S.E.* 2:288–295, 298–301). Running throughout this dominant analogy are many similes which admittedly are to a degree contradictory and bear only limited resemblance to the basic topic, but though Freud realizes that his procedure is open to objection, like a true artist he takes the risk in his mimetic endeavor "to throw light from different directions on a highly complicated [and, may we say, multidirectional] topic" (p. 291).[17]

We shall find it enlightening to consider further instances of Freud's skill in structuring (imitatively or otherwise) by means of analogies. In *The Interpretation of Dreams* he introduces a graphic simile everyone can appreciate from personal experience: "Should not the dream continue to recur perpetually, precisely as the vexatious fly keeps on coming back after it has been driven away?" (*S.E.* 5:577). On the next page Freud appropriately undertakes to settle this question and get rid of the insistent fly for good: "If it is true that the dreamer wakes for an instant, yet he really *has* brushed away the fly that was threatening to disturb his sleep." In the category of mimetic analogy, my personal favorite comes from Freud's lecture series at Clark University (*S.E.* 11:25–27). To give a vivid picture of the relation between repression and resistance, Freud draws an analogy from the very moment he is in and the very place in which he stands: an imagined troublemaker is forcibly evicted from the hall whereupon, to prevent his return, chairs are jammed against the door. Here Freud drops the analogy to continue his abstract discussion, but not for long: he interrupts himself to return to the analogy of the troublemaker, who is now represented as kicking up an intolerable racket outside the door. At the imagined request of Clark University President Dr. Stanley Hall, Freud, a deft orator deferring to his immediate audience, allows the unruly, now rehabilitated guest to be readmitted to the lecture. On Hall's authority the repression is lifted—and, we may add, the analogy is too, for Freud resolves here to "put the matter more directly."

Of a different nature entirely is a figure drawn from a piece that while small is a compendium of much deep psychoanalytic thinking: the essay "Negation."[18] Our example exhibits Freud's inventive genius at its highest. Explaining that a repressed image or idea can emerge into consciousness only if it is negated, and that therefore the intellectual substitute for repression is negative judgment, Freud asserts that *no* is the trademark of repression, a certificate of origin like "Made in Germany" (*S.E.* 19:236). If Freud had chosen a negative phrase by way of illustration, his figure would be less momentous. As it is, he rises to the occasion with a *positive* expression, "Made in Germany," which is at home in the unconscious where there is no negation; and yet, those words, being in English in an otherwise completely German text, mani-fest an expatriation to an alien clime.

If we recognize with Freud that scientific language is un-avoidably figurative (*S.E.* 18:60) and that we are condemned to rely on the inadequate language of our perceptions (*S.E.* 22:90 and 23:196), we can better appreciate his way of thinking when, having insisted that in psychology we can only describe by mo-mentary analogies that must constantly be changed, he surpris-ingly depicts the ego in an analogy that can be retained after all:

> I must ask you to picture the ego as a kind of façade of the id, as a frontage, like an external, cortical, layer of it. We can hold on to this last analogy [*S.E.* 20:195].

But it is not retained for long; Freud obliges his imagined interloc-utor with a shift in analogy:

> . . . but perhaps you will be content with a fresh analogy and an example. Think of the difference between 'the front' and 'behind the lines,' as things were during the war [p. 196].

Another fine and rare example is in the sustained description of the beleaguered ego, mimetically depicted by a series of analogies coming from all directions:

> As a frontier-creature, the ego tries to mediate between the world and the id, to make the id pliable to the world and, by means of its muscular activity, to make the world fall in with the wishes of

the id. In point of fact it behaves like the physician during an analytic treatment: it offers itself, with the attention it pays to the real world, as a libidinal object to the id, and aims at attaching the id's libido to itself. It is not only a helper to the id; it is also a submissive slave who courts his master's love. Whenever possible, it tries to remain on good terms with the id; it clothes the id's *Ucs.* commands with its *Pcs.* rationalizations; it pretends that the id is showing obedience to the admonitions of reality, even when in fact it is remaining obstinate and unyielding; it disguises the id's conflicts with reality and, if possible, its conflicts with the super-ego too. In its position midway between the id and reality, it only too often yields to the temptation to become sycophantic, opportunist and lying, like a politician who sees the truth but wants to keep his place in popular favour [*S.E.* 19:56].[19]

This analogical explanation of the nature of the ego naturally leads into the problem of portraying the id. Although nothing exists in the id that is comparable with negation, the ironic fact is that most of what Freud learned about the id was of a negative nature. Freud could only describe the id by contradistinction to the ego, which meant approaching the study of the id and the unconscious with analogies (*S.E.* 18:28 and 22:73–74). By a strange alliance, the id's elusiveness summons up the mystic Brahmans in the *Upanishads* whose constant search for God throughout their forest dwelling led only to this conclusion: "*Neti, neti, neti*" ("Not this, not this, not this").

Freud's most spectacular analogy to illustrate the permanence of psychic material is the oft-cited extended archaeological image of Rome in *Civilization and Its Discontents* (*S.E.* 21:69–70). But to appreciate its singularity, its immense originality, we must follow Freud as he composes the larger context in which it appears. To illustrate the survival of mental phenomena along with their later derivatives, Freud chooses the analogy of zoological phylogeny, but rejects it as too remote and intrinsically unsatisfactory. Then, for nearly two full pages, he sustains the analogy of Rome, only to conclude:

> There is clearly no point in spinning our phantasy any further, for it leads to things that are unimaginable and even absurd. If we want to represent historical sequence in spatial terms we can only do it by juxtaposition in space: the same space cannot have

two different contents. Our attempt seems to be an idle game. It has only one justification. It shows us how far we are from mastering the characteristics of mental life by representing them in pictorial terms [pp. 70–71].

The analogy illustrates, then, by being nonapplicable, *per negativum*. Freud continues his attack, rejecting it on a priori grounds, then switching to "a more closely related object of comparison," a person, or a human body. Thus far, his analogical procedure has zoomed in like a camera from zoological phylogeny, abandoned as too remote, to Rome, and thence to ontogeny, which is closer to home. Yet even ontogeny proves unsatisfactory as an analogy as Freud artistically concludes, "Perhaps we are going *too far* in this" (p. 71; italics mine).

Freud's analogies evince a masterful flexibility, ranging from more intellectual ones to others charged with affectivity and from static comparisons (dealing with immobile objects) to kinetic ones (dealing with transformation, movement, evolution, etc.). These analogies personalize Freud's essays, sweeping in crosscurrents across the varied currents of his substance. Critics have identified repeated image families in Freud's works from many domains: law, medicine, archaeology, physics, warfare, travel, graphics, and many more. Readers, especially those limited to English, may not realize how far some image clusters extend beyond clearly apparent areas of figurative language, subtending Freudian theory throughout. In fact, the image clusters exist as foci of brilliance in a space already aglow with light. Chemistry announces its imposing presence in the lexical derivative *psychoanalysis* (*S.E.* 21:210); in the dead r..etaphor *solution;* in *trimethalymin,* which is the most heavily condensed word in the Irma dream; and in *precipitate* (cf. the ego and superego as precipitates, *S.E.* 19:29 and 23:146). In such terms as *psychical agencies* (*Instanzen* in German, *S.E.* 5:537 fn.), we find the influence of law. And when we recall that the English borrowed term *cathexis* is really *occupation* (*Besetzung*), and relate it to *resistance*, we realize that the imagery of war is ubiquitous in psychoanalysis.[20]

Jerome Bruner sees Freud's imagery as the clue to his ideological power. Specifically, it is an imagery of necessity in which three views are combined: the *scientific*, the determinism of which is traced out in the imagery of classical mechanics, be it hydraulics or electricity; the *dramatic,* whereby the driven actors of its play are interpreted as comprising the parts of a single life; and the *tragic,* according to which a deterministic dialectic operates beneath superficial conscious experience.[21] We should extend and in some ways correct Bruner's conclusion that Freud's mode of thought and conception of man is metaphor, analogy, and drama, all understood in a deterministic sense. True enough, Freud thought in metaphors, but this statement begs for qualification; for while he may have conceived some of his psychology in military terms, he often utilized military analogies simply to illustrate the dynamism of his thinking. Besides, throughout his works, there is ample evidence of his hyperawareness of the limits of metaphorical language. Indeed, if we bear in mind that such language may spring from secondary process as well as from primary process,[22] we quickly arrive at a more accurate picture of Freud's style. Some analogies Freud posited he felt to be scientific correspondences—one of the most famous is the analogy between neurotics, children, and primitive peoples. There are other analogies that stimulated Freud's thinking and appear to have come from conscious and unconscious sources. One such example has to do with fluid flow. In *Energies of Man* (1932) the psychologist W. McDougall conceived of human energy as a fluid flow controlled by attitudes and character, which he likened to such passive natural structures as river beds and tributaries; Freud's imagery draws on man-made structures and activities, such as damming and land reclamation, which actively alter the course and speed of fluid flow.[23] This example suggests that Freud's view of man was not, *pace* Bruner, entirely deterministic but was also humanistic,[24] since the man-made draining structures convey a voluntaristic meaning and thus relate to Freud's concept of defense, the German term for which, *Abwehr,* has both a passive *and* an active sense (see Strachey's note, *S.E.* 1:xxiii).

Continuity, though not fluid flow, dominates two outstanding analogies in *Beyond the Pleasure Principle,* namely those of the vesicle and the protista or protozoa (Chapters 4 and 6). The figurativeness is exceptional, indeed unique insofar as the evolutionary link between these analogies and their referents is so minutely developed that in the resulting continuum the analogical status finally disappears. In other words, what starts out as a parallel example imperceptibly draws closer and closer to the main line of argument, so that the two finally become one. Let us track Freud on the wing as he explains that the system *Cs.*, being exposed to the external world, is not affected as other psychic systems are by excitatory processes:

> Let us picture a living organism in its most simplified possible form as an undifferentiated vesicle of a substance that is susceptible to stimulation. Then the surface turned towards the external world will from its very situation be differentiated and will serve as an organ for receiving stimuli. Indeed embryology, in its capacity as a recapitulation of developmental history, actually shows us that the central nervous system originates from the ectoderm; the grey matter of the cortex remains a derivative of the primitive superficial layer of the organism and may have inherited some of its essential properties. It would be easy to suppose, then, that as a result of the ceaseless impact of external stimuli on the surface of the vesicle, its substance to a certain depth may have become permanently modified. . . . In terms of the system *Cs.*, this would mean that its elements could undergo no further permanent modification from the passage of excitation . . . [S.E. 18:26].[25]

The long exordium on the vesicle switches over to the system *Cs.*, suddenly introduced in mid-paragraph by the words *In terms of*. The next paragraph resumes the discussion of the living vesicle and its receptive cortical layer, which gradually acquires a protective shield against stimuli, but midway in the paragraph, Freud makes another switch, this time to the receptive cortical layer of highly developed organisms. After some further elaboration on his new subject, and a digression, Freud sums up his thought, and we cannot help but notice how the two sides of the ongoing analogy join in a single condensed line of development:

> We have pointed out how the living vesicle is provided with a shield against stimuli from the external world; and we had previously shown that the cortical layer next to that shield must be differentiated as an organ for receiving stimuli from without. This sensitive cortex, however, which is later to become the system *Cs.*, also receives excitations from *within* [p. 28].

At the start of Chapter 6, Freud concentrates on the instincts and asks what critical event in the history of living substance is repeated in sexual reproduction and in its forerunner, the coalescence of two protista or protozoa. Weismann's theory of mortal "soma" and potentially immortal germ cells appears as an "unexpected analogy" (p. 46) to Freud's own theory of life and death instincts, which he fleshes out with his libido theory (p. 50). Debating back and forth about the "breaks" in his logical and evolutionary chain between the instincts, unicellular and multicellular organisms, Freud wonders whether to postulate continuity as a hypothesis when he suddenly concludes, with a brilliant negative parallelism, that the time has arrived for "breaking off" (p. 58), thus suggesting that the enclosure around the vesicle, the brain, and ego is of the same nature as the text itself, and that all of them may be broken.

In the cases of the vesicle and the protozoa, analogies function not as mere ancillaries but as centerpieces in Freud's theorizing. In the case of the vesicle the two ends of the analogy[26] flow together; the process recalls what happens in Shakespeare, whose early expansiveness (e.g., "The king is like the sun") gives way to later condensation (e.g., "The sun king").[27] On the other hand, even when Freud relied heavily on analogy, his thinking could still reassert its selectivity, as Derrida shows in his remarkable analysis of Freud's conception of writing. In the development from the *Project for a Scientific Psychology* to *The Interpretation of Dreams*, the motif of writing plays a prominent role. To describe the psychic text, Freud employs in the Dreambook a mechanical model which proves inadequate to his graphematic conceptual scheme; by the time of the "Mystic Writing-Pad" (1925) "a linguistics dominated by an aged phonologism" yields completely to a graphematic model.[28]

Throughout his writing, Freud displays an ability to think in long, sustained analogies and it is very misleading to posit irreversible developmental changes in his use of them. The content would vary, of course: if he remained fond of archaeology, he soon dropped electrical analogies, and only made extended use of chemical comparisons relatively late. Throughout his career, he would show how his analogies broke down (*S.E.* 2:290, 16:240, 21:68 ff.). It is as if Freud were tossing up clay pigeons just to shoot them down; the practice tells us much about his processive style in general, which is our topic for the next chapter. For now, however, several other remarks may be carefully ventured. Under the heading *Analogy* (which chiefly includes only extended comparisons) in the indexes to the separate volumes of the *Standard Edition*, we find that Volumes 6 to 10 (with the exception of Volume 7) contain relatively few analogies.[29] There is only one illustrative analogy in Volume 13—and significantly it does not appear in the volume's major work, *Totem and Taboo*. I suspect that since the controlling analogy Freud uses here is one he believed to be literally true (the analogy between children, neurotics, and savages), he artistically avoided flooding his text with further illustrative analogies, much as Sir Thomas Browne, in *Urn Burial*, perhaps the greatest masterpiece of English nonfictional prose, used but two Latin maxims (unlike his 17th-century contemporaries, who sprinkled them far more liberally), considering the lexicon of his essay sufficiently Latinate without them.

I have purposely reserved for last Freud's most profound use of imagery; fittingly, it occurs in *The Interpretation of Dreams*. Along with the contention that the dream is a maternal object,[30] we may bear in mind that Freud twice referred to the unfathomable core of the dream as its navel or *Nabel* (*S.E.* 4:111 fn. and 5:525; *G.W.* 2/3:116 fn. and 530), which in the latter instance is further described as an unravelable point in a "tangle of dream-thoughts." Not only did Freud return to the womb in some particular dream or in his attempts to fathom it, but the Dreambook itself, as a whole, constitutes a maternal return; the whole is thus more than the sum of its parts.

Stanley Hyman is surely right in asserting that the nature imagery, which ranges from the woods to high grounds and unifies *The Interpretation of Dreams*, symbolizes the body of a woman, that of Freud's mother.[31] First of all, there is the well-known passage in a letter to Fliess that imagistically describes the organization of the Dreambook:

> The whole thing is planned on the model of an imaginary walk. First comes the dark wood of the authorities (who cannot see the trees), where there is no clear view and it is very easy to go astray. Then there is a cavernous defile through which I lead my readers—my specimens with its peculiarities, its details, its indiscretions, and its bad jokes—and then, all at once, the high

ground and the prospect, and the question: "Which way do you want to go?"[32]

Some of this passage is echoed verbatim in the initial lines of Chapter 3 of *The Interpretation of Dreams* where Freud and the reader suddenly emerge on high ground, and he suggests pursuing one path among many. With Chapter 5, he blazes a new trail: "Having followed one path to its end, we may now retrace our steps and choose another starting-point for our rambles through the problems of dream-life" (*S.E.* 4:163). At the beginning of Chapter 7, Freud takes stock of the arduous journey: each path we have taken previously has led to light, but from now on every path will lead us back into darkness (*S.E.* 5:511); it is for no trivial reason that the dream's navel is mentioned here for the second time.

Hyman's intuition that the landscape symbolizes the mother's body may be further confirmed within the enclosure of Freud's own associations:

> The complicated topography of the female genital parts makes one understand how it is that they are often represented as *landscapes*, with rocks, woods and water. . . . And, speaking of wood, it is hard to understand how that material came to represent what is maternal and female. But here comparative philology may come to our help. Our German word '*Holz*' seems to come from the same root as the Greek ὑλη [hulē]', meaning 'stuff' 'raw material.' This seems to be an instance of the not uncommon event of the general name of a material eventually coming to be reserved for some particular material. Now there is an island in the Atlantic named 'Madeira.' This name was given to it by the Portuguese when they discovered it, because at that time it was covered all over with woods. For in the Portuguese language '*madeira*' means 'wood.' You will notice, however, that '*madeira*' is only a slightly modified form of the Latin word '*materia*,' which once more means 'material' in general. But '*materia*' is derived from '*mater*', 'mother': the material out of which anything is made is, as it were, a mother to it. This ancient view of the thing survives, therefore, in the symbolic use of wood for 'woman' or 'mother' [*S.E.* 15:156 and 159–60; cf. 5:355 and 684].

As a fusion of science and autobiography and as a product of dreams that were to some degree command performances,[33]

Freud's masterpiece is unique in world literature, scientific or imaginative; it also holds a singular place in the Freudian corpus in that the entanglement of the mother's womb was the symbolic place from which it grew. In the specimen dream analysis in Chapter 2, Freud associates his pregnant wife with Irma and looks into her mouth-vagina. In an act of self-delivery, he emerges from this uterine chapter to the outer world; thus the book as a whole is a maternal object genetically and formally, a metaphor based on the most literal fantasy. No wonder, then, that this master stylist of the German language repeatedly complained about the book's style as crude and in parts badly written; as strained with facetious circumlocution struggling for the picturesque; as tortuous and full of high-flown sentences, whose incoherence betrays insufficient mastery of the material. Of the groping Seventh Chapter he said that it was written as if in a dream, in a form unfit and a style unintended for publication.[34]

The symbolic matrix of *The Interpretation of Dreams* has been further explored by Leonard Shengold, who focuses on the journey rather than on the landscape as such, and elaborates on the journey as a metaphor of both preoedipal and oedipal involvement.[35] In this developmental journey, the wishes exposed in the Irma dream in Chapter 2 are surface, preconscious wishes, and the first descent into the hell of the unconscious occurs in Chapter 5, which significantly evokes Oedipus as traveler. Only in Chapter 7 does Freud reveal the meaning of primal unconscious wishes. Here, Freud is the oedipal conqueror, ready to penetrate into the mother's genitals, so that the trafficking back and forth in the spatial concept of the unconscious and the preconscious symbolizes intercourse.

Guided by T. S. Eliot's verses that the end of all our exploring will be to arrive where we started and know the place for the first time, we may profitably frame Shengold's insights within a larger reference. The journeying back and forth involves Freud inside and outside himself, his fantasized mother, and the extended family of dreams that he analyzes. If fantasmally *The Interpretation of Dreams* depicts an evolving mastery over dreams and maternal objects, and a development from the uterine to the preoedipal and oedipal stages, we should equally see that all three stages, and not just the oedipal one, figure imagistically in the final exploration of the mother's body in Chapter 7. For in investigating dream processes, this final chapter descends to their moment of inauguration, to the first mnemic trace and wish of the new-born child, and grandly concludes that dreams of the future are molded by indestructible wishes into "a perfect likeness of the past." Hence although Freud collapses temporal levels, he endeavors to locate a point of origin, just as elsewhere, having complained that psychology, unlike physiology or chemistry, must make do with figurative language, he goes on to say that their language, too, is figurative (*S.E.* 18:60); likewise he avers that primary symbolism, by which an idea gives rise to the sensation, may in some instances in fact restore a primary literalism.[36] As with "The 'Uncanny' " and *Beyond the Pleasure Principle*, which proceed as their own metaphors, the very unfolding of *The Interpretation of Dreams* metaphorically envelops the whole.

Whatever final stand may be taken regarding Freud's practice, we readily agree that when an author uses analogies, even in the exact sciences, there is the danger that the audience will push the analogical implications too far. But distortion is always with us: "Our understanding reaches as far as our anthropomorphism."[37] Although Freud labeled the mythologizing and personification of animism as prescientific, when he used mechanistic language, he typically lent it a high degree of animation. Some renounce Freud's mixture of the mechanical and the animated; let them ponder the paradox of those psychoanalytic writers who offer a spurious integration of cadaverous prose to describe a holistic self.

### Notes

1. Figurative language, contrary to the restrictive popular conception, may also include such patterns or schemes as alliteration, which have no intrinsic semantic function.

2. Richards handily contributed to the analysis of metaphor by differentiating two components, the *tenor* or idea, and the *vehicle* or Image.

3. *The Liberal Imagination* (New York: Viking Press, 1950), p. 53.

4. "Remarques sur la fonction du langage dans la découverte freudienne," *Psychanalyse*, 1:15 (1956).

5. *Freud: The Mind of a Moralist* (New York: Viking Press, 1959), pp. 44–51.

6. See his famous essay "L'Instance de la lettre dans l'inconscient" (English translation by J. Miel in *Yale French Studies*, 36/37:112–147 [1966], and by A. Sheridan in *Ecrits: A Selection* [New York: Norton, 1977], pp. 146–178).

7. See Chapter 5 of *A Map of Misreading* (New Haven: Yale University Press, 1975).

8. I follow traditional usage with the word *imagery*, although it tends to distort. However broadly conceived, *imagery* bears the etymological suggestion of a visual term and thus tends to exclude or minimize the participation of other senses. A more accurate term would be *sense reference*, or *percept*.

9. Quoted passage and diagram are from Laplanche, *Life and Death in Psychoanalysis*, p. 124.

10. H. Nash, "The Role of Metaphor in Psychological Theory," *Behavioral Science*, 8:336–345 (1963).

11. G. Pederson-Krag, "The Use of Metaphor in Analytic Thinking," *Psychoanalytic Qnarterly*, 25:66–71 (1956).

12. Cited by Leon Wurmser in "A Defense of the Use of Metaphor in Analytic Theory Formation," *Psychoanalytic Quarterly*, 46:466–498 (1977). In their article "Psychoanalytic Excavations: The Structure of Freud's Cosmography," E. Wolf and S. Nebel distinguish between certain recurrent metaphors in Freud's prose and "the geological-archeological, prehistorical imagery of stratified structure"; for the authors, Freud's early childhood experiences were organized into a cognitive-perceptual pattern that influenced the very conceptualization of the topographic model (*Myth, Creativity, Psychoanalysis: Essays in Honor of Harry Slochower*, edited by M. Solomon [Detroit: Wayne State University Press, 1978], pp. 178–202).

13. "Anthropomorphism: Motive, Meaning, and Causality in Psychoanalytic Theory," *The Psychoanalytic Study of the Child*, edited by R. Eissler et al. (New York: International Universities Press, 1969), 24:78–114.

14. From the (directly or indirectly) pertinent literature on this subject, three works should be singled out. By Holt: "Freud's Mechanistic and Humanistic Images of Man," in *Psychoanalysis and Contemporary Science*, edited by Holt and E. Peterfreund (New York: Macmillan, 1972), 1:3–24; and "The Past and Future of Ego Psychology," *Psychoanalytic Quarterly*, 44:550–576 (1975). By Schafer: *A New Language for Psychoanalysis* (New Haven: Yale University Press, 1976).

15. See B. Latour and P. Fabbri, "La Rhétorique de la science: pouvoir et devoir dans un article de science exacte," *Actes de la Recherche en Sciences Sociales*, 13:81–95 (1977).

16. J. Gusfield, "The Literary Rhetoric of Science: Comedy and Pathos in Drinking Driver Research," *American Sociological Review*, 41:17 (1976).

17. Through what Freud calls "ideational mimetics," a speaker combines mimetics and ideation, registering thoughts in such varied expressive signs as gesture, widening or narrowing of the eyes, or tone of voice (*S.E.* 8:193). In *The Aesthetics of Freud* (New York: Praeger, 1973), Jack Spector considers ideational mimetics Freud's potentially most valuable contribution to aesthetics and briefly establishes a link between the Freudian concept and Silberer's functional phenomenon. I might add here that Freud also pointed out a mimetically symbolic relation between the precipitating cause and the pathological phenomenon in hysteria (*S.E.* 2:176, 178–181; 3:34).

18. Only a "Joycean" translation could render this excellent text ade-

quately. Obvious problems begin with the term *'Vorstellung'* (which Strachey translates in three different ways—a sufficient warning in itself of the dangers of using the English concordance); subtler ones concern the frequent prefix *ver*, which can be used negatively or as an intensifier. There are, in fact, over a dozen translations of "Negation" in French, a partial indication of the gap between the French and Anglo-Saxon approaches to Freud.

19. In *The Tangled Bank: Darwin, Frazer and Freud as Imaginative Writers* (New York: Atheneum, 1974), S. Hyman aptly points out that to justify the absence of neatness in his representation of the psychic apparatus, Freud employs an elaborate, rambling analogy to reflect the complexity and disorder of the subject matter (p. 413; *S.E.* 22:72–73). In light of repeated examples of mimetic analogy we would wish to refine Harvey Nash's generalization (which suffers from aesthetic insensitivity to Freud's verbal designs): "His concepts are most often lucid when his images are consistent, whereas his ideas stand in need of correction or further explanation when his figures are muddled or blurred" ("Freud and Metaphor," *Archives of General Psychiatry*, 7:25 [1962]).

20. In his fine article "The Military Influence of Freud's Dynamic Psychiatry" (*American Journal of Psychiatry*, 127:167–174 [1970]), Lary Berkower traces the influence of military science upon Freud's thought, but strangely neglects to comment on the German term for cathexis. It is enlightening to note in this context that Freud on one occasion even used the word *Positionen* ("military posts") as a synonym for *Besetzungen* (*S.E.* 14:234, and fn.). On another score, Freud's frequent employment of *Spur* (cognate with the English *spoor*) rather than the relatively more abstract *Zeichen* for *trace* might be an overdetermined olfactory trace of his relationship with Fliess and the latter's theory of pan-nasal nosology.

21. "Freud and the Image of Man," in *Sigmund Freud*, edited by P. Roazen (Englewood Cliffs, N.J.: Prentice-Hall, 1973), pp. 22–29.

22. See B. Rubinstein, "On Metaphor and Related Phenomena," in *Psychoanalysis and Contemporary Science*, edited by R. Holt and E. Peterfreund (New York: Macmillan, 1972), 1:70–108. In his study of Volumes 12 and 14 of the *Standard Edition*, Holt ("On Reading Freud," p. 56) observed that analogies are used variously as conceptual models, illustrative devices, and rhetorical tools, Surprisingly, rhetorical analogies are more frequent in the metapsychological essays of Volume 14 than in Volume 12, which contains the Schreber case and papers on technique.

23. Nash, "Freud and Metaphor." However, Nash's concern with this example is descriptive and appreciative rather than genetic (see pp. 26–27).

24. Holt, "Freud's Mechanistic and Humanistic Images of Man."

25. For further fine treatment of the vesicle and Freud's analogies in general, see Holt, "On Reading Freud," pp. 56–60.

26. Cf. Gerald Levin on *Beyond the Pleasure Principle:* "The exchange of terms, different levels of generality, and the indeterminate metaphor make possible the extension of ideas in such a way that psychological and biological reality are joined to the philosophical without a delimiting of boundary" (*Sigmund Freud*, p. 110).

27. It would be interesting to trace other similarities in the development of

Shakespeare and Freud. To mention but one parallel, Shakespeare's early *Comedy of Errors* (1592) is a broad farce whereas his valedictory twenty years later, *The Tempest* (1612), is a play of lofty humor. Twenty-two years after his initial *Jokes and Their Relation to the Unconscious* (1905), Freud returned to the subject in the profound and wise essay "Humour" (1927).

28. "Freud and the Scene of Writing," in *Yale French Studies*, 48:73–117 (1972); see especially pp. 82, 84, 94, and 104. Cf. the observation of E. Wolf and S. Nebel in "Psychoanalytic Excavations" (p. 189) that in the *Studies on Hysteria* Breuer was consistently "optical" in his imagery; although such imagery appears in the telescopic model in the *Project* and *The Interpretation of Dreams*, Freud preferred "stratifying" references like depth, descent, etc.

29. In this count I exclude the analogies in Volume 8 as specimens of jokes.

30. J.-B. Pontalis, "Dream As an Object," *International Review of Psycho-Analysis*, 1:125–133 (1974).

31. *Tangled Bank*, pp. 332–333.

32. Letter of 6.8.99, in *Origins*, p. 290.

33. Mahony, "Friendship and Its Discontents," *Contemporary Psychoanalysis*, 15:55–109 (1979). Appendix A.

34. See letters of 1.5.98 (p. 254), 20.6.98 (p. 257), 11.9.99 (p. 297), and 21.9.99 (p. 298), in *Origins*.

35. "The Metaphor of the Journey in 'The Interpretation of Dreams,' " *American Imago*, 32:316–331 (1966). We may note that the *New Introductory Lectures* are also based on a journey (*S.E.* 23:7, 31, 57, 80, 110), although in this case the journey does not have the same rich overdetermination, the chapters being dedicated to widely divergent subjects.

On the other hand, such supporting travel and climbing images as "firm ground" and "shaky ground" (*S.E.* 16:367) go nicely with their chapter heading, "The Paths [*Wege*, paths, ways] to Symptom-Formation."

36. Cf. *S.E.* 2:176, 178–181; 3:34. In secondary symbolism, unlike primary symbolism, the sensation gives rise to the idea of her multiple leg pains (Frau Cäcilie selected the one in the heel, gave it a psychic value, and then lamented about not *being* "on a right footing" with other patients in the sanitarium). When primary symbolism restores primary literalism, it indicates, for instance, that hysteria and linguistic practice draw their material from a common origin. The hysteric who complains about being "stabbed in the heart" and who concomitantly has pericordial sensations may be phenomenologically correct.

37. Scientific meeting of 27.2.07, in *Minutes of the Vienna Psychoanalytic Society*, 1:136.

# 6

# The Workings of the Style

HAVING ANALYZED VARIOUS MAJOR ASPECTS OF FREUD'S STYLE SEPA-rately in previous chapters, we may now bring our results together and complement them by the construction of a final synthesis in light of which we can appreciate even more fully the fact that if we fail to question the traditional way of reading Freud, our naive attempts at understanding him will proceed to their own detriment. Some may call the claim excessive that an unquestioned, perfunctory reading of Freud is necessarily a misreading; some may conclude that it is impossible to read him without a firmly grounded theory. But the praxis of reading Freud produces different outcomes contingent upon the kind of awareness one allows oneself to bring to the text, for his writing differs radically from typical scientific demonstration with its rigorously inductive or deductive procedures. Freud avowedly wrote best when guided by an inner impulse, and we can scarcely do him injustice by reading him in a state of free-floating attention, with all that oxymoronic term implies: the relaxation of concentration demanded by free-floating responsiveness, and, in contrast, the hypercathexis required by attention. To be sure, free association and free-floating attention are counterparts, complementary terms and yet asymmetrical.[1] The argument here is not that Freud habitually wrote in the manner of a Lacan or of a freely associating patient;

for that, he was too aware of his audience and his responsibility to make himself understood. But throughout his creative career his style shows the varying influence and trace of the impulsive on rational processes. In the final analysis, Freud's Dreambook consists not just of *The Interpretation of Dreams*, but of all twenty-three text volumes of the *Standard Edition* plus his countless letters.

Apart from its physical and psychological determinants, political, social, and economic factors are implicated in the complex act of reading. In reading Freud, we must be responsive not only to the text, but also to the stamp it bears of his own character, the physicalist tradition of Helmholtzian science, and the intuitive, romantic spirit of *Naturphilosophie.* In Anglo-American circles, largely no doubt as a result of the nonbelletristic and emphatically scientific style of medical training, the prevailing reading of Freud does not, I think, do justice to the *flow* of Freud's writing. To crystallize and reify Freud's work as a mere product is a quasi-fetishization that alienates a reader from participating in the text as a process. The mode of most psychoanalytic publications is reflected thought—the processive ongoing thought, we are to believe, having been flushed out in working drafts. The *Abstracts of the Standard Edition* of Freud[2] strikingly illustrate what I mean. The *Abstracts* drop Freud's use of the personal pronoun *I*, and favor the passive voice (e.g., "The problem of anxiety is discussed" [p. 106]). The alienating philosophy behind this précis writing does away with Freud's own person and a good deal of his activity. A précis retaining the *I*, on the other hand, would involve showing an empathy or identification of the author of the précis and Freud. To put the matter another way, the openness of Freud's essays and their quality of releasing currents between the first, second, and third grammatical persons stand in marked contrast to the kind of desiccated scientific writing characterized by the use of the third person or spoken-about set within a hermetically sealed text. Generally in Freud's writings, the author and the reader are ultimately indissociable from the unraveling of the subject; in the *Abstracts* this fundamentally psychoanalytic aspect is purged—and with the first- and second-person references gone, the précis is not just condensed but grammatically displaced. Being essentially an act of the present, Freud's writing lives out ideas which are relived in our reading, and if his writing itself constitutes quasiverifications of proposed postulates, our reading experience constitutes a secondary and serendipitous verification. We do injustice to a Freudian text if we limit our flexibility in reading it to examining the way it modifies definitions and theory pertinent to other writings of the same period; and the correlation between such a fixed reading and fixed, stratified, politically affected structures would, I think, be worth pursuing.

Typically, Freud's composition is processive, not uniformly unidirectional but still progressive amid its ebbs and floods. Its essence can be to an extent appreciated by a glance at the change from the Ciceronian to the Baroque style in the 16th century, a change perceptively described in Morris Croll's classic article "The Baroque Style in Prose." In contrast to Ciceronian prose with its hierarchic syntactic structure, Baroque prose shows a greater interest in expressiveness than in formal beauty, in the motion of thought than in states of rest. The Baroque style "adapts itself to the movements of a mind discovering truth as it goes, thinking while it writes." If the Ciceronian stylists wrote *pensée pensée* (thought thought), their Baroque counterparts opted instead for *pensée pensante* (thought thinking):

> Their purpose was to portray, not a thought, but a mind thinking, or, in Pascal's words, *la peinture de la pensée.* They knew that an idea separated from the act of experiencing it is not the idea that was experienced. The ardor of its conception in the mind is a necessary part of its truth; and unless it can be conveyed to another mind in something of the form of its occurrence, either it has changed into some other idea or it has ceased to be an idea, to have any existence whatever except a verbal one. . . . For themselves, they preferred to present the truth of experience in a less concocted form, and deliberately chose as the moment of expression that in which the idea first clearly objectifies itself in the mind, in which, therefore, each of its parts still preserves its own peculiar emphasis and an independent vigor of its own—in brief, the moment in which truth is still *imagined.*[3]

Among German prose authors, Lessing was a notable master of such *pensée pensante;* and indeed Freud on one occasion acknowledged him as his conscious and deliberate model.[4]

Throughout his notes Schotte has given us a deeper appreciation of Freud's *pensée pensante* or processive style.[5] In *Studies on Hysteria*, he produced not *Krankheitgeschichten* (histories of sicknesses) but *Krankengeschichten* (histories of patients), which again confirms Freud's affinity to the writer of fiction. From the beginning of his work he refers to *Geschehen* (happening), an etymological relative of the word *Geschichte*. He had a special liking for the prefixes *her-* and *hervor-* (forth; out), prefixes that exemplify the phenomenological and processive nature of the German language; hence, his frequent use of *hervorziehen* (to bring forward, bring to light), *Hergang* (course, as in the *course* of hysteria), and *Herstellung* (setting up, restoration, or cure). German prefixes such as these have an inherent tendency processively to modulate the lexical root. In an oft-cited passage the Austrian poet Hugo von Hofmannsthal remarked that whereas the Romance languages show a certain tendency to stasis, German tends to activity and dynamism, as evidenced by the different words for reality. The Romance languages derive their word from the Latin *res* (thing); but the German *Wirklichkeit* derives from *wirken* (to act). Freud displays the ability of a literary genius to exploit his language to its limits, and he thought both in and through his language (*Sprachdenken*); we should therefore always attend to the literal as well as the literary aspects of his writing.

Surprisingly enough, *Project for a Scientific Psychology* is a supreme instance of Freud's processiveness. In view of the glaring contradictions that can crop up within a few pages, Holt has remarked:

> Concepts underwent such changes from one section to another as to be contradictory, *as he molded them to the needs of the problem under discussion at the moment.* . . . one of his saving traits as a scientist [was to allow]. . . new ideas to emerge before he was ready to fit them smoothly into the existing corpus [italics mine].[6]

Such contradictions, together with the many major developments and changes in his theories from text to text, changes he does not usually pause to point out, contribute to the kineticism of his exposition in general. Everything is in motion: science itself, the text and its self-reference, Freud the thinker, and the reader's acceptance of scientific progress, of the text, and of Freud himself.

*Pensée pensante;* processiveness; ongoing, progressive, evolving, or unfolding movement—these are various ways of describing one of the most significant traits of Freud's prose, whose movement is anything but languorous and arises from the vitality and dynamism of the instant. But his processes of mentation cohere in language; and if we may say that he was immersed in ongoing thought, he was no less immersed in language that was ongoing. As previously noted, it is Eissler's—I think, correct— belief that a psychological explanation of Freud's genius must place his powers of observation and judgment second to his linguistic capacities. Essentially, Freud's scientific *per*formance was the reenactment of what had been linguistically *pre*formed:

> By means of scientific inquiry, it became possible to present in an objectively valid form what the unconscious had hoarded and scraped together, and had already poured into exceptional linguistic forms. . . . This is also suggested by the form of Freud's manuscripts. Even in those on such complicated subjects as are dealt with in his metapsychological papers, a correction is a rarity. They convey the impression rather of a process of pouring out than of planned composition, based on careful ratiocination, which so easily goes astray and almost invariably needs improvement.[7]

Typically Freud's style centers on a series of strong nuclear statements, a kind of variegated patchwork which is ultimately left to the reader to systematize. His thought does not issue in outline form, 1 leading to 1.1, 1.2, and so on. Plunging into an idea, he can tease it out hyperbolically to nearly self-contradictory limits, proceed to an opposite or collateral idea and do it again. Like the inveterate card player he was (he played for over forty years), he could underbid and overbid his hand. He was apt to overplay a notion and gradually whittle it down; or conversely, might extend an initially fragmentary idea by tentative accretions. The reader experiences the ebb and flow of utterances whose harmonization is not preset but grasped progressively in cumulatively adjusting perspectives. I have said before that Freud subjected his mentation to primary and secondary process in a manner that gave his writing a distinctive shape; I would like now to modify that statement. Freud surrendered himself not only to impulse but also to the demands of the material he worked on. To be more concrete, parts of the Dreambook were dictated by

Freud's unconscious to such an extent that he admitted, "At the beginning of a paragraph I never know where I should end up."[8] On the other hand, as we have seen, subject matter directed the course of expository address in the *Introductory Lectures*. In an especially striking instance of the recalcitrancy of material, Freud even feels the chapter headings of *The Ego and the Id* to be somehow beyond his control:

> The complexity of our subject-matter must be an excuse for the fact that none of the chapter-headings of this book quite correspond to their contents, and that in turning to new aspects of the topic we are constantly harking back to matters that have already been dealt with [*S.E.* 19:48].

If we may posit that the ego has two masters, the id and the superego, on another level of reference we recognize that Freud's volition has two masters, apt to tug in different directions, the internal one of creative power and the external one of the subject matter:

> Unluckily an author's creative power does not always obey his will: the work proceeds as it can, and often presents itself to the author as something independent or even alien [*S.E.* 23:104].

In its departures from insistent logic, Freud's prose is witty like dreams and jokes, but with an important difference. Jokes may just as well diverge from a line of thought as adhere to it, jumble up diverse things rather than contrast them; they are very apt to proceed by invalid methods of inference, and combine words and thoughts without regard to sense. Such inefficient rational functioning produces pleasure in jokes, but elsewhere it generates feelings that are both unpleasant and defensive *(S.E.* 8:125).

Let us here break in with a couple of concrete examples to illustrate the *pensée pensante:*

> But the appearance of a significant correspondence is dissipated as soon as we discover Weismann's views on the problem of death [*S.E.* 18:46].

> At this point the question may well arise in our minds whether any object whatever is served by trying to solve the problem of natural death from a study of the protozoa. . . . Thus our expectation that biology would flatly contradict the recognition of

death instincts has not been fulfilled. . . .We may pause for a moment over this pre-eminently dualistic view of instinctual life [*S.E.* 18:49].

A statement in "The 'Uncanny' " that might simply have read "Most readers would agree" is recast to appear as a question in an evolving style:

> We have already asked why it is that the severed hand in the story of the treasure of Rhampsinitus has no uncanny effect in the way that the severed hand has in Hauff's story. The question seems to have gained in importance now that we have recognized . . . [*S.E.* 17:252].

When the *pensée pensante* suddenly breaks off and veers off in a new direction, we have what Roustang calls "diataxis."[9] At such points primary process seems more manifest, and ideas, characterized by superlatives and universal statements, are liable to be played out in a series of diverting perspectives. Sometimes the rush of the prose silently assimilates divergent ideas without so much as a connective to signal an abrupt departure. At other times Freud's style is a juggernaut, subjugating everything in its path, as in the story of a man returning a borrowed kettle, now damaged, saying that in the first place he never borrowed it; secondly, it had a hole in it long before; and thirdly, he was returning it in good condition (*S.E.* 8:62). Here Freud acknowledges some of these practices:

> Am I not confusing you by so often taking back what I said or qualifying it—by starting up trains of thought and then dropping them? [*S.E.* 16:281].

He may shut the door on a topic and in the very next gesture reopen it:

> *Slips of the pen*, to which I now pass, are so closely akin to slips of the tongue that we have nothing new to expect from them. Perhaps we may glean one little further point [*S.E.* 15:69].

Then again, in the flush and flood of thought and treatment of examples, he can quickly respond to the changes in what is sufficient for adequate explanation:

> The multiple use of the same material is, after all, only a special case of condensation . . . condensation remains the wider cate-

gory. . . . It is true that here we should not find that condensation would meet the case; but if instead of it we take the more
inclusive concept of economy, we can manage without difficulty
[*S.E.* 8:42-43].

Finally, a classic instance from *Beyond the Pleasure Principle*, which
we must not omit:

Let us turn back, then, to one of the assumptions that we have
already made, with the expectation that we shall be able to give
it a categorical denial [*S.E.* 18:44].

But here, I think, the moment has come for breaking off.

Not, however, without the addition of a few words of critical
reflection [*S.E.* 18:58-59].

With such passages in mind, we readily agree that there is often
an approximation between the inspiration in Freud's text and the
analytic situation, even and perhaps especially if this situation is
not an explicit theme.[10] In the Freudian corpus there is a submerged clinical text, a text of clinical listening and talking that
creates a unique effect; for in the world history of discourse and
ritual, the psychoanalytic clinical setting stands alone in its indispensable use of the four basic modes of discourse: the dialectical,
the rhetorical, the expressive, and the aesthetic.[11] To understand
and appreciate Freud we must have a theory of reflected praxis of
reading him, such as the one admirably outlined by Holt. In a
somewhat perverse way, a hostile reader like Natemberg followed
Freud better than scores of more orthodox critics, for at least he
paid attention to the contradictions in the text:

[Freud] must have been constantly driven by subterranean and
conflicting currents of thought for he seemed unable to maintain
a consistent position. Time and time again after making an assertion, he withdrew it in his inability to pursue a line of thought to
some logical and definite conclusion.[12]

Thus, for example, Natemberg rails against Freud's proposition
that "we shall be pleased if we can listen to the words that pass
between the analyst and his patient" and the immediate retraction
"But we cannot do that either" (*S.E.* 15:17)—which is but one
among several retractions in the first of the *Introductory Lectures*.
Critics so bent on secondary process either overlook, minimize, or

castigate Freud's processive style. A better stance is to recognize it for what it is and realize what it achieves.

If Freud's written expression constitutes open discourse, the question remains why it is nevertheless routinely treated in Anglo-American circles as if its statements were closed and declarative—nearly pharmacological prescriptions. Freud's writing is fluent, granted, but this fluency does not guarantee easy and deep understanding. The unwary reader is sure to go astray on the path of a prose mistakenly supposed pedestrian. The erroneous linking of Freud's prose with the expository discourse of a positive science is reflected in the very nonprocessive, nonprobative style of the commentators who fill English-language psychoanalytic journals. Many an Anglo-Saxon critic who endorses a conflict-free ego misconstrues Freud's elaborations as definitive—a misreading, ironically, that defies the initial premise of an autonomous ego! *Apropos*, let us ask a question: To what degree was ego psychology shaped by the fact that its leaders—Ernst Kris, Heinz Hartmann, Rudolph Loewenstein, all European-born, none a native speaker of English—resisted, in their anxious desire to assimilate, the notion that language is inherently conflictual? I would speculate further that unresolved feelings toward idealizing transferences could spill over into a reactive, repetitive desire to win Olympian fixed truths from Freud's prose. To read him properly demands ongoing self-awareness and self-analysis, as well as our hovering on the edge of free-floating attention. We go back to read and reread early texts Freud himself disowned not to capture valuable theory, but rather because our act of reading constantly affords us the pleasure of the psychoanalytic experience. Freud implicates himself into the subject of his prose, and the gradual exfoliation of its self-reflexiveness offers the applied reader deep richness and complexity. Silberer's "functional phenomenon," according to which the dream text reflects the dreamer caught red-handed in his reverie, might aptly be used to describe Freud's style.

I submit that the imminence of the present in Freud's sensibility and imagination proceeded from a rare verbal facility and memory, combined with the gift of visualization. The contention that Freud's mode of thinking and intelligence was predominantly verbal[13] must be reconciled with Nunberg's observations:

> For many years I had the opportunity to watch Freud during discussions in the meetings of the Society. When a speaker's remarks aroused his particular interest or when he was trying to make his own point especially clear, he would lift his head and look intensely, with extreme concentration, at a point in space, as if he were seeing something there. This tendency to *see* what he was thinking is reflected in his writings. They contain many pictorial elements, even when dealing with highly theoretical concepts.[14]

Freud's unique ability to verbalize the thought process and to experience as immediately present events stored in memory is perhaps best summarized in the key concept *copresence.* Rather than experiencing the *pastness* of past events, Freud could, in a manner reminiscent of hallucination though qualitatively different and controlled, summon happenings to mind and experience them reenacted in the present.

To these innate gifts we must add Freud's penchant for the rhetorical device of *enargia,* the particularly vivid and pictorial rendering of a scene. A comprehensive treatment of the critical neglect of Freud's visual powers might well begin with the distortions in the English translations of his texts in the *Standard Edition.* Freud states, for example, that the best way to present the case of Emmy is by *reproducing* the notes he made during the first three weeks of treatment (*S.E.* 2:48), yet for nearly forty pages (pp. 48–85) Strachey renders the present tense of the original case in the past tense (cf. *G.W.* 1:98–129); the English reader is thus denied the clear evidence that, when writing up the case every evening, Freud relives it and dramatically reproduces it. Nor does the English version do justice to the report on Katharina, which in the German starts out in the past tense and, at a certain point (*G.W.* 1:189; *S.E.* 2:129), begins to alternate smoothly between the present and past, continuing in this manner until the section entitled "Discussion." The write-up on Lucy is nearly wholly in the past, but two instances may be adduced to show the lack of immediacy in Strachey's somewhat loose translation:

> I find now no resistance [*G.W.* 1:176: *Ich finde nun keinen Widerstand; S.E.* 2:118: "She now showed no resistance . . ."].

> And now under the pressure of my hand the memory of a still

earlier scene emerges again [G.W. 1:179: *Und nun taucht wieder unter dem Drucke meiner Hand die Erinnerung an eine noch ältere Szene auf; S.E.* 2:120: "And now, under the pressure of my hand, the memory of a third and still earlier scene emerged . . . "].

In an earlier piece, I described how Strachey's practice of translating Freud's dreams and associations to them into the past tense not only distorts our reading of *The Interpretation of Dreams* but also flies in the face of Freudian dream theory, which traces the passage from the latent dream thoughts in the optative mood to the present indicative of the dream dreamt.[15] In fact, the predominant tense of all the dreams in the Dreambook is the present, used to achieve a replay effect[16]—striking evidence of the fictionality of that epochal masterpiece in light of the well-known fact that relatively few patients report their dreams in the present. Freud also tends to dramatize in the present the analyst-patient reaction around the dream, as the initial sentence after the hat dream illustrates: "Since nothing occurs to her in connection with the hat in the dream, I say . . ." (my translation; cf. *S.E.* 5:361).[17] Strachey's misguided use of the past tense in this sentence unnecessarily distances the reader from the immediacy of the presentation. Let us pass rapidly over Strachey's neglect of the present in Dora's dreams and associations to come to a more spectacular instance: the clinical notes on the Rat Man,[18] in which the consistent use of the present tense is splendid evidence of Freud's capacity at the end of a day's work to reexperience the past as present as he wrote up the day's notes. In 1901 Freud claimed that he no longer had his schoolboy ability to repeat almost verbatim popular lectures on scientific matters (*S.E.* 6:135), yet in 1915 to 1916 enough of his "phonographic memory" remained for him to write out his improvised lectures after delivering them (*S.E.* 22:5). The German text of the Little Hans case unexpectedly provides evidence for our understanding of the matters under discussion. Freud says he is publishing the father's notes (*S.E.* 10:5) and indeed devotes the major part of his report to giving direct quotations, yet the original text is set in the present (e.g., "On April 3rd, in the morning, he comes into bed with me . . ."), and we may well assume that such exceptional usage stems from Freud himself, furnishing just one more indication of Freud as a writer of fiction and his powers of visualized reenactment. But this gift of visualization, manifest even in the specimen parapraxis where the forgotten name is replaced by the vision of Signorelli's face that was ultra-clear (*überdeutlich*), harbored its own dangers. Freud was all too aware of them; he warned, for instance, against the inadequacy of his diagrams to convey his verbal intent (*S.E.* 19:24 and 22:79).

In focusing on the imminence Freud conveys by his use of the present tense, we have hardly exhausted the question of his manipulation of time; and much remains for us to uncover. No one can study Freud for long without realizing his recurrent efforts to orient the reader and subject along the inclusive axes of time and space. I call this hallmark of Freud's style his "scanning technique." In Chapter 5 we saw how Freud uses spatial metaphor for purposes of orientation ("Let us take another step forward," "We are on more solid ground when asserting . . ." etc.). His use of time, on the other hand, is nonfigurative as he constantly scans his own exposition to speak of what he has already done, is doing now, and will do hereafter. Thus the order of the subject matter, as it is punctuated by introspection, retrospection, and prospection, becomes an added and concurrent subject of concern. This constant scanning correlates with Freud's self-reassuring self-positioning vis-à-vis his audience; together with his argumentation, it functions as a counteractive control over his bursts of writing in which he preferred to follow impulse. If the diataxis deals above all with what is trying to be said, the scanning provides a consciousness-laden expository counterpoint, reflecting on what has been said and will be later said.

Before proceeding, I must qualify what I have said about the three temporal dimensions. The references to past, present, and future not only reflect Freud's treatment of the subject matter but also the way he feels the reader has reacted, is reacting, and will react later on. Here are but a few among superabundant examples:

> I think that, like me, you must be tired of pursuing enquiries like those we have so far been making [*S.E.* 15:97].

> I hope you will be surprised that this fact has been established and will ask me . . . [*S.E.* 15:103].

What we have already learnt from our study of the mental life of children will lead us to expect to find a similar explanation of the other group of forbidden dream-wishes—the excessive sexual impulses. We are thus encouraged to make a study of the development of children's sexual life and from many sources we arrive at what follows [*S.E.* 15:208].

The last passage with its mention of expectation in turn leads us to consider the many related terms that recur in the *Standard Edition: unsurprised, not astonished, unprepared, unintended.* Their repeated use may be subsumed under what may be called the "anticipatory device," a correlate of Freud's declared practice of giving the patient "the conscious anticipatory idea" so that the patient may find the correspondent repressed one in himself (*S.E.* 11:142 and 10:120–121). A complementary device is its opposite, a "serendipity device" by which, to the reader's delight, Freud presents as new finds turns of thought not even he himself has expected: "It was not our *intention* at all events to produce such a result" (*S.E.* 18:52). Such assertions—another would be "Unexpectedly, a hint reaches us from a direction in which we have not so far looked" (*S.E.* 15:98)—dot all Freud's works and, in their unanticipated freedom, play off with facts which are "forced" upon our notice (*S.E.* 17:237 and 18:50).

Freud's "hovering technique" introduces an additional element to anticipation, and is likewise crucial to his handling of time. By this term I mean his habit of drawing attention to an idea that is to be retained for further resolution rather than immediately elaborated. The effect is to set in motion a dual psychic process: a mnemonic retentiveness, triggered for a postponed recall, is for the time being upstaged by attention to other matters. Let us clarify by citing examples:

> . . . and it may be that I have once more entered too much into details. But you must have patience. What you have just heard will derive increased value for you from its later application. For the present you should keep firmly in mind that sexual life (or, as we put it, the libidinal function) does not emerge as something ready-made . . . [*S.E.* 16:328].

But I am obliged to keep within the framework of our discussions and to exercise restraint. So prepare yourselves for a provisional renunciation. [The renunciation takes place nine pages later] [*S.E.* 15:203].

There seems to be a contradiction here; but perhaps it is only a complication, which may be helpful to us later on [*S.E.* 17:233].

In sum, a consciousness of passing time dominates Freud's prose. His utterances are punctuated by tempo markers ranging from *at once, quickly, immediately, soon,* and *eager* to *hesitate, linger,* and *postpone,* not to mention the more common *so long as, until, hitherto, so far, yet,* and *already.* Such frequent signs, along with the devices of anticipation, scanning, and hovering, result in a time-charged text in which the chronological dimensions of the subject matter are counterpointed by the temporal features of the narration and of authorial and reader reaction.

If Glover is right in calling drive-defense the basic epistemological unit of psychoanalytic concern, Freud's style is psychoanalytic to an outstanding degree, for it constantly enacts that unit. We readily concur in the view that "Freud would probably have been a lesser thinker, most certainly he would have been a lesser man, if his ideas had come to him more easily."[19] Argument and struggle are the quintessence of Freud's exposition: he does not merely *talk about* drive and defense but dramatizes them within the text, using them self-descriptively in the context of his own reactions as well as other subject matter. Weaving id and defense derivatives into his exposition, his method creates a highly animated epistemological field. Among the verbal traces of drive are such obvious words as *drive* and *force* on one hand, and on the other hand adverbial forms like *immediately* and *at once,* which remind us of the nondelay legislated by the pleasure principle. Here are some random samples:

. . . we can say that the patient's resistance arises from his ego, and we then at once perceive . . . [*S.E.* 18:20].

I cannot resist referring, too, to . . . [*S.E.* 13:123].

Our interest is directed [*sich zuwenden*] to another point [*S.E.* 18:15].

I hasten to add, however . . . [*S.E.* 18:59].

We cannot, however, remain indifferent to the discovery . . .

which coincides in all essentials with the one that has been forced upon us by psycho-analytic work [*S.E.* 18:8].

If we decide to do so, we are bound in the end to find the courage to say . . . [*S.E.* 15:35].

Verbalizations of defense may be conveniently drawn from the *Introductory Lectures:*

But I shall resist the temptation of going further here . . . [*S.E.* 16:419].

We cannot dismiss the question of why . . . [p. 274].

No doubt you will feel inclined at first to deny . . . [p. 311].

. . . and you will not fail to see how the ceremonial corresponds . . . [pp. 268–269].

A hesitant reader may raise strenuous objections on two accounts: first, because the examples describe the activity of the conscious ego and attentiveness, and have nothing to do with the conflictual realm of drive and defense; and second, because the examples are no more than the stock-in-trade of any seasoned orator. I have overstated my point, but not entirely. The frequency and context of our examples and countless similar ones give them at least a taste of drive-defense derivatives, and by that very fact *do* set Freud apart from other orators. True enough, in traditional rhetoric we run across such formulas as "Must we not ask," "We are compelled to conclude," etc., but they are only persuasive phrases aimed at the audience and do not reflect dynamic psychic processes. The casting of these formulas and their recurrence in Freud give them a new meaning: they are turned inward, tracking and scanning endopsychic movement.

I would say, to be more exact, that the gigantic intellectuality of Freud's prose takes on an agonistic and impulsive cast, as befits an instrument that must deal with dynamic, pulsating material. *Hasten, rush, tempted, immediately, quickly,* and like lexical items suggesting impulsiveness occur often enough to make their cumulative effect a salient feature of Freud's prose; they are, to be sure, somewhat offset by the "academic," professorial tone of the researcher who *warns, is on guard, advises,* and especially *suspects,* and they are counterbalanced, too, by Freud the conquistador who *dares, ventures, has courage to,* and *risks.* The voluntaristic note of the conquistadorial vocabulary blunts the edge of Freud's determinism. But determinism is certainly present, too, enlisted in a technique of certainty by which the imperativeness of reality shades with seemingly arbitrary force into relentless, inevitable logic. Deterministic reality seems to take the part of a partially concealed protagonist who unmasks Freud's thoughts to him and to us, the readers. Freud, like us, *appears* to be a pawn of deterministic awareness and reflection:

> . . . the feelings of pleasure and unpleasure . . . act so imperatively upon us . . . we cannot avoid contact with it [the unconscious] [*S.E.* 18:7].

> The facts which have caused us to believe in the dominance of the pleasure principle in mental life also find expression in the hypothesis. . . . actually the [constancy] principle was inferred from the facts which forced us to adopt the pleasure principle [*S.E.* 18:9].

> We . . . have been led to distinguish two kinds of instincts [*S.E.* 18:46].

Freud did not comment much on arrangement or order in exposition, but the few comments he did leave are precious. In an early letter to Breuer, he wondered whether their theory of hysteria should be introduced historically by cases or dogmatically with theories, and finally opted for the latter.[20] In the rigid writing of *Three Essays on the Theory of Sexuality* he paid special attention to order, choosing a definite historical procedure, placing accidental concerns over dispositional ones (the latter coming to light only later in analytic treatment), and for the same reason attending to ontogenesis before phylogenesis (*S.E.* 7:131). When it came to writing up the Wolf Man case, Freud avoided a purely historical or purely thematic account and settled for a combination of the two (*S.E.* 17:13). For the *New Introductory Lectures* he took "the path not of a genetic but of a dogmatic exposition" (*S.E.* 22:9). In *An Outline of Psycho-Analysis* Freud's explicit aim is to state his material "dogmatically" (*S.E.* 23:144), an exclusive procedure which contrasts with "Some Elementary Lessons in Psycho-Analysis," where Freud expressly combines the *dogmatic* or deductive approach with a *genetic* one following the path earlier taken by the investigator (*S.E.* 23:281).[21] To draw an inductive conclusion: Freud proceeded deductively (the *Project*, the *Outline*, *New Introductory Lectures*), inductively (*Introductory Lectures*), and in a manner combining both approaches ("Some Elementary Lessons" and the Wolf Man case).[22]

In Freud's masterpiece, *The Interpretation of Dreams*, the architectonics are much more complicated, even apart from the imagistic unity discussed earlier. In the preface to the first edition, Freud admits that there are many broken threads in his presentation; they are due, he says, to the points of contact between dream formation and the larger problem of psychopathology and sexuality that he intends to take up on a later occasion (*S.E.* 4:xxiii; and 5:606 fn.). Even so, he owns up to his frustrations in trying to proceed according to the very opposite of a genetic approach: although he came to dreams through the study of neuroses, his attempts to reverse this course in the Dreambook often ran aground (p. 588), and en route he excuses himself for the unavoidable introduction of psychopathological matter (pp. 146 and 151 fn; see also p. 177). But there are many other contradictions on a larger and smaller scale that are easy to come by. Contrary to his express intention (p. 104), he often uses his patients' dreams. The all-important assertion that affects are not altered in dream formation (pp. 460–461) is flatly contradicted ten pages later. To Roustang's stimulating account of primary process in the writing of the crucial seventh chapter, I would add that it was Chapter 7 alone that underwent any real revision.[23] We can safely assume that the first draft of the chapter was steeped in primary process; and it is our great loss that this raw theoretical dream did not survive; it was only from 1908 onward that Freud preserved his manuscripts and working papers (see *S.E.* 1:xv).

There is, in the whole Freudian corpus, only a single detailed description of the ways a patient can associate. It has not received the widespread critical attention it deserves, and it can be used as a partial gloss on the way Freud wrote *The Interpretation of Dreams*. Associations, he says, may arise in reversed chronological order, or in a stratified concentricity around the pathological nucleus, or, most importantly, in zigzag fashion whereby the logical chain is broken and circuitous paths are taken to the deepest layers and back (S.E. 2:288–290). And yet, overriding these departures from rigorous logic and in counterpoint to them, there is an extraordinary, conscious structure, of the kind described, as Stanley Hyman shrewdly observed, in Freud's own comment on no less majestic a structure than that of *Oedipus Rex:*

> The action of the play consists in nothing other than the process of revealing, with cunning delays and ever-mounting excitement—a process that can be likened to the work of a psycho-analysis—that Oedipus himself is the murderer of Laius, but further that he is the son of the murdered man and of Jocasta [*S.E.* 4:261–262].

Similar conscious craft, Hyman brilliantly explains, characterizes Freud's classic work:

> The form of *The Interpretation of Dreams* is a controlled gradual revelation of Freud's theory, progressing from didactic oversimplification to full and rich complexity, like *The Origin of Species* or *Kapital.* . . . We can see the development most neatly in the series of summary formulations, of progressive complication, of the book's main point. The second chapter concludes: "When the work of interpretation has been completed, we perceive that a dream is the fulfillment of a wish." The fourth chapter concludes: "a dream is a (disguised) fulfillment of a (suppressed or repressed) wish." The fifth chapter adds: "a succession of meanings or wish-fulfillments may be superimposed on one another, the bottom one being the fulfillment of a wish dating from earliest childhood." By the last chapter, this becomes: "a wish which is represented in a dream must be an infantile one." Thus the simple formula, a dream is the disguised fulfillment of a repressed infantile wish, gradually unfolds over hundreds of pages.[24]

The paradoxical distinctiveness of *The Interpretation of Dreams* does not stop there. On the conservative side, it bowed to academic tradition by opening with a complete survey of the dream literature, a submissive gesture which Freud did not repeat in his later works.[25] But then, on the inventive side, the Dreambook shows us a man who more than any other deliberately revealed himself for the sake of science. In his demonstration of penetrating scientific analysis and artistic creativity, this pivotal work exemplifies what has been called, in a happy phrase, "Janusian thinking," or simultaneity of opposition.[26] The artistically creative side is clearly present in the book's genesis, for there is good evidence that many of Freud's dreams for the book were command performances. Referring to one of his dreams destined for the book and censored by his confidant Wilhelm Fliess, Freud wrote in a letter, "I can omit the topic you designate in a substitute dream, because I can have dreams like that to order.[27] The passage supports Erikson's shrewd hunch that the Irma dream bore "the historical burden of being dreamed in order to be analyzed, and analyzed in order to fulfill a very special fate."[28] Another letter sent to Fliess[29] corroborates this point and is one further indication that *The Interpretation of Dreams* occupies a unique position in the history of autobiography, indeed, in the whole of world literature, imaginative or scientific: "No masterpiece of scientific thought reveals more of its author or is written in a more personal style than *The Interpretation of Dreams.*"[30]

Contributing of course to the final impact of *The Interpretation of Dreams* is the posture Freud assumes as expositor and narrator. He is, on the one hand, like the great detective Sherlock Holmes, spoofing "innocent" dreams and giving cases intriguing labels like "The Dream of Irma's Injection" and "The Dream of the Botanical Monograph"; a second identity is that of the modest scientific worker, like Darwin.[31] We might add other identifications: the daring conquistador, the traveler and explorer, the archaeologist and historian, and more subtly and on a deeper psychic level, the human subject grappling with its own development, passing from a uterine stage to preoedipal and oedipal maturation. Associated with these identifications are the tones which we hear throughout Freud's work: those of sincerity, fortitude, irony toward himself, solicitude toward the reader, and, overall, of willingness to take the reader into his confidence. This confidence he achieves both directly, by addressing the reader, and indirectly, by using the immediate presence of an imagined interlocutor, in both ways contributing to the *semblance* of an intimate tone. (I say "semblance" since tone, which is the principal purveyor of affect, can be applied only figuratively to the printed word. Vocal tone being oral rather than visual, the simultaneity of tonal and semantic utterance balks at being compressed into the silent horizontality of printed expression.[32])

I can hardly insist enough that whatever unconscious determinants fed into the imperfect form of the Dreambook, there were other determinants besides, inherent in the material itself, as Freud was appropriately aware. He wrote his masterpiece straddling the conscious and unconscious worlds, surrendering to the whirling turbulence of the id yet at the same time standing apart, surveying the struggle. *The Interpretation of Dreams* is the product of one of the supreme minds of history, of a man who could split himself into a participating ego and a Janus-faced ego with one side ever observing himself, the other side ever attuned to the audience-reader. Hence the complaint that a voluminous dream interpretation quickly defeats heuristic ends (*S.E.* 5:405); hence the painful cognizance of the inherent inadequacy of linear exposition to render simultaneous phenomena (*S.E.* 5:588); hence the conscious and difficult curtailment of certain topics that begged to be completed (*S.E.* 5:606–607 fn.).

Freud's psychoanalytic style is a veritable psychomachia of dynamic interactions, carried on through primary and secondary process, unfolding on intrapsychic and interpsychic levels. Analysts may in general listen with the third ear; but they are still caught up in a splitting—for they do not write with the third hand, so to speak. With Freud, we feel a full authorial presence, conscious and unconscious, brought to bear on the subject matter, involving in the resultant panoramic experience Freud's unconscious and conscious, and our own; the matter under discussion, charged and vitalized by personification; the placement of a topic within the movement of a treatise as a whole; and the typically wider references and analogies (pertaining to clinical material, science, literature, history, or social questions) which lend Freud's writings their special openness and far-ranging suggestiveness. There is, besides, much talk in Freud's writing about message itself. I invite my readers to treat themselves to a satisfying surprise: Take any of Freud's texts and underline all those statements that are not strictly necessary, that talk about the message rather than constitute it; the final count of underlined words will be impressive. But this suggestion of mine is fairly perverse—for the distinctiveness of Freud's presentation is that his talk about the message is at the very heart of the message itself.

Unlike the flattened style of most psychoanalysts, Freud's writing embraces multiple perspectives. It is eminently interactional, now dramatizing part or all of the author's person, now focusing himself or the audience on the text at hand, now entering into dialogue with the audience. The animated field of Freud's style might be sketched out this way:

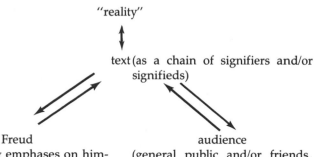

"reality"

text (as a chain of signifiers and/or signifieds)

Freud
(with varying emphases on himself as a person, psychoanalyst, writer, etc.)

audience
(general public and/or friends, enemies, analysts, etc.)

Stress may be on any single coordinate or on the influence of one coordinate on another; the distance between two or more coordinates may widen or narrow at any time, even to the point of blending or fusion, as between Freud and the audience. Contrary to the general run of analysts who merely write *about* psychoanalysis, Freud in his writing enacts and makes present, and does not just represent, the essence of the psychoanalytic experience, a constant ongoing and a becoming.

But we can think of Freud in another way. Imagine the feat of a juggler watching himself in mirrors on the ceiling and the walls around him, juggling his colored balls and at the same time describing how he catches them, why he catches them the way he does, and how he feels about it all. Imagine, too, that this handy wizard does yet more: keeping the balls dancing in air, he analyzes the spectators' feelings about his performance, even fuses magically with them in a corporate body nimble of foot and dazzling in legerdemain—but here our own lexical juggling starts to miss, and our analogy begins to limp.

Before ending, let us glance at Freud's aphoristic gift and his quotability. That he meant to be quotable we may surmise from the grounds for his dislike of a treatise by John Stuart Mill: he could find nothing quotable in it.[33] Freud's own conclusions are notably apothegmatic—and await a study. Beginnings being mythic (since starts continue), we may cherish all the more Freud's striving to conclude and yet abide. Since being absent is being still—for a symbol removed is never a symbol gone— presence and absence beat and hover at the very heart of dream and myth, and no one who has dissected them comes close to outranking Freud.

## Notes

1. They are also asymmetrical in the sense that the free floating of the analyst's attention may not coincide with the crests and dips of the patient's free association; yet sometimes it is precisely this lack of coincidence that gives rise to insight at the moment or afterwards. The phenomenon of coincidence calls for study in the light of Freud's remarks that "It must not be forgotten that the things one hears are for the most part things whose meaning is only recognized later on" (*S.E.* 12:112).

2. Edited by C. Rothgeb (New York: Jason Aronson, 1973).

3. Reprinted in *Seventeenth-Century Prose and Poetry,* edited by A. Witherspoon and F. Warnke (New York: Harcourt, Brace, 1963), p. 1066.

4. Journal entry for 17.12.34, in Wortis, *Fragments of an Analysis,* p. 109. This information flatly contradicts R. Sterba's view that Freud's style was preeminently based on Goethe's ("On Sigmund Freud's Personality," *American Imago,* 18:296 [1961]).

5. See especially pp. 110, 116–118, and 120–121 of his notes accompanying his translation of Muschg's "Freud écrivain," *La Psychoanalyse,* 5:69–124 (1959).

6. R. Holt, "A Review of Some of Freud's Biological Assumptions and Their Influence on His Theories," in *Psychoanalysis and Current Biological Thought,* edited by N. Greenfield and W. Lewis (Madison: University of Wisconsin Press, 1965), p. 100. See also Holt, "Beyond Vitalism and Mechanism: Freud's Concept of Psychic Energy," in *Psychoanalysis and Contemporary Science* 1:17–18 (1967).

7. *Talent and Genius,* p. 277. Eissler's appraisal is powerful and perceptive on a subject about which many have thought, few have written, and hardly any have commented memorably.

8. Letter of 7.7.98, in *Origins,* p. 258.

9. I cannot refrain from extending the richness of Roustang's term. *Diataxis* may be linked with the grammatical term anacoluthon, a change of syntactic construction that leaves the beginning sentence structure uncompleted, introducing a new thought in midstream. The rhetorical effect of the figure may appear quite artless, as in Matthew 7:9; it may also be used for dramatic intensity, as in *Henry V,* IV. iii. 34–36. (See the entry *anacoluthon* in *Encyclopedia of Poetry and Poetics, edited* by A. Preminger [Princeton: Princeton University Press, 1965]). On a larger scale, we might associate diataxis with the

pivotal dramatic concept of peripety or reversal of fortune (cf. Aristotle's *Poetics, passim*) and with those inner "rousing motions" felt as decisive spiritual illuminations (Milton, *Samson Agonistes,* 1381–1383).

10. An observation by R. Kuhn cited by Jacques Schotte in "Introduction à la lecture de 'Freud écrivain,' " p. 64.

11. Cf. P. Mahony, "The Place of Psychoanalytic Treatment in the History of Discourse," *Psychoanalysis and Contemporary Thought,* 2:77–111 (1979).

12. M. Natemberg, *The Case-History of Sigmund Freud: A Psycho-Biography* (Chicago: Regent House, 1955), p. 16.

13. Holt, "A Review of Some of Freud's Biological Assumptions," p. 165.

14. *Minutes of the Vienna Psychoanalytic Society,* I:xxvi–xxvii.

15. See P. Mahony, "Towards a Formalist Approach to Dreams," *International Review of Psycho-Analysis,* 4:83–98 (1977).

16. The phenomena of replay, perceptual attentiveness, and fictionalization would be worth pursuing. Consider, for example, any televised sportscast: a commentator's patter is a replay (in another medium), which can never be truly simultaneous with the images he describes, Hence a videotape replay actually gives a third (visual) and fourth (vocal) account of the reported events.

17. Here are two other random samples of Freud's present tense that Strachey renders in the past: "He adds a drawing of the tree with the wolves, which confirms his description. The analysis of the dream brings the following material to light. . . . "Why are the wolves white?' This makes him think of the sheep, large flocks of which were kept in the neighbourhood of the estate" (*S.E.* 17:29–30). "In the girl's account of her conscious motives the father does not figure at all; there is not even any mention of fear of his anger" (*S.E.* 18:163).

The endeavors in editing and translating psychoanalytic literature have been considerable, but with the remarkable exception of a few texts, serious defects persist. A case in point is *The Origins of Psycho-Analysis,* which I have shown to be severely wanting ("Friendship and Its Discontents"). Comparing the holograph and the transcript of Freud's letter that prefaces Kardiner's *My Analysis,* I detected over twenty errors—and the book is a recent title from a reputable publisher (Norton, 1977). For the scrupulous care in punctuating transcribed speeches, see the editor's note (p. xi) and translator's note (p. 277) in Jacques Lacan, *The Four Fundamental Concepts of Psycho-Analysis,* edited by J.-A. Miller and translated by A. Sheridan (New York: Norton, 1978). Compare, too, William Labov and David Fanshel's, *Therapeutic Discourse* (New York: Academic Press, 1977), p. 355: "An important part of any microanalysis is the preparation of an accurate version of the text. . . . It has been noted before that this is an open-ended process, and after 9 years we find that we still are making corrections that are by no means trivial on repeated listenings." Labov's reputation as a linguist lends the statement great weight.

18. Compare Strachey's abridged version of the notes (*S.E.* 10:259–318), again in the past tense, with the first complete and excellently edited text in *L'Homme aux Rats: Journal d'une analyse,* edited by E. Hawelka (Paris: Presses Universitaires de France, 1974). Readers without German can gain a fuller

sense of the impact of Freud's extensive use of the present tense by turning to "A Child Is Being Beaten" (*S.E.* 17:177–204).

19. Wollheim, *Freud*, p. 9.

20. Letter of 29.6.92 to Josef Breuer, in *S.E.* 1:147.

21. Cf. Freud's concern that a genetic presentation follow the chronological order of a discovery with his remarks on the structure of associations of a hysterical patient: "It was here [with Frau Emmy] that I learnt for the first time, what was confirmed on countless later occasions, that when one is resolving a current hysterical delirium, the patient's communications are given in a reverse chronological order, beginning with the most recent" (*S.E.* 2:75 fn.).

22. In the *Minutes of the Vienna Psychoanalytic Society*, there are several pertinent comments by Freud on arrangement: the scientific meetings of 10.10.06 (1:10); that of 21.4.09 (2:213); and of 21.12.10 (3:95).

23. Letter of 1.8.99 to Fliess, in *Origins*, pp. 288–289. The fact remains that in spite of the revision (*pace* Ernest Schachtel), the styles of Chapter 7 and *Beyond the Pleasure Principle* have much in common (cf. Schachtel, "Notes on Freud's Personality and Thought," *Contemporary Psychoanalysis*, 1:145 [1965]).

24. *Tangled Bank*, pp. 311–312.

25. Schachtel, "Notes," p. 141. and fn.

26. See A. Rothenberg, "The Process of Janusian Thinking in Creativity," *Archives of General Psychiatry*, 24:195–205 (1971).

27. Letter of 9.6.98 quoted by Max Schur in "Some Additional 'Day Residues' of the 'Specimen Dream of Psychoanalysis,' " in *Psychoanalysis: A General Psychology*, edited by R. Loewenstein et al. (New York: International Universities Press, 1966), pp. 74–75.

28. "The Dream Specimen of Psychoanalysis," *Journal of the American Psychoanalytic Association*, 2:8 (1954).

29. Letter of 3.10.97, in *Origins*, pp. 218–221.

30. Levin, *Sigmund Freud*, p. 63.

31. Hyman, *Tangled Bank*, p. 313.

32. A superb display of masterfully modulated tones occurs in Freud's letter of 23.3.00 to his friend Fliess (see the supplementary texts of the latter in *Origins*, pp. 313–315, and Schur, *Living*, pp. 205–206). This letter marks the turning point in a tumultuous friendship that was so crucial in the history of psychoanalysis, and is the keystone of the two men's correspondence. As I wrote else where (Mahony, "Friendship and Its Discontents," p. 96): "Its affective quality, its delicate balance and honest self-exposed fragility have a moving dignity." Referring to a recent six-month personal crisis and to his enormous longing for Fliess's company, Freud gives expression to his inner struggles and the physical toll they have taken, to his inability to make himself totally understood, and to his need to keep his woes within. With sincere frailty he concludes that to be in Fliess's company would undo the progress of his analysis. The letter records a marvelous achievement, and is also one in its own right: a stained glass window by itself and because of the rays of the sun that flowed joyfully through it.

33. Cf. letter of 15.11.83 to Martha Bernays, in *Letters*, p. 90.

# 7

# The Theory and the Man

*Thence comes it that my name receives a brand,*
*And almost thence my nature is subdued*
*To what it works in, like the dyer's hand.*
—Shakespeare, Sonnet 111

LIKE THE DYER'S HAND, THE ANALYST'S LIFE CHANGES COMPLEXION IN treating the product. Even on first reading this statement may demand qualification, but the fabric of its truth remains untinged: psychoanalysis is also the man, and on top of that, Freud is the greater man. Several years ago in Germany a well-known senior analyst told me that Freud was a cultural hero, not a personal hero. I disagree. Cultural hero he is, but also a personal one, which does not imply that he should be idolized, sanctified, or idealized. Psychoanalysis did not arise from culture alone, nor from a man alone. The psychoanalytic theory Freud proposed emerged from the interaction of a man with immense powers of intellect and observation, an intriguing personality, and a complex family history, and a particular moment of cultural and social development in European history. All too often this reality is ignored, and the epithet *applied psychoanalysis*, which designates the application of analysis to other disciplines, ironically comments on our tendency to neglect to analyze analysis. Let us recall what we have mentioned previously, that Freud was driven to write to see what would flow from his pen. Through the course of the *Gesammelte Werke*, the drives team with their rider, but a piscatory analogy may be more accurate. Many of us, gazing over the water, have had the thrill of glimpsing a fish arching into the air; so Freud, we imagine, sunk in introspection, watched for ideas to break through the unconscious, ready to seize and hold them in their transitory flight.

I am all too mindful that this chapter risks the kinds of distortions it attempts to describe; our primary instrument of communication is no total word, but a heritage of broken signs. The postlapsarian drama of the signifier and the signified continues; like Einstein's parallel lines that meet only in infinity, they truly coincide only at the hypothetical end of analysis interminable. A series of carefully researched articles on the subjectivity of personality theory is relevant to these general concerns.[1] Within the larger discipline we might call the psychology of knowledge there is the psychobiographical branch of personality theory. Every theory of personality ultimately reflects a domain of issues structured by formative experiences in the life of the theorist; particular subjective areas modify the theoretician's view of the basic human needs, of the primary obstacle in human life, and of the ideal human state. Within the framework of projection, metapsychological reification functions for the theorist partly defensively and/or reparatively.

If we agree that psychoanalysis, like science in general, is a growing body of knowledge, we should also acknowledge that "its development was peculiarly and intimately bound up with the personality of its founder."[2] Freud would be the first to admit that, in examining great issues, a subjective, distorting perspective is inevitable:

> Now every clever person comes to a point where he starts to turn mystical, where his most personal thinking begins.[3]

> And there is the further difficulty that precisely in a judgement of this kind [concerning the origin and future of a civilization] the subjective expectations of the individual play a part which it is difficult to assess; and these turn out to be dependent on purely personal factors in his own experience, on the greater or lesser optimism of his attitude to life, as it has been dictated for him by his temperament or by his success or failure [S.E. 21:5; see also scientific meeting of 20.2.07, *Minutes*, 1:124].

> Unfortunately, however, people are seldom impartial where ultimate things, the great problems of science and life, are concerned. Each of us is governed in such cases by deep-rooted internal prejudices, into whose hands our speculation unwittingly plays [S.E. 18:59].[4]

Nietzsche would readily have agreed with Freud; in a famous

passage he envisaged the history of philosophy as a series of unconscious autobiographies:

> It has gradually become clear to me what every great philosophy up till now has consisted of—namely, the confession of its originator, and a species of involuntary and unconscious autobiography; and moreover that the moral (or immoral) purpose in every philosophy has constituted the true vital germ out of which the entire plant has always grown. Indeed, to understand how the abstrusest metaphysical assertions of a philosopher have been arrived at, it is always well (and wise) to first ask oneself: "What morality do they (or does he) aim at?" Accordingly, I do not believe that an "impulse to knowledge" is the father of philosophy; but that another impulse, here as elsewhere, has only made use of knowledge (and mistaken knowledge!) as an instrument. But whoever considers the fundamental impulses of man with a view to determining how far they may have here acted as *inspiring* genii (or as demons and cobolds), will find that they have all practised philosophy at one time or another, and that each one of them would have been only too glad to look upon itself as the ultimate end of existence and the legitimate *lord* over all the other impulses. For every impulse is imperious, and as *such*, attempts to philosophize.[5]

Freud even goes a daring step further by venturing to suggest that, except in the rarest of circumstances, the history of science involves a history of parapractic error:

> Only for the rarest and best adjusted mind does it seem possible to preserve the picture of external reality, as it is perceived, against the distortion to which it is normally subjected in its passage through the psychical individuality of the percipient [S.E. 6:229].

For the Weltanschauung of primitive peoples and the similar world views of neurotics, there is an unconscious source molded by a conscious arrangement, the prototype of which is the secondary revision of dreams (S.E. 13:65). There are profound points of agreement between pathology and the great social institutions: between hysteria and art, obsessional neurosis and religion, paranoid delusion and philosophy (S.E. 13:73; 17:261; 22:160). With the coalesence of this latter pair, psychic activity is placed at the service of internal research, an activity closely allied with the functional phenomenon that may, in a very literal sense, characterize the dreams of philosophers (S.E. 14:96–97). Indeed, an analogy with paranoia also extends to religion, the endopsychic perception of psychic factors and unconscious relations being projected into a mythology and metaphysics, which science should retranslate into metapsychology (S.E. 6:258–259).

But how reliable a system is metapsychology? Did it spring like Minerva, complete and perfect, from the clear head of Freud? Have we, for far too long, extended family romance into the field of theory, and, assigning metapsychology a lofty existence, refused to see its humble roots? Metapsychology is dying a hard death; psychoanalysts, like nature, abhor a vacuum, and all the more so where Freud's monumental presence is concerned. But rather than list the growing number of assaults on metapsychology both in Europe and America, let us listen to Freud himself as he speaks of the clinical attempt to bring the drives into harmony with the ego:

> If we are asked by what methods and means this result is achieved, it is not easy to find an answer. We can only say: 'So muss denn doch die Hexe dran!'—the Witch Metapsychology. Without metapsychological speculation and theorizing—I had almost said 'phantasying'—we shall not get another step forward. Unfortunately, here as elsewhere, what our Witch reveals is neither very clear nor very detailed [S.E. 23:225].

With bewitching verbal skill, Freud (by the detour of *almost*) in fact does speak of metapsychological theory as a fantasy, and a compromising one, but we should not be surprised at this admission. We know that psychoanalytic theories offering "pseudoscientific explanations" of data are traceable to unconscious resistance,[6] and we may recall Freud's contention that Rank's own complexes were written into his book *The Trauma of Birth*.[7]

How much of the Witch's body can we lop off without killing her? "The theory of the instincts is so to say our mythology" (S.E. 22:95; cf. 14:77); the topographic approach is likewise a dispensable superstructure (S.E. 20:32–33), as is "the fiction of a primitive psychical apparatus" (S.E. 5:598). Continuing this line of thinking, we must concede that the external world as such is not directly knowable in itself, nor is the unconscious known except through its processes. Between these two unknowables is the space where psychoanalysis operates but, alas, even here we find little comfort: the science of today is the mythology of tomorrow. Such is the thunderous conclusion Freud submitted to Einstein:

> It may perhaps seem to you as though our theories are a kind of mythology and, in the present case, not even an agreeable one. But does not every science come in the end to a kind of mythology like this? Cannot the same be said to-day of your own Physics? [*S.E.* 22:211].

From the foregoing Freudian texts the following picture emerges (all the lines, and the print too, should be blurred):

| Unknowable external reality in itself | The space of psychoanalytic observation and reflection:<br>(a) today's science is tomorrow's mythology;<br>(b) means of description —inadequate figurative language (see chap. 5) | Unknowable unconscious in itself |
|---|---|---|

We shall miss a source of further inspiration and creativity if we ignore that psychoanalytic theory is processive, bearing a resemblance to "dreams from above" and marked by traces of wish fulfillment and regression. Our aim should be to direct attention to the substance embedded in psychoanalytic theory, namely the conscious and unconscious mind of its founder. Freud's dreams are the royal road to his unconscious; at least some of his theories are the service road. However, no thorough study of psychoanalytic theory has yet examined the strange and fascinating profile of traditional psychoanalytic doctrine that would emerge if we differentiated between tenets that seldom appear in Freud's canon and those that occur often. The oral tradition in psychoanalysis has popularized such clinical terms as *acting out* and *working through*, which do not often show up in Freud's writings, whereas theories he rarely postulated have not enjoyed a parallel oral reception; an added complication is that when commentators say that Freud wrote such and such for the first time, usually the word *wrote* is implicit shorthand for *wrote publicly*. On a personal note: I have often pondered this topic of orality, discussed it much less frequently, and have twice written it out, and now do so publicly for the first time.

If psychoanalytic findings risk being mythological, how is it that they become so? Simply enough: "Our understanding reaches as far as our anthropomorphism."[8] It is easy to reason to the next step that if psychoanalytic theories are anthropomorphic, they arise to that extent from our endopsychic perception, which in turn is determined by our body image. Moreover, "the ego is ultimately derived from bodily sensations, chiefly those springing from the surface of the body" (*S.E.* 19:26 fn.). The reader may be understandably hesitant about pursuing the implications of these assertions—and I sympathize with all such hesitations—but let us listen to Freud's biographer:

> During their voyage to America in 1909 Freud used to relate his dreams to his companions, Jung and Ferenczi, as they did to him; and they told me shortly after that the predominant theme running through them was care and anxiety about the future of his children and of psychoanalysis. These two ideas must have been closely associated, since there is much reason to suppose that in his unconscious his work in psychoanalysis ultimately represented some product of his body, i.e., a child. We were trustees for that child.[9]

When it comes to economic theory, psychic energy as a metaphor "can be shown to be a derivative of infantile psychosexual fantasies in which the mind is equated with an organ that can ingest, retain, and excrete substances."[10] The investigation of Freud's body image is fraught with difficulties at every turn, however, not the least of them being the limited possibility to trace it out in object relations, phasic, and developmental complexities;[11] its concomitance with social, political, economic, and cultural factors; and its persistence in apparently abstract thought. But, of course, the fact *per se* that whatever traces of Freud's body image may appear in his theory does not invalidate that theory. Here as elsewhere in this chapter, my statements are tentative, subject to the publication of as yet restricted primary sources, which will likely complicate the relationship between Freud and his theorization.

In light of the above reservation, we may make some effort to trace the roots of Freud's typically dualistic mode of thought in a constellation of phenomena, starting with certain cultural and intellectual determinants. Modern structuralism, too, operates with a binary model, which underlies such varied research as Roman Jakobson's structural linguistics and Claude Lévi-Strauss's parsing of myths. Dualism has been called the myth of our time. Be that as it may, I have noticed that whereas Saussure, the founder of modern linguistics, Freud, Jakobson, and the literary critic John Crowe Ransom are dualistic thinkers, Peirce, the father of semiotics, Hegel, Marx, and the literary critic Allen Tate are characteristically triadic. As well, a strong intrapsychic case has been presented for rooting Freud's ideation in divisible masculine and feminine identity fragments, one side representing paternal authority and the mechanistic quality of his metapsychology, the other, maternal warmth and the humanistic quality of his clinical work and theorizing.[12] The moment in Jones's three-volume biography when he unburies his best talents occurs, I believe, with his suggestion that Freud's dualism was a drive derivative stemming from his own Oedipus complex, a brilliant thought that unfortunately has not gained much currency in psychoanalytic circles:

> The dualism must have sprung from some depths in Freud's mentality, from some offshoot of his Oedipal complex, perhaps the opposition between the masculine and the feminine sides of his nature.[13]

And what link is there between Freud's dualism and the deep-rooted fragmentation we have already observed in his thought and procedure? Startlingly it announces itself at the very outset, in the very first sentence of Freud's most important and elaborate case history: "The case upon which I propose to report in the following pages (once again only in a fragmentary manner . . .)" (*S.E.* 17:7). Might not the evident refusal to produce something whole and his liking for poetic fragments as means of proof be relatable *also* to his body image? For an answer we again refer to Freud's letter to Lou Andreas-Salomé where he tells of his admiration for the feminine exquisiteness in her work, for her orderliness as opposed to his own eternal ambivalence and tendency to leave everything in disorder.[14] To what degree Freud's tolerance for fragmentary cognitive discoveries and productions exists as a derivative of his early split maternal object, mother and nanny, is a question worthy of the most serious speculation. To cite a particular: the drives are the source of psychic energy; *libido* refers to the measure of the sensual or libidinal drive. We have no corresponding term to refer to the energy of the aggressive drive.

In a rich, suggestive study, Clay Whitehead has contrasted the basic mammocentricity that runs throughout Melanie Klein's writings with Freud's theoretical phallocentricity. But in pursuing his "psychoanalysis of psychoanalysis," Whitehead sets the horizontal layering of Freud's topographic theory against Klein's vertical splitting and cleavage, and wonders about a possible relation between Kleinian verticality and the external appearance of the female genitals. It is amusing to find that the time-honored symbol of the phallus has now become bisexualized.[15] But proceeding on surer ground, Whitehead rightly recognizes that creators and students of metapsychology are liable by projection and identification to develop an overdetermined relationship with metapsychological tenets. A willingness to analyze the sources of these projections and identifications "expands our appreciation of metapsychology, places it in the creative context of the plastic arts and drama, and emphasizes the importance of exploration and moderation in psychoanalytic discourse" (p. 395).

The creations of projection, identification, and mood swings are among the milestones in the development of Freud's theory. In *The Interpretation of Dreams* Freud recognized a self-reflexiveness in what he himself censored and was defensive about: "The book proves the principles of dream interpretation by its own nature, so to speak, through its own deficiencies."[16] Years later, the uncertainty over who would win World War I crept into Freud's own clinical doubt about certain interpretations in his case history of the Wolf Man.[17] The war also cast its shadow on "Thoughts for the Times on War and Death," for it overlooked a parallel, pointed out by Abraham, that both in war and in the totem meal, the community is permitted what is ordinarily forbidden to the individual; agreeing to this parallel, Freud pertinently remarked, "It is interesting to see how the slightest trace of affect restricts the author's view."[18] If we know that in November 1923 Freud had a ligation of his spermatic ducts so as to be rejuvenated,[19] certain passages of "The Economic Problem of Masochism," finished before the end of January 1924, will appear in a very new light. If we accept that our investigations of great men are bound to be ambivalent and hide an element of hostility and revolt (*S.E.* 21:212), it follows that Freud's studies of da Vinci and Moses do the same. And finally, the change from the triumphant *Future of an Illusion* to the pronounced pessimism of *Civilization and Its Discontents* may be ascribed to his bleaker reaction to the picture of the Western world.[20]

We may now turn to the larger practical question encompassing the Oedipus complex and the relationship between Freud's life, his unconscious, and his sexual theories in general. Why was he skeptical about the potential of child analysis and about how far one could go into the unconscious and infantile life? Schur speculates that Freud's nicotine addiction (which, incidentally, Freud considered as a derivative of the "primary addiction," masturbation[21]) might have prevented him from penetrating deeper into the oral phase of development.[22] We are on solid footing when we ally Freud's hesitation about earliest infantile sexuality with his puzzlement about the meaning and desires of womanhood and motherhood. We may reflect here that Freud, patriarch of the early analysts, may not have been fully aware of his role as nursing mother to these grown-up children; that the British psychoanalytic school with its stress on mother-child symbolism and symbiosis was anticipated by Rank over sixty years ago; and that recent analytic thought has swung in favor of rooting man's sexual anxiety in his fear of the mother, an idea proposed by Rank in opposition to Freud's notion that traced such anxiety to castrating threats from the father.[23] What is more, if Freud, his mother's favorite child, consequently neglected the psychic reality of the mother's castration of her son, he likewise underplayed the son's matricidal wishes.

We are not astonished, then, to learn that the great strides in Freud's idea of woman came relatively late in his career. He recognized, for example, that contrary to his original tenets, girls' libidinal wishes during the phallic phase are first directed toward the mother;[24] during the 1920s and 30s, he increasingly departed from his belief that the young child's great protector and savior was the father; and alongside his changing appreciation of the mother's dominant role,[25] he gave mounting attention to the mother-goddess.[26] The list of changes in Freud's feminine theories is long and impressive[27] but our interest is directed rather to the reasons for those changes—other than mere increased observation. We know that Freud called his later writings part of a regressive phase. We know too that he allied death with woman and the return to the womb, as he vividly articulated in analyzing "The Theme of the Three Caskets":

> We might argue that what is represented here are the three inevitable relations that a man has with a woman—the woman who bears him, the woman who is his mate, and the woman who destroys him; or that they are the three forms taken by the figure of the mother in the course of a man's life—the mother herself, the beloved one who is chosen after her pattern, and lastly the Mother Earth who receives him once more. But it is in vain that an old man yearns for the love of woman as he had it first from his mother; the third of the Fates alone, the silent Goddess of Death, will take him into her arms [S E 12.301].[28]

No wonder that Freud wrote that he did not want to die before his mother did.[29] And the later Freud's growing sensibility to female psychology and his postulation of an independent death and/or aggressive drive—are surely not coincidental. After all, decades earlier, his collaborator Breuer spoke in an individually written section of *Studies on Hysteria* of an independent aggressive instinct *(S.E. 2:246).* It might well prove fruitful to investigate these developments diachronically, reading backwards as is allowable in dream interpretation *(S.E. 4:328);* read thus, the death drive appears as the determinant for precedent drive theories, which form a receding chain of increasingly defensive derivatives; and the death drive is a return of the repressed. Similarly, is not the conceptualization of the Oedipus complex overdetermined by the stress on the libidinal drive, which acts as a defense against attributing instinctual status to aggression, which classically is directed toward the parental figure of the opposite sex? For an answer, let us listen to Freud himself in 1929:

> . . . I can no longer understand how we can have overlooked the ubiquity of non-erotic aggressivity and destructiveness and can

have failed to give it due place in our interpretation of life. . . . I remember my own defensive attitude when the idea of an instinct of destruction first emerged in psycho-analytic literature, and how long it took before I became receptive to it [S.E. 21:120].

A recent, very thought-provoking study entitled *A History of Aggression in Freud*[30] points up the rampant aggressivity in Freud's dreams, suggests the unresolved issue of bisexuality as a possible basis for Freud's annihilatory wishes toward Fliess, shows the theoretical advance on the subject of aggressivity in the Joke Book as compared with the contemporaneous *Three Essays*, spells out personal and political reasons for Freud's rejection of the aggressive drive from 1909 to 1914, and relates two of the metapsychological essays to ego-syntonic aggression.

Freud's aggression and his quest for Woman—these are the latent forces that punctuate (I was going to say *puncture*) his writing. An equally important issue for us to consider is the relationship between Woman and the origin of his psychoanalytic discourse:

How tempting to any man habouring such latent potential for terrors and rages much [sic] be the mystical vision of regaining total bliss—of the ocean as womb! And psychoanalysis . . . may have been born of Freud's resolute determination to resist just that temptation.[31]

Wherever the International Psycho-Analytical Association in turn might be tempted to situate itself, Freud's preparatory fragment of a style is one for all time.

Speaking of the International Psycho-Analytical Association brings us to the topic of its founding in 1910, to Freud's relation to Jung at the time, and to the bearing of all this on *Totem and Taboo*, and most particularly on Freud's most famous myth, the theory of the primal horde. Briefly, *Totem and Taboo*, which in light of the following documentation might justifiably be called *The Interpretation of Psychoanalysts' Dreams*, is a commentary on various myths that have to do with the embryonic movement: the myth of Oedipus, or parricide; the myth of Cain, or fratricide; and finally, filicide, or the myth of Abraham. But the novelty of *Totem and Taboo* lies also in the perspective of discourse: it is not just expository; it also enacts its own subject matter.

In the fourth essay of *Totem and Taboo*, Freud combined

Darwin's hypothesis of the primal horde with Robertson Smith's hypothesis of the totemic meal to fabricate the following reconstruction:

> [In the primal horde] there is a violent and jealous father who keeps all the females for himself and drives away his sons as they grow up. . . . One day the brothers who had been driven out came together, killed and devoured their father and so made an end of the patriarchal horde. . . . The violent primal father had doubtless been the feared and envied model of each one of the company of brothers: and in the act of devouring him they accomplished their identification with him, and each one of them acquired a portion of his strength. The totem meal, which is perhaps mankind's earliest festival, would thus be a repetition and a commemoration of this memorable and criminal deed, which was the beginning of so many things—of social organization, of moral restrictions and of religion. . . . [Hence, according to what we now call deferred obedience, the sons] revoked their deed by forbidding the killing of the totem, the substitute for their father; and they renounced its fruits by resigning their claim to the women who had now been set free. They thus created out of their filial sense of guilt the two fundamental taboos of totemism, which for that very reason inevitably corresponded to the two repressed wishes of the Oedipus complex [S.E. 13:141–143].

Freud clearly recognized the paternal streak in his character, and so did his disciples. Several factors reinforced his paternal status: that he was literally the father of psychoanalysis; that his intellectual powers were unmatched by those of his followers;[32] that he had to supply them with patients; and that he had analyzed some of his colleagues and their intimates. As his successor, Freud chose Jung, who not only maintained residence in a more central location, Zurich, but also stood for the Christian political power that was dominant in the Western world. Fearing that psychoanalysis would die in a fratricidal war between Christians and Jews, Freud chose his inheritor from the Christian totem alone so as to prevent his new-found science from "becoming a Jewish national affair" that "would succumb to anti-Semitism."[33]

Although Freud proposed Jung as President of the International Psycho-Analytical Association, it is plain from their correspondence that Freud always remained the power behind the throne.[34] The Association was founded in 1910 at the Nuremberg Congress, but the account given in Jones's biography falls short of truth. According to Jones, Ferenczi (Jones's former analyst), true to a dictatorial bent in his character, proposed that the President be granted unheard-of censorial powers over any article written by any analyst in the world.[35] To know the truth, however, we must realize that Freud collaborated with Ferenczi in drawing up his program,[36] which indeed contained two other proposals not mentioned by Jones or Schur but found in the witness accounts of Wittels and Stekel:[37] namely, that the President was to be elected for life and would have absolute power to nominate or depose any analyst in the world. The outraged Viennese, who receive short shrift from Brother Jones, rightly rejected these proposals. Freud himself felt he was too old to take on the formal direction of the Association *(S.E.* 14:43), and his posthumous letter to Ferenczi about the Nuremberg Congress reveals his complex over aging and his awareness of a primal-horde phenomenon within the Association. Freud endeavored to avoid his symbolic death as primal father and to establish during his lifetime the rule of a fraternal band:

> I had almost got into the painful role of the dissatisfied and unwanted old man. That I certainly don't want, so I prefer to go before I need, but voluntarily. The leaders will all be of the same age and rank; they can then develop freely and come to terms with one another.[38]

Betrayal, rivalry, and secession became more pronounced in the year following the Congress, when Adler and Stekel resigned their respective posts as President and Vice-President of the Vienna Society. In 1912, as tension mounted between Freud and Jung, the Secret Committee—"a happy band of brothers"[39]— gathered around Freud to thwart such heresies as those of Adler, Stekel, and Jung. But both inside and outside that secret covenant, unrelenting Fate was silently setting the stage for a reenactment of the interflowing myths of Abraham, Oedipus, and Cain.

Between 1911 and 1913 appeared *Totem and Taboo* and Jung's *Psychology of the Unconscious,* which are both self-reflexive as well as expository treatises. The correspondence between Freud and Jung testifies amply to the overdetermination that went into the writing of these treatises: joy over cooperation, fear, jealousy, rebellion. There is also the further testimony in Jung's subsequent recollections:

> In my next book, *Wandlungen und Symbole der Libido* [*Psychology of the Unconscious*], which dealt with the hero's struggle for freedom, Freud's curious reaction prompted me to investigate further this archetypal theme and its mythological background.
>
> Like many sons, Adler had learned from his "father" not what the father said, but what he did. Instantly, the problem of love (Eros) and power came down on me like a leaden weight. Freud himself had told me that he never read Nietzsche; now I saw Freud's Psychology as, so to speak, an adroit move on the part of intellectual history, compensating for Nietzsche's deification of the power principle. The problem had obviously to be rephrased not as "Freud versus Adler" but "Freud versus Nietzsche." It was therefore, I thought, more than a domestic quarrel in the domain of psychopathology. The idea dawned on me that Eros and the power drive might be in a sense like the dissident sons of a single father, or the products of a single motivating force which manifested itself empirically in opposing forms.[40]

Casting his theory of psychic energy in terms of filial rebellion, the son Jung broke away in a single stroke from Freud, his father. Actually Emma Jung believed that her husband was working through part of his parental complex in the writing of Part 2 of the *Psychology*, and that Freud would not approve of it.[41] As for "The Sacrifice," the last chapter of *Psychology*, which posits that unconscious sexuality is merely symbolic and that the true object of psychoanalysis is the "sacrifice and rebirth of the infantile hero," Jung well said, "When I was working on my book about the libido and approaching the end of the chapter 'The Sacrifice,' I knew in advance that its publication would cost me my friendship with Freud. . . . I realized that the chapter 'The Sacrifice' meant my own sacrifice."[42]

Jung's feelings about his mythological treatise are indispensable for a full understanding of the interactional context around *Totem and Taboo*, a kind of whodunit about youthful murderers. As with his other writings, Freud felt the book to be an extension of his own body,[43] but beyond that, it also stood for the body of a woman. To realize how jealously Freud, the first patriarch guarded Lady Psychoanalysis, we need but listen in as he plans with Jung the International Congress at Nuremberg: "For the Congress I now have the following: You on the development of ψA (but mainly America, the rest is familiar to most of our people), me on the prospects for psychoanalysis, a happy combination since you represent the lady's future and I her past."[44] Freud conceived of *Totem and Taboo* as a casual liaison who subsequently took on the demanding importance of a new wife;[45] and *Totem's* cherished fourth essay in particular was a veritable "Princess."[46]

Freud's work on the last part of *Totem* served notice that his death, eagerly awaited by his Viennese opponents, had not yet come to pass; the treatise was also a lethal instrument to purge psychoanalysis of "all Aryan religiousness."[47] Nevertheless, with the completion of *Totem and Taboo* Freud's elation gave way to doubt, which Ferenczi and Jones ascribed to an inner, imaginative reenactment of the very experiences he had recounted: elation over killing and eating the father giving way to doubts; after all, it was a big step from the wish to kill the father in *The Interpretation of Dreams* to the actual murder in *Totem and Taboo*.[48] Wittels understood the book in light of the Abraham myth as wreaking "a scientific vengeance upon Jung, following the latter into the domain of folk-psychology, and there annihilating Jung on his own vantage ground."[49] Stekel agreed that Jung might have been jealous and offended at having been outdone on his own ground;[50] but the "happy band of brothers" of the Secret Committee, for their part, celebrated *Totem* by treating Freud to a dinner they called a "totemic festival."[51] Notwithstanding the Committee's displacement, Freud's work is an enactment of annihilation: Freud oedipally relives the killing of his father, and the killing of his son, Jung, according to the myth of Abraham—not to mention the annihilation of the totemic feast. In it, the sacrificing community of old, the god and the animal victim not only shared the same blood, but the god himself was represented twice over, as himself and as the totemic animal *(S.E.* 13:136,149).

Freud, in his constant involvement with the reader, as a matter of course serves up a substantial repast. Surely we are justified in seeing commensality and totemism in his writing, for he himself, his verbal offering, and the target audience are common members remembered in each text and throughout his corpus.

Notes

1. G. Atwood and S. Tomkins, "On the Subjectivity of Personality Theory," *Journal of the History of the Behavioral Sciences*, 12:166–177 (1976); R. D. Stolorow and G. Atwood, "An Ego-Psychological Analysis of the Work and Life of Otto Rank in the Light of Modern Conceptions of Narcissism," *International Review of Psycho-Analysis*, 3:441–459 (1976); "The Life and Work of Wilhelm Reich: A Case Study of the Subjectivity of Personality Theory," *Psychoanalytic Review*, 64:5–20 (1977); "Metapsychology, Reification and the Representational World of C. G. Jung," *International Review of Psycho-Analysis*, 4:197–214 (1977).

2. Jones 1:xii.

3. Letter of 15.11.20 to Groddeck, in *The Meaning of Illness*, p. 54.

4. This is another good example of the drive-influenced quality of Freud's style. After the qualification *seldom*, keynoting the cognitive weight of the first sentence, the contradictory universal *Each of us* takes over in the second. Compare the letter of 7.2.30 to Pfister; Freud at first denies that his reflection on the struggle between Eros and Thanatos is determined by emotional attitudes, only to conclude with a modified retraction: "Of course it is very possible that I may be mistaken. . . . You know that the more magnificent the prospect the lesser the certainty and the greater the passion—in which we do not wish to be involved—with which men take sides" *(Psycho-Analysis and Faith*, p. 133).

5. *Beyond Good and Evil*, in *The Philosophy of Nietzsche*, edited by W. Wright (New York: Modern Library, 1954), p. 386.

6. Jones 2:127.

7. Jones 3:69.

8. Scientific meeting of 2.2.07, *Minutes of the Vienna Psychoanalytic Society*, 1:136; cf. that of 2.20.07, 1:149. See also R. Lilleskov's report on the recent panel on "Nonverbal Aspects of Analysis," *Journal of the American Psychoanalytic Association*, 25:701 (1977): "[Furer's] own observations of children confirm the formulations of Alice Balint and Ferenczi in which identification is considered a process by which the external world becomes known and symbolized in the developing child by bodily imitation or the linkage of the external event to a bodily process."

9. Jones 3:44.

10. M. Gill, "Psychic Energy Reconsidered," *Journal of the American Psychoanalytic Association*, 25:588 (1977).

11. In a sensitively balanced essay, "L'Image du corps," François Gantheret deals with one of the most confused questions in modern psychology, that of the body. Parallel to the psychoanalytic concern with the body image (which is of an unconscious nature), he explains, runs the neuropsychiatric concern with the corporal schema (which is allied with the real body). He also draws attention to the fact that patients having undergone amputation before age five or six do not experience the phenomenon of a phantom limb. This finding indicates that the corporal schema is probably very dependent on sensorial data before this age, and that corporal schema only acquires auton-

omy later on (in *La Psychanalyse*, edited by C. Clément et al. [Paris: Larousse, 1976], pp. 63–76). In this connection we adduce a pertinent datum from another area. Visual dreams do not occur in the congenitally blind or those struck with blindness before the age of five. The "visual center" matures between the ages of five and seven; ordinarily children who go blind during this period only continue to have visual dreams for a short while thereafter (R. Blank, "Dreams of the Blind," *Psychoanalytic Quarterly*, 27:158–174 [1958]).

12. See R. Holt, "Ideological and Thematic Conflicts in the Structure of Freud's Thought," in *The Human Mind Revisited*, edited by S. Smith (New York: International Universities Press, 1978), pp. 51–98.

13. 3:267; see also 2:422–423 and 3:306–307. In the passage from the second volume, Jones relates Freud's theoretical dualism to his obsessional propensities and their attendant ambivalence. To this observation we should bring the relevant fact that Freud wrote more about obsessive neurosis than any other pathology.

14. Letter of 9.5.31, in *Andreas-Salomé: Letters*, p. 193.

15. "Additional Aspects of the Freudian-Kleinian Controversy: Towards a 'Psychoanalysis of Psychoanalysis,' " *International Journal of Psycho-Analysis*, 56:383–396 (1975). The semiotic distortions that arise in applying the body image to theory also occur in J.-B. Pontalis, "Dream As an Object," *International Review of Psycho-Analysis*, 1:125–133 (1974). After describing the dream as a maternal object, Pontalis asserts that dream interpretation is paternal since it penetrates the dream. Pontalis is misled by a submerged metaphor equating analysis with "penetration"; the tail is wagging the dog here, and the phallus gives rise to the fallacy that limits analysis to a male activity.

16. Letter of 17.2.11, in *Freud/Jung Letters*, p. 395.

17. Jones 2:276.

18. Letter of 4.5.15, in *A Psycho-Analytic Dialogue*, p. 221; see also letter of 26.4.15 (p. 219).

19. Schur, *Living*, p. 363 fn.

20. Schur, p. 417.

21. Letter of 22.12.97, in *Origins*, p. 238.

22. Schur, p. 413 fn.

23. Grotjahn, "Collector's Items," pp. 11, 20.

24. See Section 3 of "Female Sexuality," S.E. 21:235–240; 20:34 fn.

25. Cf. Schur, *Living*, p. 368 fn., and J. Harrison, "Infant-Mother Relation and Oceanic Feeling," *Journal of the American Psychoanalytic Association*, 27:402 ff. (1979). Harrison has some fine pages dealing with the effect of early maternal traumata on the later Freud's attitude to oceanic bliss.

26. H. Slochower, "Freud's *Déjà Vu* on the Acropolis," *Psychoanalytic Quarterly*, 39:96–98 (1970).

27. See especially the essays by Blum and by Schafer in *Female Psychology: Contemporary Psychoanalytic Views*, edited by H. Blum (New York: International Universities Press, 1977).

28. Cf. Freud's Dream of the Three Fates (*S.E.* 4:204–208) and his remark, "Men also picture death as a return to the womb" (*S.E.* 22:24).

29. Jones 3:152–153.

30. P. Stepansky, *Psychological Issues*, Monogr. 39 (New York: International Universities Press, 1977). See especially pp. 70–71, 84–86, 99, 141–142, 162–164, 169, and 172–175.

31. Harrison, "Infant-Mother Relation," pp. 418–419.

32. Nunberg, in *Minutes of the Vienna Psychoanalytic Society*, 1:xxx.

33. Letters of 3.5.08 (p. 34) and 2.12.08 (p. 64), in *A Psycho-Analytic Dialogue*.

34. Jones 2:69.

35. More work needs to be done on how Freud's role as an idealized father met both his own needs and those of his followers—on the process, in other words, of his accession to a mythicized ideal role. One key question here is his stature as therapist; many long monographs have been written on his theories, but there has been no comprehensive study of him as a practitioner. To begin with one small point: Freud denied ever having slept during an analytic hour in his life (journal entry for 4.8.37 in S. Blanton *Diary of My Analysis*, p. 91). However, there is testimony to his having slept in the hours of at least three analysands: Helene Deutsch, James Strachey, and John Rickman. See S. Gordon, "Helene Deutsch and the Legacy of Freud," *The New York Times Magazine*, July 30, 1978, p. 23; M. James, review of D. W. Winnicott, *The Piggle*, in *International Journal of Psycho-Analysis*, 60:137 (1979); A. Kardiner, in "Freud: The Man I Knew," quotes Rickman: "I suspect he sleeps. In fact, I know he does, because I know how to wake him. I just stop talking, and after a few moments of silence, Freud jumps in with a 'Yes, yes—go on, please' " (p. 78).

36. See letter of 16.10.10, cited in F. Alexander and S. Selesnick, "Freud-Bleuler Correspondence."

37. Cf. F. Wittels, *Sigmund Freud*, pp. 138–139; and W. Stekel, *Autobiography*, pp. 127–128.

38. Letter of 3.4.10, in Jones 2:71.

39. Jones 2:164.

40. *Memories, Dreams, Reflections*, edited by A. Jaffé and translated by R. and C. Winston (New York: Pantheon Books, 1961), pp. 154, 153.

41. Letter of 6.11.11, in *Freud/Jung Letters*, p. 456.

42. Jung, *Memories*, pp. 167–168.

43. See letter of 29.5.08, in *Freud/Jung Letters*, p. 154, and letter of 2.5.09, in L. Binswanger, *Sigmund Freud: Reminiscences of a Friendship* (New York: Grune & Stratton, 1957), p. 11.

44. Letter of 2.2.10, in *Freud/Jung Letters*, p. 292.

45. Letter of 30.11.11 to Ferenczi, in Jones 2:352.

46. Letter of 12.6.13 to Ferenczi, in Jones 2:354.

47. Letter of 13.5.13, in *A Psycho-Analytic Dialogue*, p. 139.

48. Jones 2:354.

49. Wittels, *Sigmund Freud*, p. 191.

50. Stekel, *Autobiography*, p. 143.

51. Jones 2:355. For a more detailed account of the clash between Freud and Jung, see my paper, "The Budding International Association of Psychoanalysis and Its Discontents," *Psychoanalysis and Contemporary Thought*, 2:551–591 (1979).

# 8

## Postscript: The Psychoanalytic Reading of Freud

A PERSUAL OF FREUD'S PUBLIC AND PRIVATE WORKS ENABLES US TO discover a fact that seems never before to have been pointed out: throughout his writings Freud continually lays open his reflections about writing itself, a gesture that puts him in the company of creative authors. From this observation we are immediately led to consider that Freud had various motivations for writing. Of course he wrote to convey information, to convince, or even to amuse. Sometimes too he engaged in a self-purposive, expressive writing: for example, many of his letters to his fiancée, Martha, and later to his friend Fliess read like occasions of affective release. Similar venting even attended the production of Freud's more intellectual efforts, such as the *Introductory Lectures* and the *Metapsychological Papers*, which, he said confidentially to Lou Andreas-Salomé, "suffer from the lack of good cheer in which I wrote them and from their function as a kind of sedative." Then again, writing served Freud's self-avowed end of counteracting the passivity of psychoanalyzing for so many hours of the day. His scriptive motivations also included the financial one of finishing the *New Introductory Lectures* to support his psychoanalytic publishing house[1], and the performative bonus of completing *Totem and Taboo* in order to surpass Carl Jung in his own mythological reserve and thereby subject that rebellious son to a paternally administered castration.

159

Another aim that Freud had in writing was to discover and achieve insight. Available evidence indicates, moreover, that he had those aims early in life . When he was fourteen he was given a volume of Ludwig Börne's works. Freud became so fond of this volume that it was the only one from his boyhood that he retained into his later years. One of the essays in the cherished volume is entitled "The Art of Becoming an Original Writer in Three Days" and ends with this significant advice:

> Take a few sheets of paper and for three days on end write down, without fabrication or hypocrisy, everything that comes into your head. Write down what you think of yourself, of your wife, of the Turkish War, of Goethe, of Fonk's trial, of the Last Judgment, of your superiors—and when three days have passed you will be quite out of your senses with astonishment at the new and unheard-of thoughts you have had. This is the art of becoming an original writer in three days [*S.E.* 18:265].

Apparently the young Freud took Börne's advice, yet some time afterwards the essay and the ensuing experience went out of his memory. When in 1919 his attention was drawn to that essay, he recognized that he had cryptomnesically omitted to see its influence on his discovery, or rediscovery, of free association. It is more important for us, however, to realize that Freud's early spontaneous experience was linked to writing. Freud's own commentary, contained in an epistolary fragment recently published, is resounding:

> I read him [Börne] avidly, and some of these short essays have always remained very clearly in my memory, not of course the cryptomnesic one. When I read this one again I was amazed to see how much in it agrees practically word for word with things I have always maintained and thought. He could well have been the source of my originality.[2]

It is hard to overestimate the value of the link Freud proposed between the source of his very originality and his early writing experience. But Freud's cryptomnesic reaction to that link is a nearly equally intriguing matter, for other relevant passages from Börne tellingly stayed in his memory, such as "It is not lack of intellect but lack of character that prevents most writers from

being better than they are. . . . Sincerity is the source of all genius, and men would be cleverer if they were more moral."
Börne's importance is also seen in the fact that when Freud was a
student in Paris and went to the famous Père Lachaise Cemetery,
the only graves he visited were those of Heinrich Heine (Martha's
relative) and Ludwig Börne.[3] It is no accident that when Freud
eventually published his cryptomnesia, he did so in an anonymous essay; this is even more significant when we consider it
along with two other important essays that were also anony-
mously published, "Screen Memories" (1899) and "The Moses of
Michelangelo" (1914). (We might notice in passing that, aside
from anonymity, a thread of resistance runs throughout the
subject-matter of the three essays: Freud's conflictual acknowledgment of a predecessor, his screening of his first experience in love,
and a taboo identification with a supreme hero.)

Ludwig Börne's influence even extended to the very modality
of Freud's self-analysis. It has not at all been appreciated that he
conducted his self-analysis predominantly in writing—his self-
analysis was literally a writing cure. We can hardly accuse ourselves of being trivial if we pause a moment on this point. We
know that the so-called Anna O., or Bertha Pappenheim, who
was Breuer's patient from 1880 to 1882, named her associative
kind of treatment "chimney sweeping," and the story is familiar
to us how Freud in different stages developed the "chimney
sweeping" into the free association or talking cure as the major
instrument for the psychoanalytic exploration of the unconscious.
But more relevant to our present purposes, this is how Freud
spelled out the modalities of psychoanalytic exploration in *The
Interpretation of Dreams*:

> What Schiller describes as a relaxation of the watch upon the
> gates of Reason, the adoption of an attitude of uncritical self-
> observation, is by no means difficult. Most of my patients
> achieve it after their first instructions. I myself can do so very
> completely, by writing ideas as they occur to me [*S.E.* 4:103; see
> also 4:279, 6:636 and 19:109].

The conclusion imposed by this passage upon us is inescapable:
psychoanalysis had its beginnings in a talking and a writing cure.
If we let ourselves become fully aware of this origin of psycho-

analysis, then we are prepared to make a just appreciation of the central place of writing in Freud's life.

Our attention to Freud's self-analysis as a writing cure renders us more alert to the generally ignored taxonomy which Freud made of his own works. Both in two early letters to Jung and later, during his analysis of Joseph Wortis[4], Freud distinguished those works that he had written on impulse from those written on order. Knowing Freud as we do, we are not surprised that he preferred the impulsively inspired works to those that were prompted from an extraneous source. The commissioned works, introductions or articles written for books and encyclopaedias, included such titles as "The Claims of Psycho-analysis to Scientific Interest" (1913), "An Autobiographical Study" (1925), "Dostoevsky and Parricide" (1928), and "Why War?"(1933). Though some of these exemplify a clarity worthy in its own right, both their intrusive incentiveness and the cold, formalistic requirements of article writing went against the grain of the rhythmic thrust, personalism, and essayistic bent that keynoted the best of Freud's production. To be sure, among the commissioned pieces are some that manage to be stylistically quite exceptional apart from their clarity, and upon closer look we come upon a biographical reason that explains away the unusualness of this circumstance.[5] A case in point—there are others—is the masterly essay "On Transience" (1916), in which Freud relates his memorable conversational disagreement with two towering figures of Central European culture, Lou Andreas-Salomé and the poet Rainer Maria Rilke.[6]

In his own life as a writer, Freud placed the stakes very high. Cromwell's words, "A man never mounts so high, as when he does not know where he's going,'"[7] were often quoted by Freud and indeed shed light on the conquistadorial intent behind his creative self-abandonment to unconscious impulses. The outcome of Freud's bold venture was remarkable. There exists substantial evidence showing that when in some instances Freud wrote, even from "inner impulse," he hardly needed to revise, a feat that makes us recall Ben Jonson's testimony about Shakespeare's having "never blotted a line." In some of Freud's manuscripts which have survived, we come across notably few crossings out—this is clear, for example, in the manuscripts of the process notes to the

Rat Man case (1974); some of the latter process notes were incor-
porated in with little alteration into the final case history.

We turn now to Freud's remarks on the serendipity of his
spontaneous writing. Here is Freud telling Fliess about the composition of *The Project for a Scientific Psychology*: "Yet it was only in
attempting to report it to you that the whole matter became obvious to me."[9] Next, let us listen to Freud's scattered epistolary
comments about his composing *The Interpretation of Dreams*:

> Herewith a few scraps washed ashore by the last thrust.[10] I can
> compose the details only in the process of writing.[11] It completely
> follows the dictates of the unconscious, on the well-known prin-
> ciple of Itzig, the Sunday rider. "Itzig, where are you going?"
> "Do I know? Ask the horse." I did not start a single paragraph
> knowing where I would end up.[12]

It was precisely an intellectual certainty and a corresponding absence of spontaneity that made Freud uninterested in writing out
his thoughts in 1911. As he said to Jung: "My study of totemism
and other work are not going well . . . my interest is diminished
by the conviction that I am already in possession of the truths I
am trying to prove."[13] Several years afterwards, Freud's creative
output reached its zenith, but the evidence of its spontaneity is
unfortunately somewhat indirect. In the space of a month and a
half, Freud composed his five profound metapsychological
essays—"such a furor of activity," let us repeat Jones, "would be
hard to equal in the history of scientific production." Referring to
the composition of the first three metapsychological papers within
five weeks, Robert Holt memorably exclaimed: "I calculated that it
would take me a full week merely to *copy* these three papers in
longhand—the way Freud always wrote—writing as many hours
a day as I could stand."[14]

Leaving the period from the *Project* to the metapsychological
papers, we can quickly go to the later Freud and again find him
allying spontaneity and his classic productions. Here, then, is
Freud reflecting on *Civilization and Its Discontents* (1930);

> The book does not deal exhaustively enough with the subject
> [namely, the discomfort in our culture], and on top of this rough
> foundation is put an overdifficult and overcompensating exami-
> nation of the analytic theory of the feeling of guilt. But one does

not make such compositions, they make themselves, and if one resists writing them down as they come, one does not know what the result will be. The analytic insight into the feeling of guilt was supposed to be in a dominant position.[15]

Finally, in *Moses and Monotheism* (*S.E.* 23:104), Freud asserted: "Unluckily an author's creative power does not always obey his will: the work proceeds as it can, and often presents itself to the author as something independent or even alien."

If we pause to take stock of our survey up to now, we arrive at a picture of a Freud who from his adolescence was taken by spontaneous writing and the courageous sincerity it involved, who made it central to his self-analysis, and who repeatedly adopted it throughout his psychoanalytic career. But as we continue our survey, we come upon other evidence lying not far away that unexpectedly unsettles our hard-won belief. The contrasting picture of Freud is that he merely copied out his preconceptions into perfectly finished papers. To this effect there is Freud's explicit statement about his not writing something until he had previously constructed it in his mind, down to the formulation of the very last sentence. In the context of this new revelation, Freud's writing figures as a subsequent though highly accurate report of a prior spontaneity. The sudden outcome of this new account is that Freud's writing stands as a somewhat demystified yet phenomenal achievement. One critic exquisitely clarified this phenomenon with the following description:

> But only when a train of thought, a solution to a problem, or a new theoretical concept grew in his [Freud's] head into its definitive linguistic form and when "some feeling for form, an estimation of beauty as a kind of perfection," was satisfied—only then did he sit at his writing desk. What then turned out has indeed much similarity with that process which Freud once described in a letter to Stefan Zweig: "I have already long tormented myself to find a comparison with your manner of working: yesterday I finally got the idea, conjured up by the visit of a friend who is an epigraphist and archeologist. It is the procedure occurring when one makes a paper copy of an inscription. As is well known, one lays a moistened paper on the stone and forces the soft material to fit in with the smallest depression of the writing surface."
> The chief work was consequently done before Freud actually

took to his pen. His manuscripts gave the impression of end-products and disclose little of the creative process of formulation, rejection or verification of hypotheses. . . . It must have been, as he copied, a completely worked through and wholly finished inscription stored in his memory.[16]

We are fortunate enough to have at our disposal a single contemporary account that traces how Freud used his so-called phonographic memory to couple temporally separate spontaneity and reproduction. The account, by Richard Sterba, starts out with a meeting of the Vienna Psychoanalytic Society in the late 1920's:

[Freud said:] "I have just received a letter from an American physician which I would like to read to you." . . . The letter reported on the religious conversion that the writer of the letter had experienced when he was still a medical student. . . . Freud gave us a psychoanalytic explanation of the dynamics of this conversion. I had the impression that the explanation occurred to him on the spot while he talked to us and was not in any way premeditated or prepared. Editha [Sterba's wife], who had also been present at the meeting, had the same impression. We truly observed his great mind at work.

Two days later, the manuscript of Freud's paper "Ein religioeses Erlebnis" ["A Religious Experience"] was delivered to the psychoanalytic publishing house where Editha worked as editor. The manuscript repeated almost verbatim what Freud had told us in the meeting.[17]

If we reflect further on this priceless anecdote, it will have at least partially solved our quandary about Freud's writing—after all, the two images of the authorial Freud as premeditating and as spontaneously pouring forth cannot have simultaneous validity. But a well-finished product may issue forth from either premeditation or from spontaneity, and we are familiar with such a possibility in Freud's public speaking and writing. When we dwell further on the gamut of possibilities, we are gradually led to the realization that in order to understand the quality of Freud's composition, we must make a series of further distinctions about verbal abilities. Among our friends we all single out those whose verbal gift spares them from having to grope for the right word—it's as if in their preconscious awareness, ideas and the corresponding words were sharply in focus and thus readily retrievable. A different gift, not necessarily coinciding with the first, is the ability of some who do not have to grope for syntax. A third discrete ability, the facility of organizing ideas, may variously overlap with verbal and syntactic facilities. Let us now apply these distinctions to Freud and extricate ourselves from the impasse we strayed into. Freud's compositional practice ranged from sheer spontaneity to the unusually accurate reproduction of measured preconceptions; but if his compositional practice varied between extremes, his exceptional verbal and facilities did not, so that during expressive activity of any kind, he rarely hesitated over the choice of words or syntactic structure, and once the choice was made, he rarely had to correct it.

The time has now come to let ourselves go further in investigating the characteristics of Freud's truly processive style whether it be immediately impulsive or replicatory of that impulsiveness. If we probe this style, we shall be able to pinpoint what Jones admired when he remarked that Freud could write again and again on the subject of dreams and still give the impression of revealing something new to the reader already familiar with the subject.[18] This sense of freshness stems often from Freud's genetic style, which he defined as intended for "the critical reader" and as "follow[ing] the path along which the investigator himself has travelled earlier"; precisely in that way Freud induces the reader to take a part in constructing theories and deals with his objections during the course of their "joint work" (*S.E.* 23:281). Actually there are three aspects to what Freud calls his "genetic style": its historical tracing of origins; its collaborative nature, joining author and reader; and its frequent ongoingness in the present. Hence the taxonomy of Freud's works according to the presence or absence of their impulsive origins is now complemented by their inscribed kinds of organization and relationship with the reader.

Let us take as a starting example *Studies on Hysteria*. In his introduction to its second edition, Freud counseled: "I can give no better advice to anyone interested in the development of catharsis into psycho-analysis than to begin with *Studies on Hysteria* and thus follow the path which I myself have trodden" (*S.E.* 2:xxxi). When we explore the book itself, we begin to realize its historical structure: after discussing in a letter to Breuer whether or not the book should begin historically with case histories and then terminate with conclusions, Freud decided to begin dogmatically with conclusions and then follow up with case histories, starting with Breuer's, which were largely arranged in chronological order (*S.E.* 1:147).

In its purer sense, Freud's processive text is not a closed structure of assertions but one of openness and interminability, much as dream symbols are like the language of infinitives (*S.E.* 18:212). Together with the suppleness of Freud's flexible definitions, his open-ended attitude to psychoanalysis and his engaging irony, his dominant walking metaphor was aptly to express a series of adjusting perspectives; more than Aristotle's peripatetic method in the Athenian Academy, Freud's itinerant procedure was verbally integrated into his very material. To put it otherwise, the form in Freud's prose, far from being a kind of discardable instrument as in so much of psychoanalytic writing, was organic to his thought so that form and content were unified. Not only did Freud clinically listen with the third ear, but he also wrote in attunement with it, instancing the suppleness of his discourse as responsive to the allusivity, elusivity, and illusivity of unconscious mental processes.

Harmonizing with the suppleness of Freud's processive style was his intuitive approach to fragmentary data. There were many reasons that Freud cherished the fragmentary and distrusted complete systems: psychoanalysis was a young, developing science; the unconscious content it works on is never fully knowable; also, language, the very instrument of description, will always remain inadequate before the complexities of psychic life. The suppleness of Freud's genius enabled him to understand psychoanalysis as a veritable semiotics of approximations and to insist that that very semiotics of approximations is itself approximate or fragmentary. Such a realization is reflected by the word *Stück* (piece, portion, fragment), which echoes on nearly every other page of the *Gesammelte Werke*.

It is equally to Freud's credit that he made the best of his abilities and limitations in insuring the suppleness of his science. Whereas he admittedly lacked talent for the inductivism of empirical psychology humorously dubbed by him as "the American manner" (*S.E.* 11:42), he had intuitive powers and knew how to join his courage in their service. He coupled his admiration for those "who have the courage to think something before they can demonstrate it" and his awareness of universal implications in the singular fact. He himself tells us how he saw a general relevance and applicability in the isolated case of Anna O. related by Breuer (*S.E.* 20:21). Significantly, though, for the courageous exploitation of that insight in its various ramifications, the young Freud had to await the assistance of Fliess, who, contrary to Breuer, could appreciate something of Freud's that was not yet finished.[19]

Of course Freud would subject his intuitions to reality-testing and seek supporting evidence from his own or others' experience, but what interests us here is how he would underline the flexibility of his elaborations. Sometimes, it is true, Freud rhetorically overreacted and rigidified his position—like a good rhetorician he knew that the rhetorical counterpart of the inductive proof in scientific demonstration was the example, whose logical frailty demanded the support and distraction of persuasive maneuvers. But we must not neglect the other Freud, who resorted to some verbal qualifier or even to the subjunctive mood in order to hone away full certainty from his assertions. Another verbal device of flexibility was Freud's self-irony, most of whose charm arose not from rhetorical posturing but rather from an authentic modesty about his own achievements. There is the anecdote about Freud giving vent to indifference to his sudden popularity and then citing the witty jibe of the triumphant Cromwell: "Three times as many would have come to see me hanged."[20] As a play of opposition between at least two assertions, the essential nature of irony obviously suited Freud's aim in communicating tentativeness; his self-irony had the added advantage of being able to temper any alienating impact that his gigantic intelligence might have had upon the reader. We fondly remember that Freud called his works on Leonardo da Vinci and Moses "novels" and that he wryly left it to the future to decide whether there was more delusion in his theory than truth in Schreber's delusion.

Essential to the suppleness of Freud's processive text is its temporal vividness. We especially appreciate this factor in Freud's genetic exposition when it takes place in the present rather than in the past tense. Here we should pause to reflect on this stylistic trait, for it is replete with profound implications, as we might notice in the contrast with most exploratory prose. More precisely, the general practice of exploratory writers is not at all to use the present tense—their exploration being actually an act of remembering, they use the past tense to depict the anterior exploration. How different with Freud. His genetic exposition characteristically takes place in the present tense; hence, when we are not reading one of Freud's first drafts, we are meeting with Freud's here-and-now reliving of the past, so that his representation is a re-representation. Briefly, whether in first or subsequent drafts, part of Freud's typical exploratory strategy is to present his thought as in the process of being conceived. His prose is like a manifest dream which contains a hallucinatory representation in the present tense of the optative mood of the latent dream (*S.E.* 5:534, 647–648 and 8:162). Freud made magisterial use of such temporal transformation in his case histories, for he strove to counteract the defect of those psychiatric case histories in which the aim of ostensible exactness did not succeed in being a substitute for the reader's presence at the treatment (*S.E.* 12:114). In his own case histories Freud was apt to secure our presence at the treatment by putting the life of the patient, his dreams, the treatment, and our reading experience into the one temporal plane of the present.

We should not be surprised to discover that features of oral culture contribute to the vividness of Freud's processive style. At this juncture our considerations are helped by recent research on the differences between conversational language and written formal language: the latter is typified by nominalizations, impersonalism, and the passive voice, whereas conversational, discourse (and Freud's written expression, we may add) is marked by self-references and descriptions of the speaker's mental processes.[21] To point up still another oral quality of Freud's writing, I must first draw a distinction between understandable, readable, and memorizable prose. Much of Wittgenstein's prose is very readable, but in spite of its simple words and syntax, it is not readily understandable. On the other hand, the prose of the mature Kant defies both easy understanding and reading. A few instances may illustrate. In the preface to the original edition of Kant's *Groundwork of the Metaphysics of Morals* there's a sentence running a page and a half, and in the second chapter another sentence runs on for nearly two pages; then on one of the pages of the *Critique of*

*Pure Reason* eighteen relative clauses have been jammed into three sentences, and in another sentence five genitives are strung together. But perhaps the most telling illustration of Kant's unreadability comes out of the story of how he unluckily asked how a certain friend felt when reading his work, and the friend handily replied, "Your way of writing is so full of parentheses and conditionals on which I have to keep an eye that I place one finger on this word, and then the second, third, and fourth, and even before I have to turn the page there is no finger left."[22]

By contrast, Freud's prose seems so readable, understandable, and also memorizable. This third characteristic of vivid writing, memorizability, is related intimately to the citability and aphoristic nature of orally marked prose. In this regard it is pertinent for us to know that whether as a reader or theater-goer, Freud judged a work in terms of whether it had expressions which "anyone would want to commit to memory";[23] by the same token, Freud—like another member of his household, Minna—liked to enliven conversation with aphorisms.[24] We should mind too that throughout his own works Freud coined many memorable phrases, be they conceptual throwaways or grounding points in his exposition, which not only carried the traditional authoritative ring of aphorisms but also, in their quality as verbally short, core units, could serve as exemplary specimens of the fragmented, incomplete body of psychoanalytic knowledge.

In pursuing our topic, we come to realize that Freud's citability is also due to his avoidance of piling up negatives and verbal qualifiers of certitude (e.g., "it might not often be possible to say, with too much exaggeration, that a more or less meaningful probability would tend to indicate. . ."). In this sense, Freud differs from many psychoanalytic writers who, in their pursuit of expressive exactitude, disregard Valéry's dictum that to write good prose one must reject the use of overburdening qualifiers. To use too many qualifiers, that is, is a trait foreign to aphoristic writers and militates against citability and readability. Freud rarely clusters qualifiers; instead, he prefers to spread out the qualifying statements and, in a Cézanne-like way, have layering blocks of his thought, often keyed to an aphoristic statement, offset and reorient each other. The fact that the aphorism is a *Denkersparnis*, or saving of thought,[25] comprises an appealing factor in its citability and makes us mindful that what is vividly retainable in Freud is often citable. King Solomon would have had a proverb for that.

Perhaps more than anything I have said up to now, my next contention, that the vitality of Freud's prose also comes from its playfulness, will risk provoking disagreement from my audience. In maintaining that the somber Freud neglected the healthy role of play in life, some rely for support on the following anecdote reported by Erikson:

> Freud was once asked what he thought a normal person should be able to do well. The questioner probably expected a complicated "deep" answer. But Freud simply said, *"Lieben und arbeiten"* ("to love and to work").[26]

But rather than take *love* and *work* at face value, we may wonder if Freud had intended a deeper meaning. Our perplexity proves momentary if we turn to the ready answer awaiting us in an early letter written from Freud to Pfister: "I cannot face with comfort the idea of life without work; work and the free play of the imagination are for me the same thing."[27] For Freud, then, a healthy life consists in love, work, *and* play.

It is deeply regrettable that the playwork in Freud's writing tends to disappear under the rigid censorship of Strachey's scientific prose. Freud was not one of those overserious analysts who, in a rare use of verbal wit, will apologetically demand, "Please forgive the pun." Again and again Freud insisted that the unconscious and dreams are witty; he even described the unconscious as *"der andere Schauplatz"* (the other scene, the other showplace). This witty place was also one of the scenes of Freud's writing; there he imagined himself not as the objective mirror-analyst but as the analyst endlessly reflecting in a hall of funhouse mirrors. Freud indeed played joyfully with language, and in that he awaited for unconscious connections in moments of impulsive inspiration, to that extent his enlivened prose is also a celebration of the unconscious. There are those, however, who overlook the enjoyable part of his prose and who, in kneeling before it as a block of awesome though unimaginative work, differ from retired athletes who are well aware of being subject to the tricks of their knees.

Integral to Freud's play is his understanding and screened

use of language itself. He declared himself most explicitly when he asserted that all psychological language is not literal but figurative and that it is only by virtue of that distorting figurativeness that one can describe or even be aware of psychic processes. He knew, in other words, that his verbal instrument and his content cast their shadows upon each other, and, given that epistemological trap, he opted for a language that was concrete, experientially concrete, evocative, and fluid.[28] Such a linguistic orientation is also seen in Freud's sensitivity as a translator when he strove to blur as little as possible the typically informal language of Charcot's lectures (*S.E.* 1:136). Freud's lexical usage was undoubtedly influenced by his philological conviction that "in every language concrete terms, in consequence of the history of their development, are richer in associations than conceptual ones" (*S.E.* 5:340; see also pp. 352 and 407). In light of this, perhaps we would not be venturing too much in surmising that Freud preferred a suggestive, associative language for his new science because it was a suitably flexible instrument for approximate descriptions of the ultimately unknowable, because it was more adaptable and harmonious with psychoanalysis as an evolving discipline, because it was better for his constructions written under impulse, and because it more easily engaged the reader unconsciously, preconsciously, and consciously to fill out the text with his own reflections and dynamic derivatives.

There is an admirably democratic thesis silently contained in that feature of Freud's language which I call commonness.[29] Read in the original German, Freud's texts allow us to appreciate how he lets the lexicality of the clinical material infiltrate his very critical language on that material, how with the aim of rapprochement he uses the same language when talking of the patient, the reader, and himself as analyst, and how he applies the same words to both normality and psychopathology. Moreover, whereas Strachey's translation, with its unannounced policy of lexical apartheid, stressed the difference between various aspects of reality, Freud posited now a commonness, now a complementarity. In short, without neglecting differences, Freud posited solidarity and in that way anticipated the so-called new rhetoric and its emphasis on an identification between speaker and audience, in contrast to the distancing persuasion that characterizes traditional rhetoric.

How different were the verbal choices of Strachey, who apparently endorsed Jones's rigid platform for a psychoanalytic vocabulary in English.[30] Jones's aim was to create an experientially distant technical language etymologically dependent on the dead classical languages (which survived, significantly enough, as paternal and not maternal tongues).[31] The result, Jones thought, would be the securing of precise definition and the obviating of personal associations and emotional slippage or spillage. Following in Jones's path, Strachey rejected an affect-laden writing, with the result that Freud's fluid, resonant expression acquires a rigid and abstract cast. More to the point, Strachey's *Standard Edition* turned out to be an extraordinary enterprise of defensive isolation.

There is more. In writing his psychological works from 1886 to 1939, Freud addressed them directly to the contemporary audience around him. Strachey, on the other hand, avowedly conceived of his imaginary audience as dead, as being represented by some English man of science and letters born in the middle of the nineteenth century (*S.E.* 1:xix); meanwhile, his translations were being carried out over a century later, from 1953 to 1966. In tandem with Strachey's adoption of a dead audience and dead classical language were his frequent changes of Freud's active voice into the passive; his grammatical neutralization of the personalism of Freud's pronouns; and his constant devitalization of the present tense of Freud's vivid stereophonic style into the grammatical past tense. A further problem overshadowing Strachey's heroic endeavors was that his order in translating Freud's works was drastically different from the order in which they were originally written—for example, the works in the very first of the twenty-three volumes of the *Standard Edition*, the first written by Freud, were the last to be translated by Strachey. And as if that methodological problem were not enough, Strachey compounded his difficulties by settling at the very outset on a choice of technical terms to be maintained throughout each volume, a decision that later on confessedly caused him some grief (*S.E.* 1:xviii).[32] In this connection we may cite the ever-timely proverb, *"Traduttore, traditore"* (translator, traitor); This piece of traditional wisdom defines Strachey's translation, yet the translation is nevertheless praiseworthy in many ways. On the other hand, it stands as a testimony to the greatness of Freud that his writing, like that of the

Bible and Shakespeare, transcends the limitations of translation and has been able to captivate generations in their linguistic diversity.

With a slight turn of the hermeneutic prism on its axis, we can move what up to now we beheld peripherally into the center of our vision and can turn our focus from the stylistically shaped meanings in Freud's text to their effect on us as readers. Rather being a one-sided heuristics, Freud's prose was one of collaboration bolstered by features of lexical commonness. Above all let us remember Freud's major aim in his scientific essays was to blend the thesis and proof of demonstrative writing with the characteristics of exploratory discourse through which he has us co-inquire, anticipate, accept, and reject with him (S.E. 23:281). As well, the self-stimulating, self-generative and facilitating aspects of Freud's processive discourse were part of an overall design to stimulate, to generate his audience into thinking and feeling and to facilitate their associative processes.

Significantly, in the preface to his Introductory Lectures (*S.E.* 15:11–12), while acknowledging that his readers would first be provoked into denial, Freud asked that they suspend judgment and let psychoanalysis make its impression upon them; and again, at the start of the second year's series of these lectures, Freud once more asked the members of his audience to let his material "work" on them (*S.E.* 16:243, see also 4:105-6). Years later, while telling his Viennese listeners that *Civilization and Its Discontents* promulgated a revamped theory of the drives, Freud pertinently explained, "I am like . . . someone who has to go out of the house and leaves a toy behind so that the children will have something to play with while he is absent. . . . the feeling of guilt is created by the renunciation of aggression. Now it's up to you to play with this idea."[33]

It is impossible to take full account of the endlessly varying ways through which Freud positively appeals to us: he soothes us by his empathy and the tonal qualities of his prose; he may divide his readers into the distrustful and the faithful and thereby elicit our protective feelings toward him; he enrichens us with new modes of attention; he installs in us doubts, needs, wishes, and yearnings in such a manner that we feel assured by his awareness; he might invite us into the containment of his text which, in its unfoldings, anticipations, and retrospections, constitutes its own proper temporality. Alternately, Freud might perhaps stand slightly aside, tell how he has gotten a certain idea, how he feels about it, how he goes from that idea to the next one, how he anticipates what the reader might think or feel about it, and so delightfully and unexpectedly on.

These considerations of Freud's powerful effects on the reader would not be adequate, however, if we neglected to see along with their delightful instructiveness their potential for controlling us. To clarify this control, we shall investigate how Freud weaves throughout his prose elements of suggestiveness, taming the uncanny, wit, and most importantly, aesthetic effectiveness; it will be particularly enlightening, moreover, if we are able to gloss the power of the aforementioned elements with metacommentaries drawn from Freud's own work.

First of all, a gesture somewhat reminiscent of hypnotic technique is the subject of our attention. Much as Freud transferentially used suggestion to induce the patient "to accomplish a piece of psychical work" (*S.E.* 12:106), so also through rhetorical identification he frequently utters suggestions to the reader. Also bearing on this practice is Freud's recourse to "anticipatory ideas" (*Erwartungvorstellungen*):

> There is no doubt that it is easier for the patient's intelligence to recognize the resistance and to find the translation corresponding to what is repressed if we have previously given him the appropriate anticipatory ideas. If I say to you: "Look up at the sky: There's a balloon there!" you will discover it much more easily than if I simply tell you to look up and see if you can see anything (*S.E.* 16:437; see also 10:104; 11:142 and 12:169).

The reader likewise is given through the Freudian corpus quantities of narratively anticipatory ideas too numerous for counting. Such anticipatory ideas function within Freud's overall technique of expositorily manoeuvering between predictability and unpredictability that is resonant with echoes of taming the uncanny. Freud moves us through an array of feelings from comfort to wonder as he negotiates between turning the familiar and recognizable into the estranged, on the one hand, and, on the other hand, domesticating that which seems alien. In the Dora case

Freud explicitly stressed that "what is new has always aroused bewilderment and resistance" (*S.E.* 7:11); by contrast, he spoke elsewhere of the pleasure in recognition and the rediscovery of what is familiar, adding that because of a similar relieving of psychical expenditure, remembering might also be pleasurable (*S.E.* 5:121–122). The pleasure-accruing analogies, however, are even superior, for they not only involve rediscovering the same thing but also bring out a relief of intellectual work (*S.E.* 8:210). Altogether, Freud's commentaries on familiarizing, defamiliarizing, remembering, and analogizing are applicable to these activities as pleasureful narrative techniques in his own prose. It thus behooves us even more to be aware of the potential double-sidedness of that constant pleasure as conducive to exhilarating enlightenment or to the lulling seductiveness of an uncritical attitude.

If analogies course throughout Freud's prose, so do instances of wit, and thus once more we may repair to certain analytical parts of Freud's prose to find a gloss on what is happening in the whole. A joke, Freud tells us, is "developed play" and brings about "a small yield of pleasure from the mere activity, untrammeled by needs, of our mental apparatus" (*S.E.* 8:179). Besides the pleasure stemming from the mere activity of our mental apparatus, Freud's wit through its content offers us both forepleasure and deeper pleasure (*S.E.* 8:137) and, significantly, in the process of doing so, must divert our attention in much the same way that hypnotic suggestion does (*S.E.* 8:153 and n.). Thus, in addition to ushering us into new modes of attention, Freud might by his wit divert our attention. It is not even beyond Freud's power to compound his diversionary techniques with a self-reflexivity; for example, in discussing comic relief, he calls attention to the pleasureful relief that his controlled expository process gives to the reader:

> Now that we are on the point of approaching an answer to our last question, as to the necessary conditions for the generating of comic pleasure from the difference in expenditure, we may allow ourselves a relief which cannot fail to give *us* pleasure. An accurate reply to the question would be identical with an exhaustive account of the nature of the comic, for which we can claim neither capacity nor authority (*S.E.* 8:217).

There is no question here of attempting a detailed survey of the strategic advantages brought about by the distracting forepleasure of Freud's wit throughout his opus, but were such a survey initiated, one would have to take account of the wit not only in Freud's many anecdotes but also in his attitudes to himself, his audience, and his enemies, and the content and manner of his exposition.

Finally we come to the all-important topic of Freud's sheer aesthetic impact on his readers. I suggest that Freud felt ambivalently about being called a creative writer, much as he was ambivalent about living in Vienna, constantly criticizing the city but never moving from it until he had no choice. Freud after all could have written badly if he wanted to; but perhaps that is not true— he had no choice, for he was too much of an artist to write badly merely to forestall being accorded a creative label. One may conjecture that many psychoanalysts, besides Erikson and Sterba, were first attracted to Freud as verbal artist.[34] He complained that his case histories read like pieces of literary creation (*S.E.* 2:160 and 7:9), but I would say that he did so halfheartedly, for he elsewhere declared his inclination to become a novelist in order to record better for posterity all that his patients were telling him.[35] One may even wonder to what degree Freud's artistic self-awareness had a share in the readiness with which on more than a half dozen occasions he called some of his ideas "theoretical fictions" (*S.E.* 5:603; see also 5:598; 12:220fn.; 14:231; 20:194; 23:235 and 239).

That fiction could control the reader was an issue not outside the pale of Freud's artistic awareness. In the clearest language Freud drew our attention to the craft of the fictional writer who

> can keep us in the dark for a long time about the precise nature of the presuppositions on which the world he writes about is based, or he can cunningly and ingeniously avoid any definite information on the point up to the last. . . . [T]he storyteller has a *peculiarly* directive power over us; by means of the moods he can put us into, he is able to guide the current of our emotions, to dam it up in one direction, and make it flow in another (*S.E.* 17:251).

Even more telling is Freud's description of his own "exceptional pleasure" upon reading Stefan Zweig's book of literary criticism.

It is pertinent to my general thesis that, drawn out of context, Freud's praise of Zweig would seem to concern a novel rather than a volume of critical prose:

> I have read it with exceptional pleasure, otherwise there would hardly be any point in writing to you about it. The perfection of empathy combined with the mastery of linguistic expression left me with a feeling of rare satisfaction. What interests me especially are the accumulations and increasing intensity with which your language keeps groping closer to the most intimate nature of the subject.[36]

In like manner, by virtue of the formal artistry throughout his works, Freud offers a forepleasure or incentive bonus that entices the resistant reader into unsettling realms of thought and keeps him there. Varying the pace of his exposition, Freud may immediately satisfy us, in keeping with the Pleasure Principle or, striving for the greater though postponed pleasure of the Reality Principle, he may temporarily frustrate us and promise a subsequent, satisfying resolution. Captivating us in this way, Freud has transferred the gaps that are so capital in narrative fiction to both his psychodynamic understanding of defensive derivatives and his dramatically expository presentation of that understanding. That is to say, since no personal story, fictive or real, can be told completely, the storyteller's mastery of gaps assumes paramount importance; and accordingly, Freud, like the storyteller, may talk of permanent or temporary gaps, or he may even delay both the revelation and resolution of a gap until the end of his narrative. Hence Freud's control of the emergence or disappearance over narrative stretches is simultaneously controlling the focus of our reading so that it imitates the action of the narrative. On other occasions, Freud lures us into relaxing our alertness and concluding prematurely, as we satisfyingly discover later on with his guidance. On the other hand, we may be so gratified by his democratically communal "we" as to overlook whether such indicatives as "we see" and "we observe" carry the authoritative suggestiveness of the submerged hortatives of "we should" or even "must" see and observe.

For a more substantial instance of Freud's aesthetic power, we can do no better than to consider his short paper on, "Creative

Writers and Daydreaming." To begin with, it should be noticed that the last noun of the title is a poor translation of *"das Phantasieren"* and that daydreaming is just one of several kinds of phantasying that Freud discusses, including dreams, children's play, fictional writing, myths, and legends. In the course of his essay Freud spells out the performance of creative writers: they lessen the distance between themselves and the ordinary person; they produce phantasies, that fulfill past wishes; they reveal and conceal, hiding behind their invulnerable hero, who actually represents His Majesty the Ego (*Seine Majestät das Ich*); and, finally, they bribe us by a forepleasure arising from aesthetic form. To stay on the level of these overt messages, however, we miss Freud's ludic self-reflexivity, since he also reveals and conceals; he himself is his essay's invulnerable hero—His Majesty the Ego (note that *Ego* in German is *Ich*, I); and Freud also lessens the distance between himself and the ordinary person, as is seen in the essay's very first two words, "We laymen" (*Uns Laien*). But we can best grasp Freud's hide-and-seek in the following passage, where he pronominally identifies now with the lay reader, now with the directive author:

> One feature above all cannot fail to strike us about the creations of these story-writers: each of them has a hero who is the center of interest, for whom the writer tries to win our sympathy by every possible means and whom he seems to place under the protection of a special Providence.
>
> If at the end of one chapter of my story, I leave the hero unconscious and bleeding from severe wounds, I am sure to find him at the beginning of the next being carefully nursed and on the way to recovery (*S.E.* 9:149).

In "Creative Writers and Daydreaming," besides his appealing identification with us as laymen, Freud has fulfilled before our very eyes his aesthetic wishes; in the course of their scriptive realization, they subtly become a piece of crafted and therefore enactive prose. Revealing, concealing, the essay exposes the techniques of fiction and also employs them in its very demonstration. Shakespeare might have said of this essay that while the author wore his heart on his sleeve, we don't know if the main garment is turned inside out.

All told, the force of Freud on us is such that we incur the danger of letting our experience of enlightenment in reading him drown out our critical scrutiny. But psychoanalysis as a hermeneutics of suspicion teaches us to be always vigilant, for the unconscious is inherent to the human condition, ours and Freud's. It is consequently fitting that we as agents both participate and observe ourselves in reading him; that we look for submerged intertextual shifting relationships undermining his message; that we watch for subtexts, erased quotation marks, and erased ellipses which would otherwise acknowledge the existence of gaps; that we monitor ourselves as Freud involves us in becoming the object of his text; and that in general we are aware of his efforts to guide our reading and underwriting of him. We should experience our reading as a working through or a reading through, which complements his writing through and his very willingness to write upon impulse and observe himself as a participant in that impulsively marked gesturing.

I also believe that much of our reading of Freud is determined at the outset by our textual presuppositions and attitudes. Guided by a certain paradigm of reading, some tend to conceive of Freud's texts as self-contained structures and then proceed to minimize or even disregard any textual inconsistencies; if, on the other hand, one takes it for granted that texts like crystals have fault-lines, he will be more disposed to discover strengths and weaknesses, hidden anomalies, and stresses and counterstresses. The student of Freud, and moreover the analytic student, should realize as well that he has to struggle with the sedimentation of accumulated institutional readings and discursive practices that he brings to Freud's texts. These texts, then, are not "innocent" but are already mediated and adjusted; they are given a further stabilized identity by being packaged in what is wrongly entitled the *"Standard" Edition.* To read Freud well, one must adopt self-reflexive interpretive strategies and, as the case warrants, analyze one's isomorphic needs for a rigid institution, a de-personed and static scientific text, and a canonical interpretation. In this connection one ought also to heed Bion's timely remark:

> Part and parcel of the genius's impact is the disruptive power of his communication. The Establishment, i.e., consisting of those

who exercise institutional power, strives for an appropriate containment of the genius, by partially limiting his disruptive power and by simultaneously conveying his expression to members of the group.[37]

Since it is not yet opportune to draw out the implications of my program for reading Freud, I prefer break to my expository thread in order to make an exegetical detour through some of Freud's clinical material and its reception in the psychoanalytic community. That detour might give us more ample and empirical grounds from which to judge whether a psychoanalytic reading of Freud demands more than a simple improvement in our self-awareness and our skills in textual analysis.

\* \* \*

To its merit, psychoanalysis is part of the revolutionary understanding of communication lauded by the renowned Marxist scholar Louis Althusser, who asserted in his work on *Das Kapital*: "As paradoxical as it seems to sound, we can maintain that in the history of human culture, our time risks appearing one day as marked by the most dramatic and laborious task ever, namely, the discovery and learning of the meaning of the most "simple" gestures of existence—seeing, hearing, speaking, reading."[38] In meeting that challenging statement, we shall considerably raise the stakes and thereby examine the reading of Freud's first great case history. Our choice is eminently appropriate, for Freud's great case histories "are the pillars on which psychoanalysis as an empirical science rests;" only upon their being surpassed will psychoanalysis enter into a radically new phase.[39]

We return thus to Dora, the girl who was used as a pawn by her father and by his mistress, Mrs. K; we remember too the sexual advances made by Mr. K to Dora, first when she was fourteen and then when she was sixteen. In 1961, Erik Erikson's presidential address to the American Psychoanalytic Association marked a turning point in the critical reading of the Dora case which had been published in 1905, fifty-six years earlier. For those relatively uncritical fifty-six years we might venture to take two studies as representative of the psychoanalytical reception of the Dora case. The first is Jones's biography, and it is quite to the point that he announced in the prefatory pages one of the most defensive denials in the history of modern science: "immeasurably great as was my respect and admiration for both the personality and achievements of Freud, my own hero-worshipping propensities had been worked through before I encountered him."[24] Jones's hagiographic stance, continued, of course, when he came to the Dora case: "This first case history of Freud's has for years served as a model for students of psychoanalysis, and although our knowledge has greatly progressed since then, it makes today as interesting reading as ever."[42] Significantly, the only concretely negative remark Jones expressed was an objection to Freud's contention that parental syphilis comprised a cardinal predisposing factor to neurosis in children.

Next we turn to Felix Deutsch's article published in 1957;[43] this article carries exceptional weight, for it was a write-up of two interviews that the author had had with Dora in 1922. Appearing to assume an independent position, Deutsch undertook to show whether Freud's conception of Dora was still valid or how it differed from subsequent psychoanalytic comprehension. In reality, however, Deutsch never uttered any disagreement with Freud; even more than that, he recorded as fact one of Freud's reconstructions that was adversial in tone toward Dora. Here are Deutsch's "facts" about the fourteen-year-old Dora at the hands of her seducer:

> As for her sense of *touch*, she had showed its repression in her contact with Mr. K. when he embraced her and when she behaved as if she had not noticed the contact with her genitals. She could not deny the contact of her lips when Mr. K. kissed her, but she *defended* herself against the effect of this kiss by denying her own sexual excitement and her awareness of Mr. K.'s genitals, which she rejected with disgust.[44]

To make matters worse, Deutsch's erroneous factualization is based on Freud's reconstruction, which itself tests one's credulity. Dora's own report of the original incident was rather straightforward: when she was fourteen, Mr. K on one occasion "suddenly clasped" and kissed her; at that moment she had a powerful feeling of disgust, tore herself away from him, and ran out of his place of business and into the street. Freud unwarrantably concluded that in such a circumstance favorable for sexual excitement a healthy girl would have felt a pleasurable genital sensation; he further presumed that Mr. K. had an erection pressed up against Dora and that its pressure probably caused "an analogous change" in the clitoris, whose excitement was reversed into disgust and displaced to the alimentary canal. Given, among other things, the abrupt temporality of the traumatic scene, Freud's assumptions about genital excitation are certainly gratuitous. It is also curious that when Dora said that she subsequently would avoid walking past a mixed couple engaged in "eager or affectionate conversation," Freud believed that she phobically wanted to avoid seeing a man in a state of penile excitement—this in spite of two facts: Dora's opinion that she knew nothing at that earlier age concerning the physical state of a man's excitement, and Freud's own acknowledgment that her answers were "always prompt and frank."

To repeat, then: glaring shortcomings of Freud's case history were passed over in silence until Erikson's address in 1961, which began to open the door for a more critical appraisal of Freud; still, as we all know, ritualistic deference to a nearly faultless Freud persists all too frequently in our journals. My main concern at this juncture is not Freud's limitations per se but rather the historical deficiency of psychoanalysis in suppressing part of his humanness—namely, his limitations, which in some instances were severe. In the case at hand, Freud was more censorious toward Dora than he was toward those parental adults who instrumentalized her—her father and the two Ks. We must also note the object of Freud's sympathy when he heard that Dora effected the dismissal of a governess who had instrumentalized her. Freud's association, *"die Arme"* (the poor woman, *S.E.* 7:37/ *G.W.* 5:196), was for the governess, not for Dora. Never does Dora receive such sympathy from Freud, but we do come across recurrent evidence of his aggressively pressuring, prodding, and disputing her. Note too that Freud qualified Dora's perception of her father's goings-on with Mrs. K as *"unerbitterlich scharfen"* (pitilessly sharp, *S.E.* 7:32/*G.W.* 5:190). Even more significant is Freud's brutally unfair judgment of the lake scene, where Mr. K.

made a love proposal to the sixteen-year-old Dora, who, upon hearing "You know I get nothing out of my wife," abruptly slapped him, hurried away, and told her parents about it some days later. Here now are Freud's disapproving comments about Dora in this scene:

> Her behaviour must have seemed as incomprehensible to the man after she had left him as to us. . . . Why did her refusal take such a brutal form, as though she were embittered against him? And how could a girl who was in love feel insulted by a proposal which was made in a manner neither tactless nor offensive? . . . I looked upon her having told her parents of the episode as an action which she had taken when she was already under the influence of a morbid craving for revenge. A normal girl, I am inclined to think, will deal with a situation of this kind by herself (*S.E.* 7:46, 38 fn., and 95—the pages are cited in that order).

Significantly, the actions of no one else except Dora are described as "brutal"—even the reprehensibility of her father is toned down into the understated critique that he was "never entirely straight-forward" (*S.E.* 7:109). But as objectionable as Freud's remarks are, perhaps it was no accident that after Erikson's pathfinding address it took until the middle of the last decade before Steven Marcus, an English professor and not an analyst, elaborated more extensively on the offensive incomprehension marking the management of the Dora case.[45] I offer my readers a leading question that they may answer silently to themselves: if Freud's verbal obtusenesses were remarked by such outcasts as Jung or Tausk or Stekel or Rank or Horney, how many psychoanalysts, under the self-aggrandizing defense of truth or human sensibility, would have seized the opportunity to write an easy and "safe" attacking article for one of our journals?[46] The history of silence may also be written.

It is worth further stressing Muslin and Gill's summary point that although Freud was optimistic about the therapeutic results of Dora's fragmentary treatment, Deutsch's report clearly indicated that the patient's neurosis plagued her for the rest of her life;[47] I would add that Freud's victimizing analysis not only chased Dora away from his office but also intensified her persecutory condition. In the Rat Man and Wolf Man cases as well, Freud exaggerated his therapeutic results—an exaggeration certainly arising from his own denial and possibly also motivated by the desire to remain a leader among his disciples and by a propogandistic zeal to protect his new discipline. These shortcomings and others on Freud's part were indeed all too often ignored by parasistic, pseudo-idealizing commentators on his works, as if the public image of an immortal genius were supposed to be without blemish. But my main concern at this time is not the appraisal of Freud's therapeutic accomplishments or the lack of them as such, a subject to which I have already devoted two books of comprehensive clinical, historical, and textual analysis.[48] Here I attend, rather, to our reading Freud and overcoming obstacles, both within and outside his texts, that disturb our understanding of them.

I shall offer some closing comments that start out in a new direction and I hope carry an importance in inverse ratio to their brevity. The first psychoanalytic study of reading that I consider in any way substantial is James Strachey's "Some Unconscious Factors in Reading."[49] This id-oriented essay, published in 1930, smacks of something written much earlier in this century and contains no hint of the classic, trailblazing essay about transference that Strachey published four years later, "The Nature of the Therapeutic Action of Psychoanalysis." In the earlier essay Strachey initially draws attention to unconscious factors in reading when not sublimated: scopophilia and oral and anal impulses. A little later on, however, he drops his qualification about sublimation when he says: "A coprophagic tendency lies at the root of *all* [my italics] reading. The author excretes his thoughts and embodies them in the printed book; the reader takes them, and, after chewing them over, incorporates them into himself." Given that the book is symbolically female, Strachey continues, the male author defiles the virgin page with his penis or feces; by the same token, the reader is the son who forces his way into his bookmother and extracts for himself his father's fertilizing traces.

After Strachey's article we may make a big jump, for it is only in the last twenty years that psychoanalytic thought on reading has significantly evolved. That evolution was conveniently recapitulated in a 1981 symposium centering around the transferential implications for psychoanalytic literary criticism.[50] I would synthesize several findings from the symposium and some of my comments on it in this way:

1. The concepts of transference and countertransference,

when applied by literary critics, stand as a contribution to contemporary literary criticism, which has shifted its focus from the interpretation of meanings set in a text to the processes of reading and writing. In their evaluative enterprise, critics currently differ in their estimate of how much meaning is determined by the text itself and how much by the subjective responses of the reader considered either individually or within an interpretive community.

2. The literary work in effect contains more than unconscious fantasies; preconscious and conscious ones are also worked over and subjected to play, problem-solving, and other psychic functioning, all of which in turn elicit responses from the total personality of the readership. It follows that the reader's transferential responses are but part of his total responses. This said, a virtual aesthetic experience may be disrupted by the reader''s intense emotive reaction, which may or may not be lessened by his analysis of the transference. On the other hand, as critics we may also distort the understanding of aesthetic experience by seeing it only within the framework of anti-subjective and pseudo-objective criteria.

3. One risks a danger in establishing too strong an analogy between the psychoanalytic and reading settings. To start with, one may safely assume that in the reading experience there is a reading alliance and also transference, but it would be an abuse of terms to speak without any nuance about a transference neurosis characterizing the reading event. Next, the technical criterion of an analyst's evenly suspending attention for the quintessentially unrepeatable clinical hour has no counterpart in the reader's leisurely hours and his arbitrary option to adopt shifting critical foci in returning to the same text. Finally, the critic's analysis of his transference in the literary situation, even though it may be beneficial, lacks the vital and often disorienting personal feedback and validation that keynote psychoanalytic therapy, which is based on the tenet that if self-analysis were thoroughly possible, there would be no neurosis.

Whereas the symposium concentrated on transferential implications in the reading of fictional literature, I am strongly advocating that the same approach be applied in the reading of Freud. In the first pages of the latter section I made the attempt to appraise the psychoanalytic reception of Freud's report on Dora for the purpose of showing that his distortions, displacements, scotomizations, exaggerations, and the like have been accepted uncritically in the short history of psychoanalysis. To be sure, there is a possibility that some analysts may read Freud's cases critically but, knowing the conservative position of psychoanalytic journals, have refrained from writing up their objections in a reactive gesture of self-censorship. But the other eventuality that concerns me most is that many analysts had a castrating and/or idealizing reaction to the powerful person of Freud as preserved in his prose. The history of reading Freud gives us the lesson that in the act of reading him we should, accordingly as the text necessitates, analyze our transference to his scriptive self-presentation, to the opponents he describes, to his allies, to his patients, and to his fictionalized construct of us as his readers. In addition, I personally could not have made some of my findings about Freud's case histories without having analyzed my transference to my former teachers, my local psychoanalytic society, and the International Psycho-analytic Society. But in this kaleidoscope, the analysis of our transference to Freud is most pressing in order to strive for a just appraisal of his greatness and his limitation. It is especially in indicating the latter that one is liable to be affected by anxiogenic institutional pressures, as John Sutherland reminded us.

I find it hard to overemphasize the idea that Freud's imposing authorial personality, together with its blend of intellectual and affective force, renders problematic our efforts to maintain on even keel our reading alliance with him. This reading alliance, moreover, operates under the constraint that the writer's audience is ever a fiction, much as the real author's presence in the text does not elude the reader's fictive construction. All told, the exegetic history of the great case histories demonstrates that reading Freud calls for more than heightened self-awareness or improved ego skills in literary criticism. Our analysis of transference proves crucially supplemental in reading Freud and in understanding and teaching his texts, whether outside or inside psychoanalytic training institutes. We would easily agree, furthermore, that the extent of transferential analysis will vary according to the text, with the case histories being more demanding than the rest. In that exploration of transference, the realization always awaits us that we have been and shall continue to be, unknown to ourselves, ghost writers of endless libraries with aisles on aisles of higher learning and with cellar vaults full of archival graffiti.

### Notes

1. For references in this paragraph, cf. Freud's letter of January 16, 1884 to Martha: "I note the calming influence of your gentleness as I write; in fact I already feel quite a bit calmer" (*Letters*, pp. 104–105); the letter of November 15, 1897 to Fliess: "More frequently, such one-sided letters; they allow me to forget the distance. Therewith you are only doing what I have always done—writing about what you are engrossed in and leaving aside what you cannot react to. Our conversations used to be like that: each in turn began to speak of what he had to say and did not feel obliged to respond to what he had heard" (*Complete Letters of Sigmund Freud to Wilhelm Fliess*, edited by J. Masson [Cambridge, Mass.: Harvard University Press, 1985], p. 282); and the letter of January 24, 1910, congratulating Pfister for his moderate reply to an opponent: "I could not write like that, I prefer not writing at all, *i.e.*, I do not write at all. I could write only to free *my* soul, to release *my* affect" (*Psychoanalysis and Faith*, p. 33). See also the letter of November 9, 1915, *Andreas-Salomé: Letters*, p. 35; Jones 2:396 and *S.E.* 22:3.

2. Letter of April 9, 1919 to Ferenczi, cited in *Sigmund Freud: His Life in Pictures and Words*, edited by E. Freud, L. Freud, and I. Grubrich-Simitis (New York: Harcourt Brace, 1976). p. 73.

3. Jones 1:246.

4. Letters of February 17, 1908 and April 12, 1910 in *Freud/Jung Letters*, pp. 119 and 306, and Wortis, *Fragments of an Analysis*, p. 109.

5. "Some Reflections on Schoolboy Psychology" (1914) is Freud's touching contribution to a Festschrift on the fiftieth anniversary of his high school; and for a Festschrift honoring one of his oldest friends, the ophthalmologist Leopold Königstein, he wrote up "The Psycho-Analytic View of Psychogenic Disturbance of Vision" (1910).

6. H. Lehmann, "A Conversation between Freud and Rilke," *Psychoanalytic Quarterly* 35:423–427 (1966).

7. H. Sachs, *Freud: Master*, p. 67.

8. See Strachey's textual comments on the *Project* (*S.E.* 1:286–287) and Hawelka's (1974) on the text of the Rat Man notes.

9. Letter of October 20, 1895 in *Complete Letters to Fliess*, p. 146.

10. Letter of May 31, 1897, ibid., p. 249.

11. Letter of March 24, 1898, ibid., p. 305.

12. Letter of July 7, 1898, ibid., p. 319.

13. Letter of December 17, 1911 in *Freud/Jung Letters*, p. 472.

14. R. Holt, book review of R. W. Clark's Freud: *The Man and the Cause*. (New York: Random House, 1980), in *Psychoanalytic Review of Books*, 1:9 (1982).

15. Sterba, *Reminiscences*, pp. 113–114.

16. I. Grubrich-Simitis, ed. *Sigmund Freud: Das Motiv der Kästchenwahl* (Frankfurt a/M: Fischer Verlag, 1977, pp. 40–41; the previously unpublished letter of S. Zweig dates from April 24, 1925. More recently, Grubrich-Simitis has altered her opinion and proposed the possibility that for the majority of the texts written from 1914 on, Freud composed previous drafts—I. Grubrich-Simitis, ed. *Sigmund Freud: Übersicht der Übertragungsneurosen* (Frankfurt a/M: Fischer Verlag, 1985), p. 8fn. Cf. Eissler, *Talent and Genius*, p. 277fn. My photocopy of Freud's holograph, "Analysis Terminable and Interminable," has enabled me to corroborate partially the suspicion of Grubrich-Simitis. The opening times on page 19 of the holograph were recopied by Freud onto another page mistakenly numbered 19 and then properly renumbered as 21; on this latter page Freud barred out the wrong number and the repeated lines. The mistakes clearly testify in this instance to Freud's process of drafting and copying.

17. Sterba, *Reminiscences*, pp. 124–125. Although documentation is limited, there is some indication that Freud grew more confident and bolder as a public speaker. In 1900 he prepared a lecture one hour before giving it to the B'Nai B'rith (letter of 25.4.1900 [*Complete Letters to Fliess*] p. 410); in 1909 Ferenczi would prime Freud a half hour before he gave the Clark Conferences (*S.E.* 22:227); on a still later occasion, when asked by Jones on their way to the lecture hall about the upcoming topic, Freud simply replied, "If I only knew! I must leave it to my unconscious" (Jones 1:341). Another point of consideration as that in his persona as a writer Freud might hide certain scientific doubts which he readily disclosed in his role as a semi-public speaker. As Felix Deutsch remarked about Freud's discussions at the Vienna Psychoanalytic Society in 1923: "Everything looks much more secure in writing than when he is commenting on it" (P. Roazen, *Helene Deutsch* [New York: Anchor Press, 1985], p. 210); cf. also Sterba, *Reminiscences*, pp. 106–107.

18. Jones 1:362.

19. Letters of December 8, 1895 and December 17, 1896 in *Complete Letters to Fliess*, pp. 155 and 217.

20. Sachs, *Freud: Master*, p. 127.

21. See my article "The Oral Tradition, Freud, and Psychoanalytic Writing," in *Contribution to Freud Studies*, ed. P. Stepansky (Hillsdale, New Jersey: Analytic Press, 1986), pp. 199–214.

22. See W. Kaufmann, *Discovering the Mind: Goethe, Kant and Hegel* (New York: McGraw-Hill, 1980), pp. 40, 105 and 169.

23. Cf. the letters of November 15, 1883 and August 11, 1885 in Freud, *Letters*, pp. 90 and 191.

24. Sachs, *Freud: Master*, pp. 72 and 80.

25. Sterba, *Reminiscences*, p. 120.

26. E. Erikson, *Identity: Youth and Crisis* (New York: Norton, 1968), p. 136.

27. Letter of March 6, 1910, in *Psychoanalysis and Faith*, p. 35.

28. Freud's preference for familiar, evocative words did not escape the attention of his disciplines—see Sachs, *Freud: Master*, pp. 43 and 46, and Wittels, *Sigmund Freud*, p. 130.

29. See my *Freud and the Rat Man* (New Haven: Yale University Press, 1986), pp. 180–181, 186 and 222–223.

30. See Jones's "Glossary for the Use of Translators of Psychoanalytic Works" in Supplement No. 1 to the *International Journal of Psychoanalysis*, 1924.

31. See my "Towards a Formalist Approach to Dreams," *International Review of Psycho-Analysis*, 1977, 4:83–98.

32. For a penetrating overview of this and related questions, see D. Ornston, "Strachey's Influence: A Preliminary Report," *International Journal of Psycho-Analysis*, 1982, 63:409–426; "Freud's Conception Is Different than Strachey's," *Journal of the American Psychoanalytic Association*, 1985, 33:379–412; "The Invention of Cathexis' and Strachey's Strategy," *International Review of Psycho-Analysis*, 1985, 12:391–399. A number of Ornston's pertinent publications, including "Improving Strachey's Freud," are forthcoming.

33. Sterba, *Reminiscences*, p. 116.

34. See R. Evans, ed., *Dialogue with Erik Erikson* (New York: Praeger, 1981), p. 81; Sterba, *Reminiscences*, p. 20.

35. Wittels, *Sigmund Freud*, pp. 19–20.

36. Letter of October 19, 1920 in *Letters*, p. 337.

37. W. Bion, *Attention and Interpretation* (New York: Basic Books, 1970), p. 74.

38. L. Althusser, *Lire le Capital, I* (Paris: Maspero, 1968), p. 12.

39. K. Eissler, *Medical Orthodoxy and the Future of Psychoanalysis* (New York: International Universities Press, 1965), pp. 395 and 397.

40. E. Erikson, "Reality and Actuality: An Address," *Journal of the American Psychoanalytic Association*, 1962, 10:451–474.

41. Jones 1:xiii.

42. Jones 2:257.

43. F. Deutsch, "A Footnote to Freud's 'Fragment of an Analysis of a Case of Hysteria,' " *Psychoanalytic Quarterly*, 1957, 26:159–167.

44. Ibid., p. 164.

45. S. Marcus, "Freud and Dora," *Psychoanalysis and Contemporary Science*, 1976, 5:389–442.

46. In the book I am currently writing, *Freud and His Female Patients*, I am developing at length the various comments I have made here concerning Dora.

47. "Transference in the Dora Case," *Journal of the American Psychoanalytic Association*, 1978, 26:321.

48. *Cries of the Wolf Man* (New York: International Universities Press, 1984) and *Freud and the Rat Man* (New Haven: Yale University Press, 1986).

49. *International Journal of Psycho-Analysis*, 1930, 11:321–331.

50. For the symposium's proceedings, see *Psychoanalysis and Contemporary Thought*, 1982, 5:3–53; for the perspective of self psychology on reading, see H. Muslin, "On Empathic Reading," pp. 301–316, in *Empathy: I*, edited by J. Lichtenberg, M. Bornstein, and D. Silver (Hillsdale, New Jersey: Analytic Press, 1984).

# Index of Freud References

Each title is preceded by date of publication and followed, where pertinent, by its volume in the *Standard Edition*. The numbers after the period refer to pages in this book.

# Name Index

# Subject Index